MARKETING IN THE SERVICE SECTOR

John M. Rathmell

Cornell University

WINTHROP PUBLISHERS, INC.
Cambridge, Massachusetts

Library of Congress Cataloging in Publication Data

Rathmell, John M
   Marketing in the service sector.

   Bibliography: p.
   1. Marketing—United States. 2. Service industries
—United States. I. Title.
HF5415.1.R38   381'.45'363   74-1236
ISBN 0-87626-561-1

This book is dedicated to my family:
my wife, my daughter and her husband,
my son and his wife, and my grandchildren

CONTENTS

1809420

iv

TABLES

FIGURES

vi

PREFACE

Both the demand for services and the variety of services offered are growing in the United States. Yet the marketing discipline has traditionally concerned itself with goods. Moreover, as the service sector grows, the demand for managers of service organizations grows. A recent study of MBA hiring showed that fourteen of thirty-eight industries were in the service and that four of the top five in terms of number of MBAs hired were service industries.[1]

Every product, whether tangible or intangible, which is bought and sold in the economic marketplace must be market in some form. This book is about what makes the marketing of services different. For example, some services can only be consumed with the active participation of the seller; it is unethical to advertise some services; some services are sold not for profit. It is, therefore, incremental in its marketing content.

We are not concerned with the marketing of ideas or causes (pollution abatement, for example) or the marketing of individuals (politicians, for example) or with the provision of services which are financed through donations or taxes. Marketing scholars have shown an active interest in these areas, and properly so. But the market-bounded scope of this book is sufficiently diverse and complex without venturing into nonexchange environments.

In the first place, definitions, classifications, data, and concepts are lacking, noncomparable, or unreal from a marketing perspective. Moreover as one attempts to integrate marketing terms, concepts, and practices with firms, institutions, and professions having their own traditions, customs, and practices which are quite foreign to conventional marketing (and much older), the linkage appears awkward and even improper. (What is an advertising agency's product line? What is the price of a university education? How does a dentist promote his service product? What is an electrical utility's channel of distribution?) Accountants, architects, veterinarians, and hospital, university, or public adminis-

---

[1]"B-school Grads Are Back in Demand," *Business Week,* 16 December 1972, p. 70.

trators who may be disturbed by this awkward and apparent indiscrete union need have no concern. Marketing terms such as selling, promotion, pricing, and transaction are professional in meaning and technically descriptive; they are not to be confused with the layman's perception of their meaning.

Part I introduces the service sector to marketing; Part II introduces marketing to the service sector; and Part III attempts an integration of the two in four service industries. These four industries differ sharply in the extent of their knowledge and application of marketing and in the degree to which they depart from conventional marketplace situations.

Acknowledgments are many. Students in my class in service and public marketing in many respects "wrote" this book. Over half were not marketing majors and over a fourth were not pursuing business degrees. I am particularly indebted to former students, colleagues, and professional service leaders who created original papers for this book. As representatives of various services rather than of marketing they provided restraint, balance and understanding—critical elements that would be lacking if a marketing viewpoint along were represented. Many "think" sessions were held with two doctoral candidates, Phillip A. Hines, whose major is public administration, and Michael L. McManus, whose major is human relations. The ideas resulting from these sessions with "nonmarketers" are appreciated very much. Finally, I wish to thank Mrs. Margaret Snedden for quietly, courteously, and expeditiously converting extremely rough drafts into a finished manuscript.

JOHN M. RATHMELL

THE SERVICE SECTOR

An introduction of services to marketing

WHAT ARE SERVICES?

During the next week or month why don't you conduct an experiment? Keep a record of every purchase you make in which you come away empty handed. For example, you may make a long-distance telephone call or send a telegram; since you are a student you will probably pay rent or you may lease an automobile for a short period of time; perhaps an insurance premium is due; during your travels you may pay a highway toll; you may reimburse some governmental authority for trash disposal or water service; a dental bill may fall due; or you may pay interest to a bank for a personal loan or pay tuition to your school.

In each transaction, you have "nothing" to show for your purchase. In everyday language, you have purchased a service.[1] To be more precise, you have purchased an intangible product. Upon completing the experiment you could determine your approximate total purchases for the period and from that ascertain the percentage of your expenses incurred for intangible products (hereafter called services, in keeping with conventional terminology). You will be surprised at the distribution. Commonly cited figures place consumption expenditures for services between 40 percent and 50 percent of the total; yours may be higher because of your status as a student.

A review of the preceding examples quickly discloses the great variety of organizations that market services—private profit and nonprofit businesses and institutions as well as local, state, and national public enterprises or agencies. As a result, the marketing of services involves much more than the conventional concepts of business organization and management. The first major objective of this book is to demonstrate the appropriateness of applying marketing concepts and practice to the many institutions and agencies that market services but which may have never been included under the rubric of business or marketing.

When attempting to define or describe an area of economic activity accounting for close to 50 percent of the marketplace, one encounters a dilemma: over-generalization is inaccurate and uninformative; over-specialization is unmanageable and can lead only to confusion. In this chapter, the various characteristics which differentiate services from goods are discussed. Next, all of the various meaningful approaches to classifying services are considered. Finally, appropriately discriminating classifications are identified for use in the balance of the text. This process is designed to answer the chapter title question: What Are Services?

WHY SERVICES HAVE GROWN

An extended discussion of the origin of services is not appropriate here yet the following observations suggest that historical research on the subject would contribute to understanding our current economy and prove to be a fascinating project in itself.

It appears that our ancestors purchased few services. Domestic service performed in private households is a classic example even though the transaction may not have been voluntary on the part of the seller in many instances; entertainment is another. Whether craftsmen were producers of goods only, or in addition, sold their services in the manner of the modern-day repairman is not known.

Throughout history it is likely that the need for services has been greater in urban centers than in the countryside because neither the means nor the requirement of self-sufficiency were present to the same degree in the city. So long as our society was mainly a rural one, services and their marketing remained in the background.

On the other hand, services sold to industry and trade are more evident. Private banks and insurers and goods transport are obvious examples. The services activities of the European trading companies in colonial times are also cited. The wide use of mercenaries in the military was an early service sold to governments.

From the above a tentative generalization emerges: In the evaluation of production and consumption, the *relative* importance of services as a resource input has grown more slowly on the production side than it has on the consumption side.

Consumer Services

A number of forces have fostered the growth of the service sector. At base, *consumer* services contribute to the quality of life. As societies advance, the marginal utility residing in additional increments of goods declines. Of course, the quality of food, clothing, and shelter improves, but the consumption of goods is finite. This decline in the desire for more goods has been accentuated in recent years by a reaction against materialism in our life style. The search for more meaningful experiences, more vivid activities is in the ascendency. The acquisition of more and more artifacts is no longer the only or primary goal, although it has by no means disappeared. In the vernacular of the day, "doing (not owning) one's own thing" is an appropriate description. Reduction in family size means a reduced need for goods and increased time for cultural activities, recreation, and travel. The increase in leisure or discretionary time encourages the purchase and consumption of services whose consumption is a function of time such as participation and spectator sports, education, and travel. Conversely, the consumption of most goods is seldom perceived as a function of time. Higher levels of education stimulate an awareness of opportunities for self-fulfillment; it is submitted that self-fulfillment results from experiences rather than ownership. Utility lies in experience rather than possession. At the same time, more mundane activities are contracted out or delegated to others who offer their services in a productive capacity. Existence is more complex. Just as the ultimate consumer cannot possibly be an expert on every *thing* he buys, he cannot be an expert on everything that must be *done*. He must buy the services of experts. And this is not a bad idea. Economies in scale of operations and specialization are possible in many services—with some restraints, of course: if such economies were pushed to their ultimate, there would be no service. Finally, in our political-economic system the leverage public agencies have for advancing the well-being of their constituencies lies in the performance of services rather than in the production of goods. The growing acceptance of the need for assuming this responsibility is self-evident.

Nonconsumer Services

Three major reasons can be mentioned for the growth of services purchased and consumed by other than ultimate consumers: *industry, institutions,* and *government.* The benefits from specialization is one reason. Thus, an educational institution delegates housing and feeding to a service organization specializing in housing and feeding. And a business organization delegates advertising to an agency that specializes in advertising. The second reason is the combined impact of rapid technological change and the knowledge explosion. Business organizations are engrossed in the day-to-day crises of the firm and the need for achieving short-term success. In order to keep abreast of technical breakthroughs and newer understandings, business enterprises and nonprofit institutions turn to service organizations whose "stock-in-trade" is knowledge, typically the consulting firm. Third, the desire for flexibility points to the purchase of many nonconsumer services as they are needed rather than to their institutionalization within the enterprise in the form of fixed cost departments. For example, most organizations contract with marketing research firms to do field surveys rather than staff up to do it themselves. Similarly, the organization may call upon the services of an executive search agency when the need arises rather than institutionalize this type of sporadic activity within.

CHARACTERISTICS OF SERVICES

Aside from the common element of intangibility, services have other characteristics which differentiate them from tangible products and so imply that the concepts and practices of marketing in the service sector differ from those in the goods sector. Put another way, the common statement, "the marketing of goods and services" is imprecise since the expository material which follows the statement typically focuses on the marketing of goods. Thus, a second major objective of this book is to ascertain the extent, content, and practice of marketing in the service sector.

Primary Characteristics

First, since there is no transfer of ownership in the sale of a service, relationships between buyer and seller and control over the use of the product are indeterminant. Upon transfer of possession in the sale of a tangible good, the buyer's control over the use of the product is absolute, except for some rather limited restrictions imposed by lenders in credit sales. Buyers of food, clothing, appliances, machine tools, and stainless steel are not dependent upon the seller in their consumption or industrial use of the goods purchased. In service transactions buyers are often dependent on the seller during the consumption and industrial use of purchased services. Whether the seller be a professional football team, a hospital, a public utility, or a lawyer, for example, the buyer is never completely independent of the seller until the service has been consumed or used. Consumption or use is not possible without the participation of the seller.[2]

A second and related differentiating characteristic of services lies in the interrelation of production and consumption. Goods are produced, sold, and consumed. Services are sold and then produced and consumed simultaneously. (This does not deny long-term benefits.) Consider the production and consumption of: electricity; a telephone call; a visit to a physician; an insurance policy; or a college education. Because of this concurrency of production and consumption there has been a commonly held belief that services are not marketed. This belief derives from the sequential view of production, marketing and consumption. In fact, as Figure 1.1 shows, in place of the one interface between buyer and seller of goods—marketing—there are two interactions between the buyer and seller of services—marketing and production. This concurrency in production or performance and consumption dictates a word of caution for marketing. Innovation and change in how services are marketed require close interaction between marketer and producer or provider of services.

A third characteristic is what might be termed the *in-being* nature of services. Whether the service seller be a university, a bank, a port

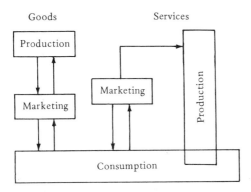

Figure 1.1   *BUYER-SELLER INTERFACE: GOODS AND SERVICES*

authority, a hospital, or a beauty parlor, the capacity and capability to produce a service must exist before any transaction can take place. Note that the word is *capacity,* not *inventory*. Services are not stockpiled and the flexibility inherent in inventory is absent. Peak-load, excess capacity, and production scheduling are important factors, since service marketers are faced with fluctuating demand. Unused service facilities are perishable products.

Fourth, with the exception of a few machine-intensive service industries such as electrical utilities and automated telephone systems, uniform performance standards are difficult to attain. Not only do performance standards vary from one service seller to another (compare television stations, consulting firms, and health care agencies, for example) but the quality of a single service seller may vary from buyer to buyer. (Consider variations in the performance of advertising agencies, transportation facilities, and psychiatrists in the performance of their services for various buyers.) A moment's reflection shows that the difficulty in achieving performance standards derives in part from the inherent inflexibility of the service sector discussed above and in part from the "human-intensive" nature of many services. However, performance standards become more plausible as services convert from human- to machine-intensive categories. Support goods which must be in place before a service is sold, such as an x-ray machine or a telephone exchange, and facilitating goods, such as a physician's thermometer, the golf player's clubs, or programmed learning machines are examples. Professional requirements for entry and possible government licensing are also designed to reduce variations in performance.

Fifth, there is a need to reconsider the traditional functions of marketing as they relate to services. The functions of *exchange* (buying and selling) are present, of course, even though the means of establishing contact, negotiating, and contracting vary widely within the service sector and in comparison with the exchange of goods. The functions of *physical supply* must be recast: transportation is viewed as a concept of location of the service facility and storage is conceptualized as available capacity to perform a service. One of the *facilitating* functions, risk-taking, warrants particular attention. Because of the simultaneous nature of performance and consumption and the very intangibility of the service, the service seller is much more dependent upon the good faith of the buyer. Most services are paid for after they are performed; they cannot be repossessed; possession cannot be maintained until payment; and services are not available as collateral. For example, advertising media and space and time buyers have financial problems if advertisers and their agencies are slow in paying for print and broadcast advertising which has been created and communicated and no longer exists. Sellers of professional services face the same problem. Educational institutions have been quite successful in shifting the risk to the buyer; hospitals view the patient as collateral as a means of risk reduction although insurance has largely eliminated this practice.

Secondary Characteristics

In addition to these primary characteristics of services, secondary or derivative differentiating characteristics can be identified. Services cannot be purchased and resold although service sellers are often represented by agents—insurance and travel agents for example. One seldom speaks of the price of a service. Rather it is expressed in terms of fee, rate, tuition, or premium. Similarly, a service buyer is seldom referred to as a customer. Rather, he is a depositor, client, policyholder, spectator, patient, or student. With the exception of utilities and transportation, services are nonpolluting relative to the production and consumption of goods. Some would argue that this characteristic alone makes expansion of services over goods mandatory if environmental disaster is to be avoided. Finally, since services cannot be owned there can be no pride of possession but there very well can be pride of performance. That is, there must be some symbolic value for the buyer in watching a leading baseball team, in attending a "name" university, or in being the client of a nationally recognized legal firm.

Some aspects of the service sector are characterized by heterogeneity rather than commonality in contrast with goods. (1) A much greater variety of institutions offer services, as noted earlier. Almost all goods are purchased from profit-making private enterprises. Services are purchased not only from these conventional organizations, but also from professional people, from private nonprofit institutions, from craftsmen-entrepreneurs, and from public agencies. (2) Price-making procedures may be highly regulated or they may derive from a policy of pricing according to ability to pay; the actual price may result from highly sophisticated analysis or pure hunch. (3) The capital equipment needed to provide one unit of service varies from that of a public utility and railroad to that of the teacher and consultant. (4) Because of the heterogeneity of the institutions which market services, quite varied promotional media are utilized ranging from a university's announcement, to the lawyer's formal business card, to the more conventional advertising of the television network, the bank, and the insurance company.

The thrust of this section has been to suggest that the marketing of services is sufficiently different from the marketing of goods to warrant special consideration. The service product is different; the reasons for buying services are different; and the means of marketing them are different. Put another way, if there is agreement that "goods and services" are marketed then it must be accepted that services are products, that they are priced, and that they are promoted; that marketing programs for services are planned, executed and evaluated; and that the marketing effort of a service organization is organized and staffed. That these conclusions apply to consultants, nonprofit "think-tanks," baseball teams, banks, and beauty parlors suggests some of the conceptual difficulties which will emerge on subsequent pages.

The Service Sector Market for Goods

Even though the differentiating features of services as contrasted with goods have been emphasized it should be noted that there is a substantial *support* goods component in the production and consumption of services, varying, of course, from service to service. Many service industries require heavy investments in capital goods before a single unit of service can be sold. Utilities, transportation, education, and communications fall in this category. The professor's books, the motel's rooms, the bank's lending resources, and the railroad's rolling stock are not inventory but means of services production.

In addition, many services require *facilitating* goods, usually provided by the seller but often by the buyer. The house that is rented and the automobile that is leased, the telephone receiver, the student's books, and the great variety of recreation equipment are examples. In fact, services can be ranged on a continuum of need for support goods and facilitating goods: extremes of the former are illustrated by the telephone system and the professor-consultant and of the latter by the physician and the concert singer.

Thus, as the service sector grows in importance demand will also grow for goods which must be installed before services can be offered and for goods which are used up in the provision and consumption of services.

CLASSIFICATION OF SERVICES

By Type of Seller

Three major ownership arrangements are evident among the marketers of services. The great majority are owned by private individuals who share in the profits and bear the losses. Another group of organizations which sell their services are also privately owned but not for profit. Private educational institutions, artistic groups such as symphony orchestras and museums, and some insurance companies are examples. Finally, some enterprises which market their services are owned by the public and managed by government. These include many public utilities, local transportation systems, state and national parks, and some forms of insurance. In addition to these major types of ownership, hybrid or mixed ventures where private and public ownership and management are intermixed are becoming increasingly common—COMSAT and AMTRAK, for example.

Sellers of services can also be classified according to their source of income. Private profit-making enterprises, be they corporations, partnerships, or proprietorships (the latter two, based on professional or craft skills, predominate in a number of service industries) are dependent upon the sale of their services for income. The income of private nonprofit enterprises is derived in part from the sale of their services and in part from donors.[3] Public enterprises may receive all of their income from the sale of services, or, if that source is inadequate, from taxation. In the case of these enterprises, steps are being taken to convert them from a condition of partial dependence on the public treasury to a fully self-supporting status.[4]

Trends are apparent in the movement of service organizations from one income-producing category to another. Private nonprofit organizations are shifting to the public category, universities and hospitals, for example; private profit-making enterprises are entering services traditionally assigned to other types of organizations, private mail service and technical education are examples; and, as has already been noted, publicly owned service organizations are competing in what were formerly private enterprise areas: transportation, insurance, employment and recreation, for example. Major social issues proceed from the intersects of private and public services: health care, education, and health insurance, for example, in terms of both product and price. On one side market forces are the prime determinants, on the other, political and moral forces. Where they intersect there are discontinuities of major proportions leading to confusion and unrest. Resolution of these issues, short of abolishing the intersects, is not easy.

By Type of Buyer

Individual and household consuming units make up one major type of service buyer. Most personal services and recreational services are purchased by individuals; household operations and consumer financial services are typically purchased for household consumption. Insurance, legal services, and transportation may be purchased and consumed by either individuals or households.

Industry is the second major type of service buyer. The word "industry" must be given a very broad interpretation: it includes agriculture, mining, manufacturing, trade, other service establishments, both profit and nonprofit, and government. Some industrial services are intended to improve or facilitate functional performance: transportation, utilities, building maintenance and industrial feeding, for example. Others make their contribution to industry at the decision-making level: business consulting, legal services, advertising agencies, and engineering services, for example.

By Buying Motives

Why people buy what they do has commanded the attention of behavioral scientists and marketing people for many years, yet no unanimity has been achieved. The rational-emotional dichotomy is the most widely enunciated but it is being increasingly questioned; the objective and symbolic characteristics of various types of goods have been cited as influential factors in decisions to buy; and others see consumers as buying from habit, out of impulse, or after planning a purchase.

To what extent generalizations regarding consumer motivation in the purchase of goods apply to service purchases is unknown. Services are not visible; they are performed for or by the buyer. Decisions to buy some services are so universal that motives to buy are irrelevant: electrical or postal services for example. Because services are not owned, cannot be accumulated or displayed, and because of the buyer's greater dependence on the service seller, the purchase of both consumer and industrial services is likely to proceed from rational buying motives rather than emotional and to be planned rather than on impulse.

The so-called emotional motives play a role in decisions to buy personal care, health care, and recreation services. And certain "visible" services are undoubtedly purchased for their status or prestige symbolism: where one travels or the forms of entertainment in which one indulges.

Certainly, this is not the last word in classifying services according to buying motives. Much more must be learned about both buying motives, per se, and the nature of service products.

By Buying Practice

Services may be contracted for or purchased on a unit-by-unit basis.

Under the former arrangement, service facilities are in being to meet the concurrent production-consumption characteristic. Many communication and utility services at both the consumer and industrial levels are so characterized.

Some contractual purchases of industrial services anticipate production and consumption at regular intervals: industrial feeding, building maintenance, employee health check-ups, for example.

At the consumer level the use of contracts is more common in the purchase of services than of goods. In addition to typical communication services (telephone and television cable) and utility services (electricity, water, and garbage disposal), other consumer services such as financial and insurance add to a substantial share of consumer services purchased on a contractual basis.

Services which are purchased as needed typically do not make use of the contractual arrangement. Most personal services and business services of the managerial type are in this category. Shoe repairs, personal care, entertainment, and automobile repair services are examples at the consumer level; industry and institutions purchase consulting services and other specialized talents as needed. (Consulting on a retainer basis is an exception.) Similarly, some services are purchased on a unit-by-unit basis to meet unanticipated needs: unscheduled medical help, legal, and funeral services are examples.

If any trend is evident, it is in the direction of an expansion of contractual arrangements, particularly at the industrial level. The invisible nature of services and the buyer's typical unfamiliarity with them lead to the conclusion that a contractual arrangement is more productive than the necessity for repeated buying decisions.

The purchase of services may or may not vary seasonally. A review of some of the above examples discloses services whose demand knows no season. On the other hand, others are characterized by demand patterns which fluctuate with changes in the climate. The demand for still other services is derived from goods whose production or consumption have seasonal characteristics. Industrial demand for financial and transportation services falls in this category; at the consumer level the preparation of automobiles and real estate for climatic strains are examples.

Many consumer goods are purchased for gift-giving and thus have extreme variations in demand as occasions for giving gifts come and go. Because our culture tends to associate a gift with a good, variations in the demand for consumer services for this reason are not common. Recreational travel is an expanding exception to this generalization.

The familiar classification of goods into convenience, shopping, and specialty categories is applicable to buying practices in the service sector. The reader can quickly identify low-priced services and those involving a minimum of skill as "convenience services." The appellation "shopping services" includes only a modest segment of the range of consumer services relative to its goods counterpart. Inability to inspect, lack of pleasure in shopping for services, and lack of the symbolism in ownership incentive may account for this. On the other hand, "specialty services" are relatively more common than specialty goods. It is not uncommon for consumers to go out of their way to purchase services from specified banks, entertainers, physicians, lawyers, and personal care establishments. Industrial services, on the other hand, are more likely to be treated as "shopping services." Advertising and consulting services are purchased in this way; many functional services are purchased on a specification-bid basis, also a manifestation of a "shopping service."

In addition to the temporal and spatial characteristics of buying practices in the service sector discussed above, they can also be classified according to buying responsibility characteristics. At the consumer level, personal services are, by definition, purchased by the consumer of them. Consumer services which are consumed by the household are purchased either by the head of the household or jointly. The view of the housewife as "purchasing agent" for the family does not hold for services to the extent that it may in the purchase of tangible goods. Similarly, seldom is a consumer service purchased by one person for consumption by another. Where industrial services are purchased frequently and involve substantial funds, functional departments have responsibility for buying: finance, transportation, insurance, and advertising are examples. Infrequently purchased industrial services and those involving small amounts of money may be purchased by the user department (the marketing department purchasing the service of an employment agency for example). In the case of industrial "convenience services," the purchasing department will have responsibility for acquiring them.

By Product Characteristics

Most services are found at two extremes in terms of their product characteristics: either they are completely uniform as in the case of public utilities or each service product is patterned to the needs of each purchaser. Relative to the goods sector there are few services with product "lines" from which to choose. Life insurance is an example of the exception and the range of choices offered by motels or hospitals is another.

By Degree of Regulation

Some of the characteristics of services discussed previously and the reader's own experience attest to the substantial dependence of the buyer on the seller's performance in a service transaction. The mystery of the service, the difficulty of comparing and inspecting alternative service offers, the rather nebulous nature of just what performance is in the case of many services, and the impossibility of recalling ineffective services are some of the barriers to equality between buyer and seller in the service marketplace. To redress this imbalance, regulations have been enacted and more are being proposed.

At one extreme are services which are subject to extensive public regulation, much more extensive in fact, than that encountered in the goods sector. These services include the various utilities, many financial services, transportation, and communications. Within each of these classes of services the incidence of regulation varies: compare telephone and television, electricity and bottled gas, commercial banking and installment loan companies. A second class of services is generally subject to the same public regulations imposed on the marketing of goods: hotels and motels, theaters, for example. A third group of services are currently largely unregulated by any public body. These include personal and business services of a craft or professional nature: repair services of all kinds, legal and medical services, and the services of professional athletes.

The trend is toward more public regulation. While the overall subject of services and public policy will be treated in a later chapter it should be noted here that the high level of buyer dissatisfaction in the performance of many currently unregulated services is likely to expand the requirements that services be licensed, that minimal service skills be demonstrated before they can be offered for sale, that standards of performance be established, and that provisions for redress be promulgated.

In the case of professional services such as accounting, medicine, and law, most constraints are imposed on practitioners by the profession itself rather than by statute. The right to remove professional practitioners for failure to meet standards established by the profession has no counterpart in the marketing of goods.

It should also be noted that both the public and self regulation of services apply only to private profit-making service enterprises. Services which are sold by nonprofit institutions are outside the jurisdiction of regulatory bodies. From a marketing standpoint, there is no reason why this should be so, especially where they compete with regulated profit-making enterprises. Public enterprises are subjected to a different type of regulation. Since they are operated for the public, are "owned" by the public, and are financed to some degree (unless completely self-supporting) by the public, provision is made for some form of accountability to the public. Unfortunately, accountability is limited to the use of public funds and not to the quality of the output of the public enterprise.

Finally, local and state regulation is more common in the service sector than in the goods sector. Relatively few service enterprises are interstate in scope because size incentives are absent (communications and transportation services are obvious exceptions). Personal services are primarily intrastate because of the nature of the product sold. Similarly, since services are neither inventoried nor transported, their sale and purchase tend to be localized.

A Synthesis

The preceding discussions of various approaches to the classification of services have drawn heavily on traditional concepts of marketing and, therefore, marketing as it pertains to tangible goods. Even when services are extracted from the traditional approach and environment with their goods orientation, some conventional classifications are still appropriate, some are discarded, and new ones must be created. The following service classifications appear to be the most discriminating and will be used throughout the balance of this text. In order to present a rounded synthesis, some redundancy is unavoidable. Table 1.1 seeks to integrate these various classifications as nearly as possible.

First, some services are exclusively or primarily performed for consumers; others are exclusively or primarily performed for nonconsumers, that is, businesses, institutions, and governments. For example, many household maintenance and personal care services are exclusively of the consumer variety; passenger automobile repairs and life insurance are *primarily* consumer services; the services of consulting firms and advertising agencies are *exclusively* nonconsumer in nature; and financial and legal services are *primarily* devoted to the nonconsumer area.[5]

Second, services may be primarily human-centered or primarily machine-centered. That is, the utility of the service to the buyer derives largely from the performance of a human being or a machine. Legal, medical, spectator sports, and many other entertainment services fall in the former category; utilities, transportation, and communications services in the latter.

Third, services may be classified as large, medium, or small in such absolute terms as dollar investment, sales volume, or number of employees. Compare a utility with a law office, for example. Within each service category the same division can be applied. When looking at the service sector in total, either very large or very small enterprises seem to predominate.

Fourth, the classification of services into private profit, private nonprofit, and public enterprise categories will prove important as the various crosscurrents at work are considered. For example, private nonprofit educational institutions are converting to public status while private profit-making enterprises are entering the education service field. In urban centers private profit services such as transportation are giving way to public enterprises whereas at the federal level increasing efforts are being made to shift responsibility for services from the public to the

Table 1.1

PREVAILING CHARACTERISTICS OF SERVICE SECTOR

Nature of Service	Type of Buyer		Character of Service Producer		Character of Selling Enterprise			Absolute Size		Type of Regulation		
	Consumer	Non-consumer	Man-Centered	Machine-Centered	Private Profit	Private Nonprofit	Public	Large	Small	Public	Self	None
Communications	X	X		X	X		X	X		X		
Consulting and Business Facilitating		X			X						X	X
Educational	X	X	X			X	X	X	X	X		
Financial	X	X	X		X			X	X	X	X	
Health	X		X		X	X	X	X	X	X	X	
Household Operations	X		X	X	X		X	X	X	X		
Housing	X	X	X	X	X				X			X
Insurance	X	X	X		X		X	X		X	X	
Legal	X	X	X		X				X		X	
Personal	X		X		X		X		X			X
Recreational	X				X	X	X		X			X
Transportation	X	X		X	X		X	X	X	X		X
Miscellaneous	X	X	X	X	X	X	X	X	X	X	X	X

private profit sector. Political philosophies and performance efficiencies are, of course, intertwined and the pendulum shifts back and forth with the ebb and flow of various views of the political economy. Since the Depression of the thirties the production and marketing of services by public enterprises has been in the ascendency. Currently the balance shows a mixed pattern. The future is uncertain.

Fifth, it can prove useful to keep in mind the groups of services which are rather sharply differentiated in terms of the extent and nature of regulation. Some are highly regulated by government agencies; others function within formal group regulations relating primarily to ethical conduct and performance; others are subject to regulations applying to all enterprises; some (nonprofit) are unregulated; and public enterprises must account for the use of public funds.

Finally, services can be classified according to their function: communication, consulting and business facilitating, educational, financial, health, household operations, housing, insurance, legal, personal, recreational, transportation, and miscellaneous. In the next chapter exactly what is and what is not included in these 13 classifications will be detailed.

In examining Table 1.1, it should be stressed at this stage in our understanding of the service sector that the characteristics of each type of service as shown by the Xs are intuitively determined. A single X on one row under any major column heading signifies inclusion of the total service category. Two or three Xs indicate that the service category is found in a variety of situations.

FOOTNOTES

1. Because service marketing has not achieved the structure and acceptance of conventional marketing, our terminology, concepts, and general understanding are imprecise and incomplete. Accordingly, the author intends to avoid doctrinaire approaches and leave to future marketing students the rewarding project that the process of redefinition, reformulation, and refinement offers.

2. In the consumption of some services, the proficiency, knowledge, and experience of the consumer can substantially affect the quality of consumption. This is particularly true of education, music and the performing arts, spectator and participant sports, and consulting services.

3. See Benson Shapiro, *Marketing in Nonprofit Organizations* (Cambridge, Massachusetts: Marketing Science Institute, 1972), p. 5.

4. For example, the Bay Area Rapid Transit District is required by law to cover its operating expenses out of sale of its transportation service. Also, it is the intent of the new Postal Service to finance its operations from sale of its services.

5. For most services, consumer or user statistics identifying type of consumer are not available; therefore, distinctions between consumer and nonconsumer are largely deductive. For some they can be approximated where gross and personal consumption expenditures are computed by the federal government.

THE CHANGING FACE OF UTILITIES MARKETING

David K. Hardin

Illustrates the need to utilize marketing and particularly marketing research in a regulated service industry.

It takes no great brilliance to have noticed that public utility marketing functions are undergoing dramatic changes. No longer is the utility marketing objective one of maximizing the utilization of a particular energy product, be it electricity, natural gas, bottled gas, or some combination. Today, it is harder and a lot more challenging. Today's utility marketing job is one of increasing profitability and long-term customer satisfaction with limited available resources.

Today's utility marketer faces the difficult task of having to make *choices* between various markets and services to promote. Historically, the marketing problem has been more simply to seek enlarged revenues from new and existing customers.

The purpose of this discussion is to look at these two basic questions: (1) What is the role of marketing in today's public utility? (2) How can the conflict between rising customer needs and limited energy availability be handled to insure long- and short-term profitability?

The New Role of Marketing

Today's utilities marketer has to decide not only whom to satisfy, but what specific customer groups and markets to *risk losing* due to resource limitations. Does he seek the new residential development business or the new industrial business? Does he meet current customer growth needs or seek new customers? And, at the same time, how can he best maintain favorable consumer attitudes to insure voter support for rate increase requests. In other words, the public controls profits in two ways—first, as a customer affecting volume and, second, as a voter affecting prices.

The author is Chairman, Market Facts, Inc. and was President, American Marketing Association, 1972-1973.

The problem is compounded by rising costs and increasing frustrations at the customer end resulting from poor service worker performance. Profit levels will increasingly be a function of consumer acceptance or rejection. It is obvious with today's cost pressures and consumer resistance to higher prices that the maintenance of current levels of customer service will not be possible. Yet, consumer goodwill has never been more important.

Thus utility management faces the need to make more efficient marketing decisions as never before. The average consumer will not support public utility profitability unless he is favorably disposed toward the utility and what it is doing for *him*. In making judgments on what areas and services are going to be maintained, enhanced, and reduced, management must keep this in the forefront of their minds.

The Need for Effective Communication

Clearly, if management is to maximize consumer benefits and minimize the frustrations with fixed available resources, there is a real need for effective communication with the market. The communication must provide for good feedback to the company.

At the very time that utilities need more customer contact, the contact is diminishing. Personal contacts via company stores, contests, and bill paying are declining. The computer has added a further impersonal note. For example, can a customer win a fight with *your* computer over a bill?

Management needs to keep current market segments happy enough to avoid losing them as permanent energy customers and, at the same time, to stay involved in those new markets, such as new housing where capital commitments in terms of energy source are not readily reversible. Once a new office building is heating with oil, it is lost as a gas customer. Basically, management has to have the answers to questions such as:

1. What benefits will the customer give up most happily?
2. What ecological stress will he permit?
3. What kinds of communication will do the best job of building credibility, acceptance, and understanding of the utilities' needs?
4. How can we reach the ecology enthusiasts who are disproportionately effective with rate commissions (and stockholder meetings)? How can we get on their team or, at least, off their *hate* list?

Determining What the Customer Wants

The problem of allocating limited resources to excessive demand calls for the judgment of Solomon. Top management today doesn't have the answers. More important, it doesn't know how to get them. Fortunately, however, the answers are available.

The problem is one of showing management that the market research technology is available to answer their questions. Market research today has powerful tools that are available to answer these key strategic questions, yet market research is too often looked at as a tactical statistical function—not a strategic planning tool. Moreover, it is too often true that researchers are not brought into the strategy issues and as a result, management doesn't know they can really provide the answers.

What are these techniques? How do they work? One basic technique is consumer tradeoff analysis. Tradeoff analysis measures the value system of each individual in the market. It is a proven method of finding out what people value most, and, more important, what they will be most willing to give up to get it. This technique has been applied already to a wide variety of marketing strategy problems.

The tradeoff method is based on a simple model of consumer choice behavior, representing an application of "conjoint measurement." It can be used to predict consumer response to new or modified levels of service.

Techniques of conjoint measurement have generated much interest in the field of mathematical psychology in the last few years, where the notion was first enunciated by Luce and Tukey (1964).[1] Green and Rao (1971)[2] describe the application of such methods to marketing research problems. The basic idea is that by providing consumers with stimuli from among which to choose, we can make inferences about their value systems based upon behavior rather than upon self-reports. The word "conjoint" has to do with the fact that we can measure relative values of things considered jointly which might be unmeasurable taken one at a time.

This establishment of value systems and the ability to measure them for populations of consumers has many advantages. First, it will permit management to find out what people are willing to sacrifice in order to keep something else. Second, and very important, it will provide a basis for giving an objective view to internal management and governing bodies about the real feelings of the population. All too often, extremists or involved groups, such as the ecology enthusiasts, have a disproportionate effect on government behavior.

This technique also provides management a balanced view of the willingness of the public to accept alternatives (brownouts in contrast to thermal pollution). Is the average person willing to give up some electricity or is he willing to risk nominal thermal pollution? How far will he go in each case? Or, would he rather pay a higher price for his electricity? The elasticity of each of these areas is measurable. The goal is to maximize satisfaction with fixed available resources. This technique, tradeoff analysis, is an established and vital tool in government and industrial circles, although the utility industries have largely ignored it.

Hypothetical Example

Let us suppose that electric utility services to consumers could be described adequately in terms of four attributes, each with three levels, as shown in Table 1.2. We assume that the "utilities" shown reflect the personal value system of a single individual. For each attribute these numbers show relative values to him of having each level of each attribute. They are obtained from preference data of a type to be described shortly.

Now our model says that this individual's relative acceptance for a utility service with the specific levels of each attribute is obtained by multiplying together the corresponding utilities. For instance, his relative acceptance of a 25 percent higher electric bill with occasional brownouts, only rural nuclear power plants, and limited free light bulb service (Service A) will be .33 x .34 x .42 x .31 = .0146. This is only a relative value, and only has meaning when compared to such values for other options. For instance, an electric service with today's prices, occasional brownouts, no nuclear power, and unlimited free light bulbs (Service B) has relative value of .57 x .34 x .31 x .49 = .0294. Therefore, according to the model, this respondent would prefer Service B to Service A.

Table 1.2

FOUR ATTRIBUTES OF UTILITY SERVICES

Electric Utility Bill	Same as today's	.57
	25% higher	.33
	50% higher	.10
Brownout Frequency	No brownouts	.51
	Occasionally during pro- longed hot spells	.34
	Frequently in the summer	.15
Presence of Nuclear Power Plants	Prohibited	.31
	In rural areas only	.42
	In metropolitan areas where power plants are now	.27
Light Bulb Service	Unlimited light bulb service	.49
	4 free bulbs a month only	.31
	No light bulb service	.20

We have now described the model, which depends on a set of "utilities" for each respondent, but we have furnished no hint of how to obtain these values. Certainly the respondent can't be asked to simply write them down for us, and in fact there is probably no direct way of obtaining them since he may be quite unaware of them. Fortunately, we are able to take rank-order preference data as input and from such data to produce estimates of service acceptance.

Consider services differing only in price and brownout frequency, and suppose a respondent were to state his rank order of preference for a set of these. Such data can be arranged as in Table 1.3

If we were to examine these data one attribute at a time, we would conclude that this respondent prefers no brownouts and lower prices. By looking at comparisons of two attributes, thereby we see that while this respondent's preferred service will cost the same as today's and have no brownouts, his second choice shows that he would accept occasional brownouts rather than pay more. Thus by considering these two attributes jointly, we can learn something about their relative importance in influencing his preferences.

Application

These kinds of data, developed for samples of each type of customer (consumer, industrial, etc.) can tell utility management what is needed in order to obtain the goodwill of their customers and maximize their acceptance and profitability. Thus, an effective allocation tool can be developed for each of the markets that management is trying to serve that will give them solid and unquestionable criteria for maximizing customer satisfaction and return on investment over the long run. Yet, how many managements today can say that they are doing anything but guessing?

No group today, neither utilities management, nor the government, nor any other group involved in making key decisions about energy applications, can long do without this kind of information. These kinds of data provide a basis for meeting the market's needs with minimum painful adjustment. They can be essential not only in determining the appropriate course of action, but also in determining utility

Table 1.3

ONE RESPONDENT'S RANK ORDER OF PREFERENCE: BROWNOUT FREQUENCY

Electric Utility Bill	No Brownouts	Occasionally During Prolonged Hot Spells	Frequently in the Summer
Same as today	1	2	5
25% higher	3	4	7
50% higher	6	8	9

marketing strategies (what performance areas to stress and emphasize to what markets) and also as evidence before rate commissions about the potential willingness of the public to accept alternative resources.

Unless the utilities can truly improve their marketing efficiency so that they can maintain the goodwill needed for the acceptance of continued profitability, while the public is being forced to give up some of the benefits to which they have become accustomed, the industry faces severe problems.

Marketing research can make a real contribution. This contribution potential must be communicated to top management in a convincing and impactful way. Achieving this goal is a real challenge for effective marketing and marketing research management.

FOOTNOTES

1. R. D. Luce and J. W. Tukey, "Simultaneous Conjoint Measurement: A New Type of Fundamental Measurement," *Journal of Mathematical Psychology* 1 (1964), pp. 1-27.

2. Paul E. Green and Vithala R. Rao, *Applied Multidimensional Scaling* (New York: Holt, Rinehart and Winston, Inc., 1972), pp. 1-292.

2

DIMENSIONS OF THE SERVICE SECTOR

No attempt has yet been made to inclusively and precisely define the service sector and establish its boundaries. Yet this is essential in the introduction of a relatively new area of marketing. Such an exercise could be unchallenging and distressingly austere. However, this should not be true here for we will be pushing back the frontiers of our concepts of production, marketing, and consumption.

For example, let us pursue the illustration which introduced the first chapter. Not all of the consumer's income is spent directly for the purchase of goods and services. Aside from that which is saved some of it is dispensed in the form of membership fees to a great variety of organizations. Another portion of income is channeled into voluntary contributions to religious and charitable organizations. In addition, a substantial percentage of earned income is paid out by the earner in the form of taxation. Are services purchased? Do transactions occur? What is purchased and what is sold? Certainly these income disbursements compete with goods and conventional services for the consumer's purchasing power.

Producers also pay taxes and make contributions and both accounts are likely to loom larger in the financial books of the firm as greater stress is placed on the social responsibility of business.

BOUNDARIES OF SERVICE MARKETING

It is clear from the above that boundaries must be established, albeit somewhat arbitrarily. Yet, in addition, an inclusive and internally consistent description of the service section is equally essential. The problems are manifold. Services are variously defined so that real-life descriptions are noncomparable. For example, some definitions include only the labor-intensive variety; most confine their concept of services to those purchased by ultimate consumers only; typically, only services sold by private businesses are considered; and still others view services as a residual economic activity after extractive and manufacturing industries have been accounted for.

Definitions and the Limitations

A service may be defined as any intangible product purchased and sold in the marketplace. The nature of the buyer and seller is a matter of indifference: the buyer may be an individual or household, a business, a nonprofit institution, or a government agency; the seller may be a business firm, a professional, a nonprofit institution, or a government agency. The important criterion is that a market transaction occurs. Intangibility means that the buyer comes away from the transaction with "empty hands." (As noted in Chapter 1, many tangible support or facilitating goods are usually necessary on both the seller and buyer side of the service "production-consumption" process.) That which is tangible or intangible is a sensory determination—there is nothing hidden or esoteric in the concept. A good can be handled; a service cannot. This type of definition minimizes the gray area.[1] Natural gas cannot be seen but it can be contained, therefore it is a tangible good; music can be heard but it cannot be handled and therefore is a service. When one purchases an automobile, he comes away from the transaction with ownership of steel, rubber, aluminum, and other materials; he has purchased a good. When one leases an automobile, he has purchased the right to use it, and this right is an intangible product or service; when the right of use which was purchased is consumed, the automobile returns to the possession of the lessor and the lessee (or buyer of the right of use) comes away "empty handed."

If not already evident, it should be noted that all definitions, interpretations, analyses, and viewpoints are expressed in a marketing context. Views of services which are based on economic, legal, or statistical conventions, on professional concepts, or simply on custom are superseded by those which are consistent with marketing thought and practice. The use of quotation marks is one evidence of a break with convention and custom. At times this attempt to integrate services and marketing will result in awkward and even improper expressions or concepts such as viewing Beethoven's Ninth Symphony as a product; quoting the price of a college semester; describing the promotional activities of an accounting firm.

"Services" Which Are Excluded

Various authorities have included certain activities and expenditures under the rubric "services" which do not square with a marketing approach and will therefore be ignored in the remainder of the book.

First, noneconomic transactions are excluded. These include the current wave of political, religious, social, and ecological causes which the consumer is urged to accept, support, or join. It is true that the cause might be viewed as an intangible product; it is also abundantly evident that a substantial amount of promotion is carried on to influence the public. The total effort might be described as a marketing analog because there is a partial similarity to marketing but it is not a marketplace phenomenon and would unnecessarily complicate the service concept offered here.

A second type of activity or transaction which is excluded is the voluntary contribution. It is, in a sense, a marketplace transaction in that funds are transferred and, presumably, some service is purchased. However, the "price" is determined by the buyer and not the seller, the amount varies from buyer to buyer, and the nature of the intangible purchased is difficult to identify. What does one buy when he places his contribution in the collection plate on Sunday? When he contributes to the United Fund? Is the service purchased some external, objective intangible such as the services of a Boy Scout executive or is it some internal, subjective satisfaction?

A third and substantial category of services excluded here are those which are supported *exclusively* through various forms of local, state, and federal taxation. The services of policemen and firemen, of the military, of public school teachers, of social service case workers, are so categorized. A transaction of sorts does occur and a service is certainly rendered. However, the transaction is nonvoluntary and the value of the service is not determined in the marketplace. And the relationship between payment made and service rendered is most tenuous; for example: (1) services purchased through the mechanism of the income tax and (2) the services purchased by a retired couple when they pay their school tax defy description. Both "transactions" bear little resemblance to the marketplace.

However, two caveats should be entered. First, many services which are purchased from public enterprises or agencies are included such as those rendered by publicly owned utilities, toll highways, and publicly owned museums, convention halls, and stadiums where admission is charged even though tax subsidies are also present. As a general rule, any service offered by a public institution wherein there is a direct relationship between the price paid and service rendered is included. Second, it is of interest to note that certain services flow in and out of the marketplace. Tax-supported police protection can be augmented by purchases of police and detective services in the marketplace, and private schools whose services are purchased by the user or the parents of the user are an option in place of tax-supported schooling. It is likely that this flow of services in and out of the tax-supported category will increase as more precise analytical techniques and systems approaches become more widely adopted. For example, home loan insurance was once the sole domain of the federal government. Now, private companies carry about as much insurance as the FHA evidently because they are more efficient and because they meet market needs.[2]

A fourth exclusion is that which the federal government identifies as "owner-occupied nonfarm dwellings." The government definition follows:

> The owner-occupied nonfarm dwelling—space rental value is one of the imputation items in the National Income and Product accounts. It is made to provide comparable treatment between rented and owner-occupied housing. It assumes that home ownership is a business producing housing services which are sold to the homeowners. The sales are estimated in terms of the sum for which the particular type of home could be rented, and the expenses of the home owners are deducted to obtain imputed net rent. The imputed gross total becomes consumer expenditures and imputed net rent becomes a part of the rental income of persons.

Government estimates place personal consumption expenditures for services in 1970 at $262,538,000,000. Of this total, $59,554,000,000 are allocated to this category.[3] Therefore, its exclusion is a major one.

However, from a marketing standpoint the need to provide comparable treatment between rented and owner-occupied housing is not present. When a family buys a house, it is buying a tangible good—just as tangible as food and clothing; on the other hand, a house rental transaction is the purchase of a service in the same category as an automobile leasing transaction.

A fifth "service" excluded from consideration is that which economists categorize as wholesale and retail trade.[4] The reason for including manufacturing in the goods sector accounts but wholesaling and retailing in the service sector accounts is obscure. It may derive from the ancient custom of treating trade as a tertiary economic activity; it may derive from the practice of considering sales clerks as service workers who add no form to the product in contrast with factory workers who do give it tangibility. In any event, marketers universally consider the wholesale and retailing of goods as part of the production process. Marketing economists would state that the extractor adds value and sells the good to the manufacturer, who adds value and sells the good to the wholesaler, who adds value and sells the good to a retailer, who adds value and sells the good to the consumer. Thus, the wholesaler and retailer are part of the goods production sector, not the service sector.

CONTENT OF THE SERVICE SECTOR

It is now possible to attempt a *marketing* description of the service sector. At the risk of redundancy, attention is focused on private, whether profit or nonprofit, and public enterprises and institutions which create intangible products which are priced and promoted in a great variety of practices by the creator of the service or his agent for sale in the American marketplace. A review of the data that follow shows that some services are sold to the ultimate consumer market exclusively, others are sold to the nonconsumer market exclusively, and still others are sold to both markets. In addition, it will be noted that some services are vertical in nature in that they are designed to meet the needs of a very specialized consumer or nonconsumer market segment whereas others are horizontal in that their demand is almost universally distributed throughout all segments of the American market.

Table 2.1 shows that approximately one-third of the nation's wages and salaries, proprietors' income, rent, corporate profits, and interest were generated in the service sector in 1970. The figure is overstated to the extent that income generated by the sale of real estate is included as income from a service when it is not. On the other hand, many services to industry of the vertical type are not included in the services total but are incorporated in the extractive and manufacturing accounts.

Were the practice of economists followed to include wholesale and retail trade in services computations, national income generated in the service sector would be over 48 percent.

Table 2.2 shows how consumers distribute their expenditures between services and other products, that is, durable and nondurable goods. Excluded from the service component are the rental value of owned homes and gas utility payments. These are expenditures which the government classifies as services whereas they are excluded here because they are not intangible services but tangible goods. Were they included, the services component would account for 42 percent of consumer expenditures.

Data on the purchase of services by industry and government are sketchy. One source estimates that 17.8 percent of manufacturing sector purchases in 1963 were from service industries and that 40.7 percent of all service sector outputs are sold to "other industries." Wholesale

Table 2.1

SERVICE COMPONENT IN NATIONAL INCOME - 1970*

(Millions of dollars)

	$	%
All industries, total	$795,887	100.0
Transportation	29,455	3.7
Communication	16,929	2.1
Electric, gas, and sanitary services	14,412	1.8
Finance, insurance, and real estate	87,033	10.9
Services	103,159	13.0
Government*	12,166	1.5
All services	$263,154	33.1

*Government enterprises only. General government excluded.
Source: *Survey of Current Business*, vol. 51, no. 7, pt. 1 (July 1971), p. 17.

Table 2.2

SERVICE COMPONENT IN PERSONAL CONSUMPTION EXPENDITURES - 1970*

(Millions of Dollars)

	Non-Service Component		Service Component	
	$	%		
Food and tobacco	142,945	100.0	0	0.0
Clothing, accessories, and jewelry	56,548	90.8	5,730	9.2
Personal care	6,059	60.0	4,042	40.0
Housing	62,412	68.4	28,812	31.6
Household operation	54,783	64.0	30,835	36.0
Medical care expense	8,584	18.2	38,684	81.8
Personal business	0	0.0	35,497	100.0
Transportation	59,978	77.0	17,893	23.0
Recreation	27,901	71.5	11,148	28.5
Private education and research	0	0.0	10,353	100.0
Foreign travel by U.S. residents	0	0.0	5,445	100.0
All expenditures	419,210	69.0	188,439	31.0

*Excluded: All services purchased through taxation; voluntary contributions to religious and welfare activities; and several accounts representing transactions by individuals between countries.
Source: Derived from *Survey of Current Business* (July 1971), p. 24.

and retail trade and real estate are viewed as services. Were they excluded, nonconsumer service sales would account for a larger percentage.[5]

Based on the classification system adopted in Chapter 1, a list of service industries is shown in Appendix A. The Standard Industrial Classification (SIC) list is not complete; many of the four-digit classifications are shown in the source to be made up of as many as 20 or 30 quite distinct services. In addition, the list is not precise; some services may be misclassified. But more importantly, the matter-of-fact listing suggests a false balance or equality of importance between services. For example, SIC 7392 includes business consultants and economists, computer programming services, marketing research, public relations counselors, and patent consultants to name a few. SIC 794 includes the many professional athletic clubs, sports promotion, and stadium operations. SIC 8221 is probably the most important service category of all for college students.

The reader is invited to scan Appendix A stopping at random points, and concentrating on the types of services which come to mind. He will be impressed either by the newness of the idea that these are opportunities for marketing management careers or by the fact that the particular service industries noted have never thought of themselves as being involved in marketing and therefore are likely candidates for a strong infusion of marketing know-how.

Finally, Table 2.3 shows various government service enterprises at

Table 2.3

LIST OF GOVERNMENT SERVICE ENTERPRISES

Federal:

 Alaska Railroad
 Army-Air Force Motion Picture Service
 Bonneville Power Administration
 Commodity Credit Corporation
 Direct Loan Program of Veterans Administration
 Emergency Credit Fund (Farmers Home Administration)
 Export-Import Bank
 Federal Deposit Insurance Corporation
 Federal Home Loan Bank Board
 Federal Housing Administration
 Government National Mortgage Association
 Federal Savings and Loan Insurance Corporation
 Housing and Urban Development Department
 Officers' and Enlisted Men's Clubs
 Panama Canal Company
 Post Office
 Postal Savings System
 Rural Electrification Administration
 St. Lawrence Seaway
 Southwestern Power Administration
 Southeastern Power Administration
 Tennessee Valley Authority

State and Local:

 Air and water transportation terminals and facilities
 Highway toll facilities
 Housing and community development activities
 Local housing and urban renewal
 Local public utilities
 Workmen's compensation funds

the federal, state, and local levels. Services are sold by them in place of, or in competition with, private enterprises. Some provide services for which private operations are not suited, particularly where the need for profit would conflict with the goals of legislation establishing the service.

Services and Consumption

The business school student may have been confused thus far by the repeated references to taxation, public enterprises, nonprofit institutions, and other institutions and activities normally outside the context of business operations, particularly outside the conventional concept of the marketing function. It has been necessary to broaden the concept of marketing in this way because services *are* provided by a much more varied set of institutions. At this point, an attempt will be made to integrate services into the totality of consumption.

Figure 2.1 shows the source, flow, and destination of all that is consumed by our society, giving "consumption" its broadest interpretation. The figure and accompanying notes are self-explanatory. Briefly, what is consumed is, in part, the result of marketplace transactions (voluntary exchange) and, in part, the result of political decisions as to how tax monies will be distributed (nonvoluntary exchange). The purveyors of goods and services are private or public institutions, agencies, and enterprises. All arrows end with the consumer; in other words, consumption is the end of all production no matter how remote it may be. The complex of lines at the top of the chart illustrates the great variety of transactions which take place in the production process.[6]

Unfortunately, the chart is not drawn to scale. This is the responsibility of the macro-economist. Were this to be done at periodic intervals, the growth and decline of various segments and flows could be discerned. The one constant would be, of course, the consumer.

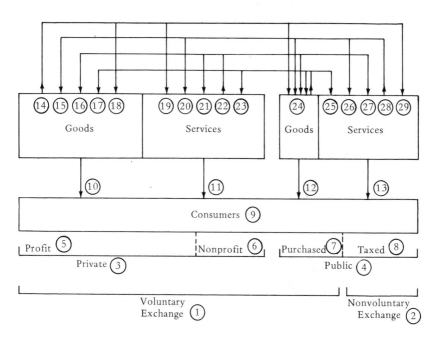

Figure 2.1   *SATISFACTION OF CONSUMPTION THROUGH VOLUNTARY AND NONVOLUNTARY EXCHANGE (NOT DRAWN TO SCALE)*

Satisfaction of Consumption Through Voluntary and Nonvoluntary Exchange

Key to Chart

1 All market transactions
2 All purchases through taxation
3 Transactions between consumers and private sellers
4 Transactions between consumers and public bodies
5 Transactions between consumers and retailers or lawyers (ex.)
6 Transactions between consumers and private universities (ex.)
7 Transactions between consumers and public bodies (postage, ex.)
8 Services rendered by public bodies: financed by taxes (protection, ex.)
9 Ultimate consumers
10 Food; automobiles
11 Telephone service; Red Cross
12 Government publications
13 Highway tolls; sewage treatment
14 Goods sold to other than ultimate consumers (computer hardware, ex.)
15 Commercial purchases of government services (voluntary or nonvoluntary) by goods-handling firms
16 Commercial purchases of private services (goods handling)
17 Voluntary or nonvoluntary purchases of government goods
18 Purchases of goods for resale or industrial use
19 Commercial purchases of goods by private services
20 Purchases of government services (voluntary or nonvoluntary) by private service firms or institutions
21 Purchases of private services by private services and institutions
22 Services sold to other than ultimate consumers
23 Voluntary or nonvoluntary purchases of government goods by private service firms or institutions
24 a. Purchases of private goods and services and government services by government goods producers
   b. Sale of government goods to private goods and services and government services producers
25 Purchases of government goods by government services
26 Purchases of government services by government services
27 Purchases of private services by government services
28 All sales of government services to other than ultimate consumers
29 Purchases of private goods by public services

NOTES:
1. Many services are offered by both private and public bodies: utilities, insurance, and outdoor recreation for example.
2. Mixed ventures (partly public and partly private) are not reflected on chart.

SERVICES IN OTHER COUNTRIES

Although our concern is with service marketing in the United States, its reality throughout the world should be acknowledged. Here, again, the problem of defining the boundaries of the service sector is present. In other countries there is a strong dependence on the primary, secondary, and tertiary industry classification with the third class including everything but agriculture and industry.

In terms of employment, a study of certain member countries of the Organization for Economic Cooperation and Development identifies four groups of countries classified according to the importance of the "tertiary sector" (commerce and services).[7] (1) Agricultural countries: growth of services is slow. (2) Partial industrialization: manpower shifting from agriculture to both industry and commerce and services. (3) Industrialization completed: manpower shifting from agriculture to commerce and services. (4) Agricultural manpower low: major employment shifts are from industry to commerce and services.

Data from the United Nations pertaining to market economies show that North America accounts for 46.1 percent of gross domestic product and 56.3 percent of "other" domestic product (financing, insurance, real estate and business services, social and personal services, and public administration and defense). Corresponding percentages for Europe are 30.4 percent and 26.4 percent and for East and Southeast Asia are 11.4 percent and 7.4 percent.[8]

These studies indicate the growth of services as economies move through various stages of development. Unfortunately, both are concerned with effects, not causes. They do suggest, however, that the "take off" phase of growth in services is to be found abroad.

FOOTNOTES

1. There is a gray area, though, and attempting to account for every product—good or service—can become ludicrous. For example, restaurants are not considered a service; they are, in reality, an alternative channel in food marketing. But is not the restaurant's product a service—that is, does not the utility of the restaurant's service rest in its intangible element rather than in the physical product? Similarly, how would one classify *The Executive Voice,* a management intelligence service on tape cassette from *Fortune* magazine? One can only say that the existence of exceptions in marketing classifications must be accepted. We are not dealing with immutable physical characteristics.

2. "Karl the Magic Man," *Time,* 17 January 1972, p. 59.

3. *Survey of Current Business,* vol. 51, no. 7, pt. 1 (July 1971), p. 24.

4. See, for example: Victor R. Fuchs, *The Service Economy* (New York: National Bureau of Economic Research, 1968) and Colin Clark, *The Conditions of Economic Progress* (London: Macmillan & Company, 1960), Ch. 9.

5. Thayer C. Taylor, "Selling the Services Society," *Sales Management,* 6 March 1972, pp. 23-30.

6. Goods received as gifts and services performed voluntarily are not included. Goods moving, and services rendered, within households and enterprises are not included even though the practice of transfer pricing is in effect.

7. Maurice Lengelle, *The Growing Importance of the Service Sector in Member Countries* (Paris: Organization for Economic Cooperation and Development, 1966), pp. 8-9.

8. *Statistical Yearbook 1971* (New York: Statistical Office of the United Nations, 1972), pp. 12-13.

KNOWLEDGE: THE BIGGEST GROWTH INDUSTRY OF THEM ALL

Gilbert Burck

Introducing new concepts and highlighting the problem of establishing the boundary and content of a complex and growing service industry.

. . . [T]he nation's measurable outlays for knowledge are bound to grow faster than the national product. Note the word "measurable." Much of man's exchange of knowledge, including his most interesting and original as well as his most intimate and deplorable communications, goes unmeasured. Only when people exchange money for knowledge can it be statistically measured and does it become part of GNP. Primitive man probably spent most of his time gabbling, haranguing, arguing, and otherwise exchanging information, often with the help of a club, but of course none of it was measured. As civilization overtook him and schoolmen and other information mongers began to be paid for their work, the measurable production and distribution of knowledge began to be significant; and with the invention of the printing press and the advent of the industrial revolution they really began to expand.

The production of measurable knowledge goes on expanding faster than the economy because it generates as well as feeds on economic growth. People spend more and more for information they feel or hope will help them cope with a rapidly changing and increasingly complex world, and they also spend more and more for information whose value to their economic well-being is marginal and tenuous. They can afford this increased outlay only because the economy is expanding faster than the population, and because their living standards are consequently rising. And by a happy but logical coincidence, the biggest single factor in the nation's rising productivity is the growth of the knowledge industry.

Extracts from Gilbert Burck, "Knowledge: The Biggest Growth Industry of Them All," Fortune *70 (November 1964), pp. 128-131, with publisher's permission.*

The whole U.S. knowledge industry may be conveniently divided into seven main groups:

1. Research and development, the business of unearthing "new" (mainly technical) knowledge and of putting it to use, has grown no less than fifteenfold since 1930, and now accounts for 10 percent of the industry.
2. Education, the business of retailing old knowledge and inculcating the habit of acquiring further knowledge, has nearly quadrupled since 1930, and accounts for about 45 percent of the industry.
3. Publishing and printing, mostly the business of selling timely, important, or amusing information in the marketplace, has grown tenfold since 1930, and accounts for 12 percent of the industry.
4. Entertainment, an omnium-gatherum that includes broadcasting, movies, spectator sports, plays, concerts, and phonographs and records, has grown 240 percent since 1930, and accounts for 6 percent of the industry.
5. Information machines, which enable industry to communicate knowledge and include everything from typewriters to computers, have grown about fourteenfold since 1930, and account for 8 percent of the industry.
6. Professional services, which contribute accounting, architectural, medical, and legal information mainly to business, have increased nearly threefold since 1930, and account for 9 percent of the industry.
7. The communication industry (to the extent it handles knowledge) has also grown threefold since 1930, and accounts for 7 percent of the industry.

1809420

The entertainment industry includes plays and concerts, spectator sports, movies, phonograph records, and broadcasting, and so encompasses a good deal more than mere entertainment by contributing a wide variety of items to man's store of knowledge. The theatre and concert hall are relatively insignificant in dollar volume ($433 million together in 1963), but they exert a pervasive influence by functioning as pilot plants of a sort for dramatic and musical culture that is broadcast or recorded; moreover, their gate over the past decade has been improving at close to 8 percent a year, twice as fast as that of spectator sports. The growth of local repertory theatres, such as Tyrone Guthrie's project in Minneapolis, appears to be only in its early stages.

The growth in the number of symphony orchestras, without benefit of state subsidy (which they enjoy in West Germany and Italy), has been phenomenal. Before the war, according to the American Symphony Orchestra League, there were some 600 orchestras; today there are 1,350, counting only organizations that perform an authentic symphonic repertory. They do not include chamber-music groups, whose precise number is large but unknown. The number of live symphonic performances seems bound to rise as people acquire the knowledge and understanding they need to enjoy a serious musical performance. Abetting this tendency is the phonograph and record business, which tripled in the past decade and grossed $1.6 billion in 1963. Americans buy nearly 60 percent of the world's records, and at least a third of the money they spend on them goes for what might be called non-junk.

Movies and broadcasting also contribute a great deal, worthwhile and otherwise, to man's store and exchange of knowledge. Radio-station revenues increased 16 percent between 1954 and 1958 and 30 percent since then; in 1963 they stood at $680 million. TV-station revenues rose 74 percent between 1954 and 1958 and 55 percent since then, and in 1963 stood at $1.6 billion. How much or whether the quality of these activities has improved during the past few years is, to say the least, debatable, but whether they will improve in the future is perhaps less uncertain. It is hard to imagine better-educated audiences putting up with some of today's fare.

The rest of the knowledge industry is accounted for in the main by services and machines that promote the nation's productivity by disseminating information efficiently and effectively. Professional services help business and individuals to use both the country's resources and its finished production with rising effectiveness. They include legal, financial, engineering, accounting, and medical advice, for which the U.S. laid out no less than $17.8 billion in 1963. The communication industry got paid $14.6 billion for transmitting knowledge in 1963, and without it the whole economy would be as crippled as if it were strikebound. It is true that the industry transmitted a great deal of useless or marginally useful information; Machlup estimates that a third of all telephone conversations are devoted to exchanging "pastime" knowledge—e.g., what Susie wore at the party. But the telephone provides another example of the fact that most information is a consumer product, not specifically calculated to advance any productive process. Both the communication and professional-service industries may well continue to grow, as they have been growing, faster than the national product.

. . . [T]he steady expansion of the knowledge industry will very likely go a long way toward eliminating many bothersome aspects of the unemployment problem. One of the convictions that animates many prejudices about the problem is that productivity will rise so much that men will have to work only three or four hours a day to produce everything they "need," and very soon will be confronted with the necessity for reducing working hours and for thinking up things to do in their new leisure.

This kind of extrapolation sounds a little absurd, and it is. Note the word "need." Man's appetite and capacity for buying things may be unlimited, but his physical needs are strictly limited. He can eat only so much by weight, can be only one place at a time, and can wear only one outfit at a time. His need for knowledge, however, is practically unlimited. If education teaches him anything, it is how much he has to learn and how to learn it; and the more he knows, the more he is driven to find out. The educated man is hard put to keep up with what is going on in his world, to say nothing of other interesting worlds. There is no "saturation point" for this need, and therefore no foreseeable ceiling on the number of people that can be employed in satisfying it.

3

INDUSTRIAL STRUCTURE AND PUBLIC POLICY IN THE SERVICE SECTOR

Table 3.1 shows changes in size and income of representative services over the past two decades. (Note that several of the time series do not cover 20-year periods.) Both in absolute and relative terms the data show some of the broad shifts in American tastes and goals. Consider: higher education income; health care expenditures; visits to national parks; and number of overseas travelers. Other figures reflect the rapid growth curve of relatively new service industries. Consider: revenue of commercial broadcasting stations; assets of savings and loan associations; attendance at professional football games; and the revenue of scheduled airlines.

Only about half of the service measures in Table 3.1 increased at a greater rate than the gross national product, current or constant dollars. Several reasons can be suggested for variations in the rate of change. (1) Most result from changes in demand. Consider the statistics for education, upholstery and furniture repair, hotels, recreation, and transportation. (2) Undoubtedly some of the variations reflect supply conditions. Note the statistics for health services and rental housing. In a number of instances the relatively slow growth rate reflects a lag in supply response to changing demand: the time needed to expand supply of medical and legal services can be shortened but risks are incurred. (3) Since the service sector has been treated as a residual by both economists and public administrators, supply has failed to keep pace with demand because evidence of growing demand simply was not available. (4) Both public and private nonprofit service providers are less sensitive to changing demand; this type of commercial sensitivity is often viewed as inconsistent with the nature of their enterprises. (5) Finally, it is argued that the regulated services—whether publicly- or self-regulated— are slower to respond to changing demand because of constraints imposed on the decision-making processes of the service provider.

As a matter of fact, each service is made up of its own unique conditions of demand and supply. Some of the variations in service trends are

Table 3.1

TRENDS IN SERVICES

($ in millions)

	1950	1970	Percent Increase
Communications:			
Postal service revenue	1,677	6,473	286.
Bell Telephone Companies: revenue	3,342	17,369	420.
Independent telephone companies: revenue	270	2,791	934.
Commercial broadcast stations (radio and television): revenue	550	3,945	617.
Consulting and business facilitating:[1]			
Advertising: number	7,706	8,185	6.
Business and consulting services: number	9,470	14,252	50.
Equipment rental and leasing: number	5,926	6,916	17.
Educational:			
Institutions of higher education: selected sources of income:			
Student fees	395	3,814	866.
Federal, state & local gov'ts	1,078	7,932	636.
Private gifts and grants	119	605	416.
Financial:			
Commercial banks: assets	170,500	581,500	241.
Mutual savings banks: assets	22,385	79,227	254.
Savings and loan associations: assets	16,893	176,183	943.
Health:			
Personal health care expenditures	10,400	58,752	465.
Physicians: number	232,697	348,328	50.
Dentists: number	87,164	115,610	33.
Hospitals: number	6,788	7,123	5.
Household operations:			
Electric utilities for public use: production (bil. kw.-hr.)	329	1,532	366.
Laundries: number[2]	30,269	111,926	270.
Upholstery and furniture repair: number[2]	13,305	19,418	46.
Housing:			
Renter occupied units	19,266	23,565	22.
Hotels: number[3]	16,741	13,947	(17.)
Motels and motor hotels: number[3]	21,310	26,213	23.
Insurance:			
Life insurance company premiums	6,249	21,679	247.
Legal:			
Lawyers: number	184,000	355,242	93.
Personal:[4]			
Barber, beauty shops: number	169,684	291,706	72.
Funeral services: number	18,387	20,191	10.

Industrial Structure and Public Policy in the Service Sector **39**

Table 3.1 (cont.)

	1950	1970	Percent Increase
Recreational:			
National parks: visits (1,000)	33,253	172,005	417.
Baseball: attendance (professional)	17,659	29,000	64.
Football: collegiate attendance	18,962	29,466	55.
NFL attendance	2,008	9,913	394.
Broadway shows: performances[5]	8,917	6,865	(23.)
Off-Broadway shows: performances[5]	1,883	8,819	368.
Major symphony orchestras: number[5]	28	28	0
Community symphony orchestras: number[5]	761	1,021	34.
Overseas travelers: number (1,000)	676	5,260	678.
Transportation:			
Railroads: operating revenue	9,924	12,500	26.
Scheduled airlines: operating revenue	558	7,131	1,178.
Motor carriers: operating revenue	4,276	15,437	261.
Gross National Product: current dollars	284.8	974.1	242.
Gross National Product: constant dollars (1958)	355.3	720.0	103.

( ) = Decrease

[1]U.S. Bureau of the Census, Census of Business, 1967, *Vol. V Selected Services—Area Statistics: 1963-1967.*
[2]See Footnote[1]: *1954-1967.*
[3]*1958-1967.*
[4]See Footnote[1]: *1954-1967.*
[5]*1955-1970.*
Source: U.S. Bureau of the Census, *Statistical Abstract of the United States: 1972* and *Historical Statistics of the United States: Colonial Times to 1957,* 1960.

easy to explain: railroads vs. scheduled airlines; hotels vs. motels; or amateur football vs. professional football. In most cases, however, explanations require careful appraisal by both the market analyst and the managers, professionals, or technicians within various service categories.

INDUSTRIAL STRUCTURE

The service sector is generally unconcentrated.[1] Table 3.2 reveals both the prevalence of noncorporate ownership and the ability of proprietorships and partnerships to generate substantial receipts in the service sector. Table 3.3 indicates that the extent of the corporate form varies within the service sector, and implicitly, suggests that concentration varies. Thus, the motion picture industry would be viewed as more concentrated than personal and repair services.

Central administrative offices serve as another surrogate measure of concentration. They are defined by the Census Bureau as offices whose primary functions are to manage and administer the activities of other establishments of the company. Within the "selected services" category consisting of 1,187,814 establishments in 1967 there were only 929 central administrative offices.[2] During the same year, 305,680 manufacturing establishments were served by 3,584 central administrative offices.[3]

Table 3.2

LEGAL FORMS OF BUSINESS: NUMBER AND RECEIPTS - 1969

(Percent)

	Corporations		Proprietorships	
	Number	Receipts	Number	Receipts
Manufacturing	50.	98.	50.	2.
Wholesale and retail trade	20.	78.	80.	22.
Transportation, communication, utilities	18.	94.	82.	6.
Financial, insurance, real estate	34.	82.	66	18.
Services	9.	50.	91.	50.

Source: Computed from U.S. Bureau of the Census, *Statistical Abstract of the United States: 1972*, Table 745.

Table 3.3

CORPORATE FORM OF ORGANIZATION: SELECTED SERVICES - 1967

	Percent Corporate Form
Hotels, motels, etc.	18.
Personal services	8.
Business services	21.
Auto repairs, etc.	15.
Miscellaneous repair services	8.
Motion pictures	56.
Other amusements and recreation	17.
All selected services[1]	13.

[1]Commercial services only. Discrepancy in prevalence of corporate form between this table and Table 3.2 is accounted for by inclusion of professional services such as physicians and lawyers in the latter.

Source: Computed from U.S. Bureau of the Census, *Census of Business, 1967, Selected Services: Miscellaneous Subjects, BC67-SS8*, 1971, Table 25.

Assuming the appropriateness of this measure, a much lower level of concentration in the service sector than in the production sector is evident.

Among service *corporations,* the overwhelming majority are privately held. Publicly owned service corporations are concentrated in the communications, transportation, and utility industries. Only recently have some of the consulting and business facilitating firms "gone public." Typically, publicly owned service firms are also capital-intensive services. The need for capital is greater and the investor has the visibility of physical assets. Where assets are principally in the form of people or ideas, and this applies to most services, public investors may be more reluctant to risk their funds.

Monopoly and Competition in Service Industries

The various concepts and philosophies of competition and monopoly reflect a predominantly goods orientation. This results naturally from the concurrent development of economic theory and the Industrial Revolution—a revolution in the production and marketing of goods. Thus, understanding of the theory and role of monopoly and competition in the service sector is fragmentary.

In general, to the extent that the variables and practices involved in the performance and marketing of services coincide with those of goods there need be no special treatment. However, services differ from goods in three major respects that can be only identified here. They do represent factors having a significant impact on the nature of monopoly and competition in service industries which are absent from the goods sector.

1. Formal and legal regulation substitutes for the marketplace. Regulation may authorize a monopoly in the case of utilities or an oligopoly in the case of transportation. No such condition formally exists in the goods sector.

2. There are ethical constraints on competition in professional services. The codes of ethics governing marketing activities of various service providers such as certified public accountants, lawyers, and the medical professions have explicit statements regarding the implementation of various price and nonprice competitive practices; certain of them are expressly "prohibited." No such prescriptions are found in the goods sector and if they were applied they would undoubtedly be viewed as collusive practices by state or federal antitrust agencies. Moreover, for a number of professional services, prohibitions against certain types of marketing activities are enforced by the state. For example, were a lawyer in the state of New York to advertise his services in a local paper, offering to prepare standard wills at a special discount price, to make the illustration extreme, he would be cited before the state's appellate court and, if found guilty, would be disbarred, that is, lose his license to practice. Subsequently, were he to continue to practice law he would be performing a criminal act. No such private regulation cum public support structure exists in the goods sector.

3. The nature of ownership and control in the service sector is quite mixed. As noted in Chapter 1, services are provided by private enterprises and institutions both for profit and not for profit and by publicly-owned agencies. Further, the extent of this mixed character is expanding. The purely public nature of mail service and the purely private profit character of rail transportation are being challenged both in concept and practice. Among the regulated services, regulations apply equally to publicly-owned and privately-owned enterprises even though their

accountability differs. Increasingly, all three types compete in varying combinations. (1) Private and public universities "compete" with each other and educational ventures owned by profit-making firms are a small but growing element; at the primary and secondary education level, the use of the education voucher is intended to inject market competition into the system, while performance contracting removes education from the tax-supported to the private profit category. (2) In communications, COMSAT and NET with their combinations of private and public control and financing compete with private enterprise. (3) Private and public health services and facilities find themselves increasingly competing. (4) Many people today rent from public housing authorities, a private service until recently. (5) Public participation in insurance may grow and eventually compete with private insurers to varying degrees. (6) In the area of entertainment and recreation, the ultimate consumer may buy these services from the three types. On the other hand, with almost no exception (retail operations on military bases is one) goods are manufactured and marketed by private enterprises for profit.

As the service sector takes on an increasingly mixed character new understandings of monopoly and competition are mandatory; generalizations from the goods sector do not suffice. For example: (1) Private testing laboratories for profit compete with private nonprofit testing laboratories, and to some extent, compete with the National Bureau of Standards, a public agency. One must earn a profit and pay income taxes thereon—the others do not. (2) Nonprofit hospitals seeking exception from the price freeze, in effect as this is written, protest that "they [Cost of Living Council] are treating us like a business."[4] Our contemporary views on competition and monopoly and industrial structure just do not accommodate such a heterogeneous institutional setting on the supply side.

PUBLIC POLICY AND SERVICE MARKETING

Services and government policy interact in interesting and unusual ways having an impact on marketing issues and practices. One is a cornerstone of the free market system: Ease of entry—should it be facilitated in order to encourage competition or should it be constrained in order to protect the consumer? Competition is a second cornerstone. How intensive should it be and in what forms among the various services? Does intensive competition improve or injure the quality of service performance—business consulting, auto repairing, or major league baseball, for example? The presence of innovative ideas both in product and practice is still a third characteristic of the free market system. Does public policy in the service sector encourage innovation or support the status quo?

At the strategic level, does public policy support service product specialization or diversification? Should *systems* of health care, or transportation, or communications, or entertainment be facilitated or restricted by public policy? Should price competition be encouraged or discouraged by public policies: consider, for example, education, air freight, advertising, or barbering. Should public policy strengthen or weaken contractual understandings between service providers and their agents and between service franchisors and franchisees?

Public policy in the service sector takes on a variety of forms which are quite similar to those found in the goods sector, but there are several exceptions. (1) Some services are restricted to public ownership: the Postal Service. (2) Others may be performed by private enterprises subject to varying degrees of restriction on marketing efforts, particularly pricing: consider public utility and telephone services. (3) Increasingly, public agencies are participating as partners with private enterprises in the performance of certain services: property insurance. (4) Some services are subsidized by government: ocean shipping. (5) As noted previously, some privately determined professional standards have the support of public policy: certified public accounting and dentistry.

The Regulated Services

As already noted, a substantial segment of the service sector is subject to regulation primarily by statute rather than regulation by market competition. In essence, the marketplace is accepted as an adequate protector of the public interest in the production and marketing of goods and in the performance and marketing of many services; however, for a variety of reasons which cannot be detailed here, public policy requires that statutes and public regulatory bodies are necessary to protect the public interest in the performance and marketing of certain services. Services in interstate commerce are regulated by the Interstate Commerce Commission, the Federal Communications Commission, the Federal Power Commission, the Civil Aeronautics Board, and the Federal Reserve Board. Counterparts are found at the state level to regulate the performance and marketing of intrastate services. The regulation of insurance has traditionally rested with state agencies.

A particularly vexing public policy issue is the unequal incidence of regulation of competing service providers. Compare, for example, the regulation of scheduled and nonscheduled airlines; of community antenna television and network television. Problems also arise from the fact that regulated services buy from unregulated suppliers.

While the incidence of regulation varies from service to service, marketing activities most likely to be regulated include the following: First, in some regulated service industries there are no competitors, electric utilities and domestic telephone services, for example; in other industries the number of competitors must be consistent with public need as determined by the regulatory body, broadcasting and air transport, for example. Second, regulated firms are often constrained with regard to their product line. In general, this restriction is a price paid by the regulated firm for the shield of regulation which protects it from the rigors of competition. Not all regulated firms support either the protection or the price. Third, pricing as an element of marketing strategy is invariably severely circumscribed.

A better understanding of the impact of regulation on marketing practice can be obtained from direct quotations of relevant passages in the act regulating rail transportation. Marketing interpretations are enclosed in brackets.

From the Interstate Commerce Act: (1) Before instituting interstate transportation for hire . . . , all regulated carriers must now obtain proper authority from the Commission . . . . [This is a barrier to entry or a restriction on growth through geographical expansion. Consider its implications were this requirement to apply to a manufacturer or a retail chain.] (2) . . . [A]ll carriers must strictly obey their own tariffs [that is, prices] which, upon being properly published, have the binding force of a statute. [This means that any deviation from a published tariff, or price list, is a law violation.] (3) The construction, operation or abandonment of a rail line is made unlawful unless approved by the Commission . . . . [This means that any attempt to expand or simplify a product line requires the Commission's approval. The reader can readily visualize the effect of this type of regulation were it to apply to the marketing of goods.]

The Restricted Services

Earlier, the rather widespread practice of formal self-regulation was noted. In some professions, self-regulation is sanctioned and supported by law, in others the degree of statutory support is more limited, and in others, self-regulation is purely a private matter. For present purposes these three types of self-regulated services are identified as restricted, semi-restricted, and nonrestricted services. The basic justification for restrictions of any kind is the necessity to assure the public, or market, that minimum standards of performance can be expected. Given the inability to examine and evaluate the service in advance, the critical nature of professional services, and the dependent role of the buyer, the need to restrict practice in some fashion is evident.

The legal and medical professions are the best examples of restricted services. Performing or practicing these services without the sanction of the state is illegal. Public accounting is an example of a semi-restricted service. Anyone can practice public accounting but only those who have successfully completed a prescribed educational program and passed professional tests can claim to be *certified* public accountants. Depending on state laws, architects, engineers, barbers, and funeral directors may be classed as semi-restricted services. A number of professional services are nonrestricted in that there are no private performance standards or ethical codes or, if there are, they do not have the support of statutes. In this category are found advertising, business consulting, marketing research, and life insurance underwriting.

Looking at economic activity in general, Friedman identifies three levels of restriction, in ascending order: registration, wherein nothing more than a fee or special tax is required as in the case of a taxi operator; certification, wherein a state agency certifies to the competence of the practitioner but initiative for obtaining certification rests with the individual as in the case of certified public accounting; and licensure, wherein the individual is licensed by the state to perform a particular service or he does not perform it at all.[5] It is of interest to note that in the case of some services, registration with the state is required in order to practice while private associations of professionals establish educational requirements and performance standards. For example, a life insurance agent must be registered in order to sell, while the right to be identified as a Chartered Life Underwriter is granted by a private institution, the College of Life Underwriters.

Antitrust Laws and Services

Traditionally, conventional marketing has been concerned primarily with the public policy issues of monopoly and restraint of trade, unfair competitive practices, and, recently, consumer protection. Antitrust has not been a particularly important regulatory issue in the service sector. The regulated services have their own statutes and regulatory bodies as has already been indicated. Many services are performed by small, intrastate proprietorships and so would hardly be charged with monopoly or attempts to monopolize. In addition, there is a real question as to the commercial nature of many services—entertainment, dentistry, and education, for example. The status of professional sports vis-à-vis the antitrust laws has just recently come under scrutiny. (Are the exclusive franchises granted by various professional leagues monopolistic practices? Are the various contractual arrangements which tie individual players to specified teams trade restraints?)[6]

Assuming the question of what is commerce and what is not is resolved, the Federal Trade Commission Act's Section 5, declaring that unfair methods of competition and unfair or deceptive acts or practices in commerce are unlawful, is wholly applicable to services. Correspondence schools, credit collection agencies, home repairing services, and employment agencies among others have been cited.

On the other hand, two areas of regulation widely considered in conventional marketing are not relevant in the service sector. (1) The McGuire Act and state resale price maintenance laws are inapplicable since services are not resold. (2) At the present time, the Robinson-Patman Act does not apply to services because they are not viewed as "commodities" by courts that have faced this issue.

Incidentally, a clear distinction should be drawn between the Federal Trade Commission and the regulatory bodies cited earlier. The FTC attempts to *maintain* competition in a free market; the others are a *substitution* for competition in a free market. The FTC acts only if it believes competition is injured; the others must approve management decisions before they are implemented.

Public Policy Issues in the Service Sector

Because of the relative recency of services as a major economic factor, public policy posture is even more confused and conflicting than that found in the goods sector. Some favor more hard competition in services, others view hard competition as a destroyer of performance quality.[7] There are those who argue for more regulation by commission at the federal or state level and others who support "regulation" by the marketplace. Some argue for more government intervention through subsidy, joint venture, or outright takeover and others argue for greater contraction of publicly provided services. And others enter the arena representing neither practitioner nor government but the consumer, asserting that his interests should dictate public policy regardless of where this might lead. In short, economists, public officials, and practitioners disagree with and among each other—disagreements seldom encountered in the goods sector.

In at least three services, there is the possibility of conversion to a status similar to the regulated utility: health care, property insurance, and professional sports. Were this to occur, all the trappings of regulation would be imposed: commissions, hearings, and reports. Freedom of entry would be restricted, innovative ideas would be stifled, price competition would be outlawed. The politician has rightly perceived that these three services offer sensitive issues. The reasons for voter (that is, consumer) sensitivity are indeed real. The problem is whether a shift from private to varying levels of public regulation will improve the situation. It might be argued more appropriately that these services need a heavy infusion of the marketing concept.

Efforts are being made to strengthen self-regulation practices, to expand formal self-regulation to new services, and to supplement self-regulation with public certification and licensing procedures. For example, the marketing research profession is in the process of developing codes of conduct leading ultimately to some form of certification. Whether such certification would be made by a public body as in the case of public accounting is not clear. Certainly there are many similarities in the practitioner-client relationship and in the nature of the services performed. Many argue for publicly imposed restrictions of nonprofessional services, currently devoid of any meaningful self-regulation, in the public interest. For example, many would argue that certification or licensing should be required in the household and automotive repair services. Levels of training and performance standards would be established by local or state authorities. These would be mandatory in the case of licensing or would provide a basis for distinguishing approved service establishments from unapproved ones in the case of certification. In addition, there is the strong possibility that restrictions are promoted by practitioners currently under no form of self-regulation not so much to protect the public but to protect themselves from unrestricted entry or hard competition.

An entirely different viewpoint is taken by truly liberal economists and supporters of the antitrust laws. They argue for more open competition and less self-regulation whether or not it is supported by public certification and licensing. And they not only argue against expanding the use of regulation by commission but favor a more intensive application of the antitrust laws to professional services. They would challenge, for example, the legality of suggested minimum fees published by bar associations and the activities of rate-making bureaus in the property insurance industry. Once jurisdictional issues are resolved, it is likely that antitrust laws will be applied more generally in the service sector.

Added support for a shift from self-regulation to more open competition can be drawn from alleged events leading up to the resignation of the Vice-President of the United States, Spiro Agnew. "Ostensibly, the design specialists serving the construction industry adhere to a code of ethics emphasizing integrity. Moreover, they supposedly sell their services, like doctors or lawyers, on the basis of qualifications and experience rather than the price competition of the marketplace. In fact, however, architects and engineers have increasingly resorted to 'buying' jobs from politicians."[8]

In the face of these crosscurrents, it is difficult to articulate a clear and consistent public policy regarding the performance and marketing of services. Various forces are at work and, ultimately, in the marketplace of ideas, their dimensions and implications will be exposed and a viable public policy emerge. This goal might be reached in the following three ways:

First, total, not just economic cost, must be weighed in determining public policy in the service sector. It may very well be that some services must be performed "decently and in order" within the framework of rules of conduct and ethical standards determined by the practitioner rather than in the "chaos" of the uncontrolled marketplace. The criterion should be the critical nature of the service to the patient, client, or consumer. For example, quackery in medicine, law, or finance would be intolerable. The cost of a decline in confidence in the quality of these critical services would be greater than that resulting from any alleged monopolistic pricing. On the other hand, services which are not critical in terms of economic cost or functional significance to the buyer should be offered in a freely competitive market.

Second, the public, or the consumer, or the market, must receive greater recognition from the supply side of the service sector. If service providers and practitioners would talk more to their market and less to each other, there would be less pressure for government intervention. This assumes, of course, that "talking" would be a serious business and not merely window-dressing. This acceptance of the marketing concept or, more appropriately, the "consumption concept" offers a bridge between private and public control of the marketplace. With the advent of militant consumerism, regulated monopolies and oligopolies have a critical need for the marketing concept. The "safety valve" of competitive options is lacking or inadequate. The alternatives seem to be a real sensitivity for the consumer's concerns or more intense regulation or even government takeover. The interaction visualized here might include the presence of user businessmen and representatives of the public on the boards of directors of regulated public utilities; representatives of the business community might be included in the governing boards of the accounting and consulting professions; the inputs of parents would be of value to professional boards managing local hospitals; and bar associations could benefit from including local businessmen in their deliberations. In addition, many of the local personal and household services could learn from the market for their services through formal dialogues sponsored by chambers of commerce or better business bureaus. Otherwise, some form of public regulation is a reasonable certainty.

However, and this is the third point, such revolutionary action should be the last resort. The history of public intervention in private affairs has demonstrated to this author that it is the wrong solution, an excessive remedy, or one with no provision for disengagement once the need for intervention has been satisfied. Monopolies, oligopolies, and trade restraints are repugnant whether they are the result of private understandings (which the antitrust laws are designed to prevent) or are imposed by public ownership, participation, subsidy, regulation, or licensing. Where these steps are proposed, the burden of proof should be on the proponent, whether he be a businessman seeking protection or a politician or public administrator seeking power. It should be reiterated that public involvement *may* be required, particularly in the consumer's interest, but this solution should be one of last, not first resort. An understanding and application of marketing practice is a far superior solution; the extent of public participation in the service sector relative to the goods sector may very well be a reflection of relative lack of marketing competence.

FOOTNOTES

1. For one example, of 2,400 moving and storage companies grossing almost $2 billion annually, only 40 receive more than $1 million. "When Moving Men Show Their Worst Side," *Business Week,* 21 August 1971, p. 86.

2. U.S. Bureau of the Census, *Census of Business, 1967, Selected Services: Miscellaneous Subjects, BC67-SS8,* 1971, Table 26.

3. U.S. Bureau of the Census, *Census of Manufacturers, 1967,* Volume 1, *Summary and Subject Statistics,* 1971, Table 4, p. 44.

4. "Where Nixon's Freeze Is Starting to Hurt," *Business Week,* 30 June 1973, pp. 21-22.

5. Milton Friedman, *Capitalism and Freedom* (Chicago: The University of Chicago Press, 1962), pp. 144-149; E. T. Grether, *Marketing and Public Policy* (Englewood Cliffs, New Jersey: Prentice-Hall, Inc., 1966), pp. 13-14.

6. See "Antitrusters Take On Professional Sports," *Business Week,* 9 October 1971, pp. 60-61f. and "Legal Developments in Marketing," *Journal of Marketing* 37 (April 1973), pp. 78-79.

7. A recent FTC report on talent and modeling agencies in Southern California distinguishes between licensed and nonlicensed agencies. The former are legitimate, the latter, "suspect" and "fly-by-nights." How should questionable practices be contained while competition is strengthened?

8. "Correcting a Drift Toward Corruption," *Business Week,* 20 October 1973, p. 34.

WHY NOBODY LIKES THE INSURERS

Jeremy Main

How a service industry invites government intervention because of a real or perceived failure to meet its market responsibilities — a failure which could be corrected through innovative marketing.

It is the insured, of course, who pay the heaviest penalty for the insurers' burdens: the person, living alone in the big city, who cannot get burglary insurance at any price; the California specialist who pays $3,000 a year for malpractice insurance, eight times what he paid a decade ago; the good driver who loses his insurance simply because his insurance company decides to quit doing business where he lives; the downtown drugstore owner who—if he can get coverage at all—must pay $827 for $7,500 in crime insurance that cost him only $325 eight years ago.

Since an ample and reasonably priced supply of property and liability insurance is as essential to the economy as credit, government is bound to step in when private companies fail to provide coverage. For years the insurance industry enjoyed a unique freedom from federal interference because the Supreme Court consistently held that insurance was *not* in interstate commerce. When the Court reversed its position in 1944, Congress passed legislation to keep the states predominant in regulating insurance. The federal role was confined to a few special situations—e.g., insurance on crops and bank deposits. But lately Congress has seemed far more willing to permit massive federal intervention. Within the last two years the government has begun to underwrite flood insurance and inner-city riot insurance. Federal regulation is now clearly in the offing for several types of insurance—notably for auto insurance, which the Department of Transportation has been studying intensively for two years.

Extracts from Jeremy Main, "Why Nobody Likes the Insurers," Fortune *82 (December 1970), pp. 83-87ff., with publisher's permission.*

Insurance companies quarrel among themselves about what is wrong and what should be done. They divide into three main groups—stock companies, mutual companies, and "independents"—each of which has a trade organization to fight its battles, and a retinue of dependents. The stock companies, which write two-thirds of the property and liability premiums, are mostly old eastern establishments that sell through outside agents. Most of the remaining business is written by client-owned mutual companies. The mutuals were established, many of them in the Middle West early in the century, with a system of agents working on lower commissions. Both stock and mutual companies have generally let industry rate-making bureaus establish their prices.

The independents, which include both stock and mutual companies, are called "independent" because they are free of the rate-making bureaus. Many of them sell directly by mail or through their own salaried agents, rather than through outside agents. On the strength of low-priced direct sales, the two biggest independents, State Farm Mutual and Sears, Roebuck's Allstate, have taken first and second place, respectively, among all casualty-insurance companies in terms of total premiums. The independents, by and large, are content with things as they are, and so are many of the mutuals. It is the old stock companies that are most eager for change these days. They see in innovation a chance to win ground back from the mutuals and independents.

The industry will have to reorganize itself and its thinking as it attempts to deal with the problems of property and liability insurance. The days are long past when insurance executives could sit peacefully in their offices and let others make decisions for them—the bureaus setting the rates, the agents getting the customers, and the lawyers determining the payments. The grip of the agents and of the rating boards has been loosened. With the spread of open-rating, the industry has become more competitive, more flexible.

There are fresh winds blowing through management. In the brocade-curtained offices of the newly diversified Insurance Co. of North America, seventeen of the top twenty officers have come to their jobs in the last two years. "As a rule the insurance business has been pretty sleepy," says Charles K. Cox, president of the firm. "Here, there has been a management upheaval down the line." The entry of Prudential Insurance Co., the biggest life company in the country, into property and liability in partnership with the Kemper group of Chicago creates another kind of stimulant. Prudential sees some prospects of profits, and believes that the industry has passed the worst of its crisis. But the Pru moved principally to provide a whole variety of additional financial and insurance services for its agents to sell.

The insurance industry must also turn outward to the problems of society as a whole, for insurance problems cannot be solved purely within an insurance context. "The industry," says the Wharton School's Denenberg, "has always viewed itself as sitting in the background and spreading risk over the environment over which it has no control. This doesn't work any more."

Society is also beginning to help the insurance business solve its problems, or to intervene where the industry falls down. Clearly some of the burdens the insurance companies carry are bound to be unprofitable. For instance, insurers must accept their portion of poor-risk drivers from each state's "assigned-risk" pool. Some risks the business just will not underwrite: therefore the federal government has undertaken an exposure of $2.5 billion in flood insurance and $7.4 billion for riot damage in central cities. Now Congress is considering federal crime insurance in the cities and seventeen senators have even introduced a national health-insurance bill. Other kinds of government-provided insurance are likely. Some find it hard to accept the government's new role, but there is no other choice when the industry withdraws from whole areas of vital insurance. As HUD's Bernstein says, "The question of where insurance comes from is less important than that people get it."

II

SERVICE MARKETING

An introduction of marketing to services.

4

PRODUCT DEVELOPMENT AND PRODUCT POLICIES IN THE SERVICE SECTOR

The overriding importance of the product in determining a seller's success is a fundamental premise of marketing. It applies to a service as well as a good and to a public agency as well as a profit-making enterprise. The ways in which intangible products are developed or improved and the success criteria vary both within the service sector and when services are contrasted with goods, yet the need for product policies and product strategies loses none of its significance in the case of services.

A few illustrations to orient the reader are appropriate at this point. Some new service products include: closed-circuit and cable television; the servicing and maintenance of "orphan" computer installations; rental housing for the elderly and low income families; the provision of legal services for the disadvantaged; campgrounds; and urban transportation systems. Both private and government institutions are contributing to these new products either separately or jointly; some require large financial investments, others, very little; some are subject to intense regulation, others are regulation-free; and both consumer services and "industrial" services are included.

In this chapter, conceptual matters will be considered first: (1) characteristics of services or their marketing as they relate to the service product which differ markedly from conventional goods marketing and (2) the meaning of certain widely accepted marketing concepts when they are applied to service products. The way in which service products are developed is a second consideration. The productivity level of services probably has received more attention than any other aspect of the subject. Because it is intimately related to service product policy and strategy, productivity is the third subject of this chapter. Finally, attention will be focused on a fundamental shift in the organization of production in this country. Until very recently, diversification by manufacturers and intermediaries was limited to tangible goods; today an increasing number of both groups are diversifying into services. The implications of this trend for systems marketing will be explored.

CONCEPTS

1. It must be acknowledged that service product development, policies, and strategy occur in a great diversity of settings, some quite novel. For example, consider the service products (their development, policies, and strategy) of the following: a television network; an advertising agency; a university; an electrical utility; the Veteran's Administration; a law partnership; a barbershop; a symphony orchestra; or the Federal Reserve Board. As a generalization, the more human-centered the service, the more it departs from conventional treatment of the product element in marketing. Similarly, the more regulated or more professional the service is, the greater the difficulty in relating the service product to the conventional marketing concepts.

2. Whereas goods are *produced,* services are *performed.* Thus, the quality of a service product derives from its performance, not from its physical characteristics. Furthermore, as was noted earlier, the performance of many services requires the active participation of the buyer. Accordingly, success or failure in service product performance may be dependent in part on the buyer: consider for example the role of the student, the patient, or the consultant's client. The concept of performance will be referred to again in the discussion of productivity in services.

3. In some respects, the service product is an *idea.* For many services the most important resource input (a raw material) is a good idea. (This, of course, does not necessarily apply to machine-intensive services.) The success leverage in a good service product idea is enhanced by the fact that the need for the service is often unrecognized by the buyer until he becomes aware of the service. The expression "why didn't I think of that," is particularly apt here. This is what seems to be happening: In a relatively affluent society, consumers prefer more and more to delegate to others the performance of activities viewed as conflicting with higher levels of consumption. On the production side, firms are delegating peripheral and sporadic activities related to the production process to business facilitating services. In other words, both consumer and producer are moving from self-sufficiency to more selective consumption and production. Successful service product ideas are found increasingly in these essential yet (perceived to be) extraneous and peripheral activities of consumption and production.

4. Assuming a good service idea has been identified, then professional, technical, or entrepreneurial skills are the major inputs necessary to convert the idea into a marketable service. Excepting the giants in communications and utilities, the majority of services require only modest infusions of capital other than that necessary to acquire appropriate skills. As we move into a service-oriented economy, ideas plus skills will offer increasing opportunities for careers. Success will be

determined by the appropriateness of the idea and the level of skill. This latter factor is a major issue today because, as noted in Chapter 3, standards for certain skills are low or non-existent. Almost everyone can offer his "services" in some form. Even though charlatans in the service sector may not remain in business long, substantial waste and disappointment can result. In view of the growing opportunities in the service sector, the need for standards throughout to protect both buyer and skilled services seller is evident.

5. On the other hand, in those services which do require heavy capital investment or whose standards demand heavy investment of time in order to qualify to perform a service (the medical profession, for example), a balancing of supply and demand becomes a critical issue.

The preceding discussion leads to a consideration of two widely accepted concepts which must be reformulated to apply to services. (1) Value added by manufacturing refers to the value of goods shipped less the cost of materials and supplies plus other physical inputs, and value added by marketing refers to the spread between sales and cost of goods sold plus other supplies and materials consumed by intermediaries. Thus, value added is the difference between input and output at various levels on the supply side. Since services are not resold there can be only one level of value added, and the concept of input must be recast to represent only supplies consumed and the depreciation of capital goods used up in the production of a service. (2) A related concept which must be noted is that of utility. Services certainly do have time and place utility, but form utility must be replaced by some concept of performance utility. This utility may be high or low depending on the level of professional, technical or artistic skill of the service provider. Just how possession utility can be defined to include services is not clear; perhaps satisfaction utility is a meaningful substitute.

6. Services, like goods, have life cycles. Undoubtedly, there are fads and the fashionableness of service styles grow and ebb. Services in the growth segment of the life cycle curve include telecommunications, health maintenance delivery systems, leasing, and forms of outdoor recreation. Services which appear to have passed their peak of growth include motion pictures and vaudeville, rail passenger service, watch repairing, domestic services, and unisex higher educational institutions. Note that both technological and sociological changes have had their impact on services which are currently in decline yet each could have a rebirth of popularity if life styles or technological changes increase their social acceptance or economic feasibility. Because marketing practice in the sevice sector has not achieved the level of proficiency attributed to its counterpart in the goods sector, shifts in service product performance, pricing, and promotion to reflect changing status in the life cycle have not been much in evidence.

7. In the marketing literature, goods are classified in various ways. The same classifications apply to services. There are consumer and industrial services just as there are consumer and industrial goods. Examples are self-evident. While consumer purchases are typically distributed between durable goods, nondurable goods, and services, more realistically, the durable-nondurable dichotomy should apply to services as well. For example, both health care and insurance meet the criteria of a durable service, whereas a haircut or an evening's entertainment would be of a nondurable variety. The criterion is the length of time during which benefits are derived from the performance of a service. Some services are of a specialty nature and others are classified as staple services. A firm specializing in oil exploration illustrates the former and a machine shop offering its services to manufacturers to repair machine tools is an example of the latter. Finally, there are both shopping and convenience services, as well as shopping and convenience goods. Legal, medical, and business consulting are typically a shopping service, whereas low-cost and elementary services in both the personal and household operation classes are likely to be of a convenience category.

Two caveats should be entered regarding product classifications. First, the classification of the service is determined by the buyer, not by the intrinsic nature of the service. Second, because a service cannot be observed or inspected, and because the buyer is likely to be more dependent on the service seller, it can be generalized that services are viewed by most buyers to be of a durable, specialty, shopping nature.

8. The marketer of services is faced with questions regarding depth *versus* breadth in his service product line and with the related issue of "make or buy" in decisions to broaden the line. Commercial banks offer a classic example of increasing breadth in services offered—a type of financial department store—whereas physicians and lawyers have tended to specialization, that is, depth. The regulated services are limited in breadth of services which they are permitted to offer whereas business consultants are in a period of product diversification. In the advertising agency business, breadth *versus* depth of services offered is a currently controversial subject. Some favor the full service agency which might be viewed as a "marketing agency"; others prefer a purely advertising role. In recent years there has been some movement in the direction of agency specialization *within* advertising: creative ad-making services, independent media buying agencies, public relations specialists, "jingle-makers," and others depending on the advertiser's requirements. Providers of services whose demand is seasonal are attempting to broaden their line in order to reduce peaks and valleys in their demand (ski slope operators, for example). The same can be said for educational institutions. The trend toward service systems, of course,

encourages breadth in the service product line. The question of "make or buy" is, for the most part, a question of whether to develop new service competencies within the firm or acquire qualified personnel from outside.

The preceding is not the final word on product concepts in the service sector. The commentary should be viewed as a point of departure for further discussion or research.

SERVICE PRODUCT DEVELOPMENT

A brief state-of-the-art review of formal and organized research and development in the service sector leads to the conclusion that it is at a very elementary stage today, with exceptions, of course. New service products "happen"—they are not formally developed. They happen as a result of vision, entrepreneurship, hard work, and willingness to risk. Consider the following:

1. Family-oriented amusement parks along superhighways
2. Campgrounds
3. Gymnasiums for businessmen
4. Property appraisal
5. Catering in the home
6. Concert booking for small towns

The limited financial and manpower resources of the great majority of service firms prevents indulging in the "luxury" of organized service product development. Government agencies which sell their services to the public lack the motivation to innovate although the new Postal Service is a marked exception to this observation. Services which are subject to intense government regulation often find that attempts to introduce new service products are forbidden or seriously circumscribed by regulatory bodies. Finally, it may be that the newness or immaturity of the service sector relative to manufacturing may be sufficient to explain general lack of sophistication in the development of new service products.

However, one must distinguish between a new service and a new method of delivering a service. Whether the latter is, in fact, a new service product is a question which cannot be answered here. For example, the Bell Laboratories is one of the most sophisticated and successful research and development facilities in the world. Is it developing new services or new means of delivering services? Physicians and hospitals have at their disposal a growing number of sophisticated instruments. Do these instruments represent new service products or improved means of delivering these products?

Table 4.1

EXAMPLES OF SERVICE PRODUCT INNOVATIONS

Nature of Service	New Service Product	Service Product Improvement
Communications	Communication satellite	Free-standing public telephone
Consulting and business facilitating	Equipment leasing	Overnight TV rating service
Educational	Three-year degrees	New curricula
Financial	Bank credit cards	"Bank by mail"
Health	Treatment with lasers	Intensive care
Household operations	Laundromat	Fuel budget accounts
Housing	Housing for the elderly	Motel swimming pool
Insurance	National health insurance	No-fault insurance
Legal	"Divorce Yourself" kit*	Legal services for the poor
Personal	Physical fitness facilities	—
Recreational	Dual cinema	New play
Transportation	Unit train	Flight reservation system

*Under court injunction in New York but being appealed.

Are the new and improved service products listed in Table 4.1 really new or improved products or are they new or improved means of delivering an already existing product? Perhaps there is no "new" service, only new and better means of production/consumption. Parenthetically, one may take exception to the "newness" of the specific examples in Table 4.1 as well as with the decision to classify certain innovations as improvements rather than new products.

Organization for Service Product Development

Organizational responsibility for new service products varies substantially. If the service organization is small, specialized, and professional, responsibility will rest with the owner, practitioner, or principal. On the other hand, new product departments or their equivalent may be found in large and diversified service organizations. For example, firms in the entertainment-communications areas conduct formal searches for new program ideas and have fully developed research and development procedures. Undoubtedly, large commercial banks have assigned responsibility for new ideas resulting from the wave of diversification which currently characterizes the commercial banking field. The actuary department of an insurance company is, in reality, a new product group. Curriculum committees at educational institutions have as one of their responsibilities the development of new curricula. There are undoubtedly very few "R&D" or new product groups or departments in the service sector; however, they do exist under a variety of titles and forms.

Development Steps

The conventional steps of exploration, screening, business analysis, development, testing, and commercialization apply to services as well as goods. They may be implicit, fragmentary, and imprecise, or they may be explicit, thorough, and scientific. Assume an airline wishes to expand its product line by adding a new scheduled service between two points currently not served. Through exploration it identifies a number of possibilities and then screens out most of them on the basis of competition, lack of physical facilities, or regulatory constraints. Through a business analysis, number of flights, schedules, flow of traffic, number of departures and arrivals will be determined and narrow further the potential new products. Because the new product is an intangible, the development phase is bypassed, and a market test is conducted for a limited time period before the commitment to offer scheduled service between the two points is made. It should be noted that the behavioral sciences are relatively more important in the development of a new service product whereas the physical sciences are relatively more important in the development of new means of delivering a service.

PRODUCTIVITY IN SERVICES

Productivity is a ratio relating output and input: outputs in the form of goods and services and input in the form of resources, particularly labor. Normally, levels of and trends in productivity are not one of the great marketing issues. It is included here because of the simultaneous nature of production and consumption and the intimate participation of the buyer in the production or performance of many services. Moreover, the *qualitative* element in service products is an overriding factor in any attempt to measure their productivity. (Quality of output is not unimportant in the goods sector but present measures of productivity have stressed measurable and visible units of output.)

It has been argued that the rate of growth in productivity in the service sector is lower than that prevailing in the goods sector. As an increasing quantity of resources is shifted from the goods to the service sector this slower rate of growth in productivity, if true, has serious implications for economic welfare. Reasons cited for the poor performance of the service sector include: a slower increase in the quality of labor; fewer opportunities for labor-saving devices; less rapid technological change; and fewer opportunities for economies of scale.[1] To this list one could add: fewer opportunities for labor specialization and inadequate attention to the need for good management in some of the newer and less business-oriented services such as the arts, health care, and in the nonprofit and government services industries.

Problems in Measuring Productivity

Our knowing whether or not the services are not keeping pace in productivity improvement is increasingly open to question. Attempts to apply productivity measures in the goods sector to services are in many cases erroneous. For example, in conventional productivity terms, what is a physician's input or a business consultant's output? Where the error has been recognized, rather than seek new measures, output has simply been assumed to be equal to input and therefore productivity growth has been zero, as in the case of government services. As more funds were appropriated to a particular government agency, output appeared to increase proportionately, never more or less rapidly.

Certain characteristics of services and their marketing should be noted before any assessment of productivity is made. First, it should be reemphasized that services are performed, not produced. Therefore, we are not so much concerned with productivity as we are with "performability" of the service sector—higher performability or lower performability. Second, there is buyer participation in the consumption of services, or at least, a high degree of dependence on the seller. Third, service facilities must be in being before they can be used. Consider an ambulance service, for example. The more it is used, the more "productive" it is. Fourth, services cannot be stockpiled thus denying one of the most useful techniques for improving productivity in the goods sector. Fifth, services are produced and consumed simultaneously and therefore difficult to inspect in advance and evaluate subsequently. This characteristic is particularly significant if one accepts the proposition that quality of output is a significant criterion in determining productivity. Finally, since no title passes, that is, no "thing" is bought or sold, ethical values on the seller's part are relevant; in other words, it is easier for a charlatan to sell a service than a good.

At this point, it should be clear that productivity is a function of the quantity and quality of both input and output. This is true for goods but it is even more so for services. In fact, to ignore the qualitative aspect of productivity is to ignore the only really meaningful component of many service products. Basing assessments of productivity on measurable factors in service performance is widely practiced today and can lead to highly questionable policies.

Speaking of medical care, Fuchs says:

Traditionally, output has been measured in terms of the number of physician visits, or number of patient days in a hospital. This approach is roughly comparable to measuring the output of the automobile industry in terms of the number of cars produced without regard to size, durability, performance characteristics, and so on.[2]

Figure 4.1 shows a hypothetical positioning of the major classes of services according to the quantitative-qualitative mix in their respective outputs. Conventional measures of productivity would be most inappropriate for those services appearing to the right of the figure. For example, more operations per physician's hour, more cases per lawyer, more advertisements per copywriter's hour, more students per teacher, more concerts per musician's practice hour, or more permanents per beautician would reflect greater productivity. However, the buyer would not necessarily agree, and rightly so.

Improving Productivity

How can the productivity of services be improved? The question is not academic, for improvement in productivity is equivalent to improvement in the service product itself. At the macro level, services have contributed more than their share to inflation with the result that options are narrowing: either greater productivity or greater regulation or public ownership. At the micro level, there is another challenge to greater productivity not found in the goods sector: because of the high labor content of most services, the buyer always has the option of "do-it-yourself." This option is open to the advertiser, to top management, or to the ultimate consumer as he contends with the high cost and low productivity of household operation services, automobile repairs, and even education and health care.

One recommended approach to improved productivity in the service sector is through greater standardization of performance and mass production.[3] Just as goods evolved from custom production to mass production, Regan anticipates the mass production and impersonalization of services. This has already occurred in capital-intensive services: public

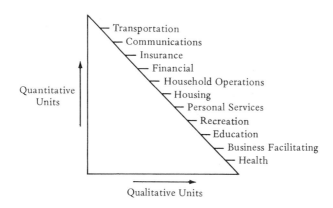

Figure 4.1 *PRODUCTIVITY OF SERVICES: OUTPUT MEASURES*

transportation, utilities, and communications. The replacement of the meter reader with remote meter reading is an example. The typical concert series, group travel tours, the use of teaching machines, and the speedup in treatment of patients by doctors and dentists are examples of this trend in services of a more personal nature. Questions open up concerning quality if this trend continues.

Improvement in the technological *means* of performing services is a second approach to improving the productivity of services. This does not refer to mass production or impersonalization. It does mean greater proficiency in performance. In other words, technology can strengthen the personalized nature of many services. Improved technology in the means of service performance improves the quality component in productivity. Consider the diagnostic tools now available to the physician, to the automobile repairman; the benefits of audio visual aids to the professor; the benefits of the computer to the business consultant. Implicit in the preceding proposals is some measurable unit of input—labor hours, labor cost, or total factor costs.

A third approach to determining and improving the productivity of services, particularly those that are human-intensive, is to shift attention from measurable units of input and output to *custom* measures, if you will, for each service, made up of two elements: a clear statement of just what the objective or purpose of each service is and an identification of surrogate measures which relate a particular service's productivity to its purpose or objective: mortality rates; length of applause at the end of a concert; waiting time for car repairs; before and after measures of client profitability for business facilitating services; repeat sales of personal services; or starting salaries of college graduates. These are suggestive only; perhaps multiple measures would be desirable, some measuring quantitative and other qualitative productivity trends.

In summary, improving the productivity of service performance is equivalent to improving the service product. Its intangible nature requires that the qualitative rather than quantitative output of the services be stressed. Advances in technology of the means of performing services increase their productivity substantially. While trends in the productivity of capital-intensive services can be measured as they are in the goods sector, in human-intensive services, quantitative and qualitative surrogate factors which relate to the objective or purpose of the service may be used.

DIVERSIFICATION

Until recently, few firms carried on inter-sector operations. Manufacturers diversified laterally or vertically in the goods sector and service organizations remained in services. The latter is generally still true, whereas the former pattern no longer holds. As late as 1966, the author could identify but one clear example of diversification from goods into services—Sears, Roebuck and Company's entry into the insurance field.[4] Several reasons for this entry into the service sector can be cited. First, industry has recognized the growth potential. Second, the extended period of profitable operations has provided many manufacturers with financial resources to support ventures into the "unknown" world of intangibles. Third, with the advent of systems selling, manufacturers are required to think in terms of services if they are truly going to market a system.

Patterns of Diversification

Several patterns of diversification into services can be identified. First, conglomerates have not hesitated to acquire service businesses. A review of the financial reports of larger conglomerates shows that very few have failed to invade one type of service industry or another. A second pattern is a selective and judiciously planned entry into services, not by conglomerates, but as a strategy of product line extension. Third, the systems selling pattern is becoming increasingly evident as firms manufacturing capital goods enter into long-term contracts with customers to service the capital goods they sell. Fourth, some firms are capitalizing on internal know-how: if skills work for the firm, and are of a non-proprietary nature, they are a marketable intangible product. Finally, some manufacturers have broken into the service sector for a variety of reasons ranging from social responsibility to public relations.

In varying combinations, these patterns are evident in the following illustrations:

1. ITT, U.S. Industries, Inc., Bell and Howell Company, Lear Siegler, Inc., and Litton Industries, Inc. operate business and technical schools.
2. Quaker Oats Company, Bristol-Myers Company, Mattel, Inc., and AVCO Corporation are participating in a variety of ways in motion picture production.
3. In addition to motion pictures, AVCO Corporation operations include financial services, broadcasting, and real estate. Textron Inc. has also entered the financial services industries.
4. Because of the recent drastic decline in demand for their products, aerospace firms are diversifying into computer and communication services and leisure-time and recreational activities.
5. Firestone Tire and Rubber Company is now in the investment banking business.
6. Manufacturers of recreational vehicles are establishing "land

marinas" where motor homes can be stored and serviced, are establishing rental operations, and are looking to the recreational vehicle campground business as they move into a systems concept for recreational travel.

7. In addition to manufacturing electrically oriented products, General Electric Company's subsidiary, General Electric Credit Corporation, is in the equipment and fleet-leasing business, commercial and industrial time sales plans, capital loans and real estate, accounts receivable and inventory financing, and consumer credit. In addition, this manufacturer has entered, or is considering entering, the following services: entertainment, community development and housing, industrial and personal services, medicine, and education. For example, General Learning Corporation is a subsidiary of GE and Hurok Concerts, Inc., is now part of Tomorrow Entertainment, Inc., another subsidiary of GE.

8. DuPont now markets industrial training courses originally prepared for the company's own employees. This company also markets an energy management program originally developed for its own plants to companies where energy is a major cost item.

9. Xerox is producing films for children.

10. Union Camp Corporation, a manufacturer of paper products and packaging, has opened five integrated service station-recreation area-motel units at interchanges on Interstate 95 located on the company's land.

11. General Mills has introduced "Counterweight," a diet-and-exercise program for weight reduction and Pet Incorporated provides frozen food warehouse and distribution, a logical extension of its food manufacturing and retailing operations.

Regardless of other reasons for entry into the service sector, it should be stressed that the profit motive is common to all, no matter how unusual the combination may appear to be.

There are problems to be considered. Some of the service ventures are far removed from the firms' areas of competence and reputation and for that reason acquisition rather than growth from within may be the wiser approach. Second, the production and marketing of intangibles calls for a different order of expertise; the transferability of goods manufacturing and marketing competence to services can be properly questioned. Finally, antitrust questions may be raised, particularly where the systems pattern is evident. If service industries presently characterized by competition among small businesses attract large manufacturers, regulatory agencies are sure to investigate for evidence of incipient concentration.

Intra-service sector diversification is also occurring. This is especially true of commercial banking (see Chapter 9). Insurance firms are searching out related services, particularly in finance. Although constrained by regulation, freight carriers are attempting to provide more integrated services through diversification. For example, the Federal Communications Commission has authorized the Southern Pacific Company to sell the services of an 11-state common-carrier microwave network formerly limited to its own operations. Transamerica Corporation is probably the only major service conglomerate: over 90 percent of its revenues are from services such as life insurance, property insurance, real estate, leisure time, airlines, lending, and investment.

From a marketing standpoint, inter-sector and intra-service sector diversification growth is indicative of the acceptance of systems marketing, one of the most exciting and promising marketing developments of recent times. Professor Kaven's paper in Chapter 7 presents the recreational travel system. "The Meeting Planners," a joint service of American Airlines, American Express, and Hertz make *all* necessary arrangements for business group meetings. DuPont sells paint to industrial plants, subcontracts the painting, and maintains paint protection standards and appearance for a specified period. The barriers which have traditionally separated goods production and service performance are surely coming down with the advent of the system of products—goods *and* services.

FOOTNOTES

1. Victor R. Fuchs, *The Service Economy* (New York: National Bureau of Economic Research, 1968), pp. 4-5.

2. *Ibid.,* p. 116.

3. William J. Regan, "The Service Revolution," *Journal of Marketing* 27 no. 3 (July 1963), pp. 57-62.

4. John M. Rathmell, "What is Meant by Services?" *Journal of Marketing* 30 no. 4 (October 1966), pp. 32-36.

AIR TRAVEL AS A COMMODITY

John R. Klug and Robin A. Brumwell

An important marketing concept — the product life cycle — is shown to have application in the service sector.

The Life-Cycle Theory

The concept that individual products, industries, and, in fact, international trade follow a fairly predictable life cycle has been convincingly set forth by Professor Louis T. Wells, Jr.[1] of the Harvard Business School. While Professor Wells' work has been primarily concerned with *products,* considerable work is being done by Professor W. Earl Sasser, of Harvard, to extend Wells' work to include services such as air travel and tourism.

Life-Cycle Air Transportation

Early Phase. If we apply the model in Table 4.2 to the transatlantic airline industry, we can say that the "early phase" was from the end of World War II to 1958. During this time the airlines industry was in an embryonic stage and competed essentially with sea travel, on the basis of speed and convenience rather than price.

Growth Phase. With the advent of jets and the introduction of the economy air fare in April 1958, the cost of transatlantic air travel was reduced to only $71 more than the cost of sea voyage. As a result air travel became a sharp competitor with sea travel. The "growth" phase for transatlantic air travel was the period 1958-1970.

Mature Phase. The shakeout in the airline industry, begun in the early '70's, is still continuing. In the mid and late '60's

John R. Klug and Robin A. Brumwell, "Air Travel as a Commodity" in The Tourism Gap: Can It Be Bridged? (Philadelphia: Leventhol Krekstein Horwath & Horwath, 1972), pp. 39-40, with publisher's permission.

Table 4.2

LIFE-CYCLE PHASE

	Early	Growth	Mature
Demand structure	Low-price elasticity for aggregate demand	Growing price elasticity Price competition begins	Basis of competition is price, or product differentiation through marketing techniques
Industry structure	Small number of firms	Large number of firms, but many casualties and mergers	Number of firms declining
Nature of product	Highly differentiated specialty		Nondifferentiated commodity

charter operators obtained an increasing share of the North Atlantic traffic as the concept of air travel progressively lost its uniqueness and increasingly became a price-sensitive commodity in the eyes of the consumer. The flight had increasingly less appeal to the airline traveller, who was instead more interested in what he would do when he arrived at his destination.

Summary. These results support the contention that *pleasure* air travel is progressing along a life cycle toward a commodity, differentiated primarily by price.

FOOTNOTES

1. Louis T. Wells, *The Product Life Cycle and International Trade* (Cambridge, Massachusetts: Harvard Graduate School of Business, Division of Research, 1972).

5

PRICING IN THE SERVICE SECTOR

This discussion of the role of pricing in services begins with an anomaly: the word "price" or "pricing" is seldom used in practice. Consider Table 5.1 for a moment. One doesn't ordinarily speak of the price of a semester of education; the price of a loan; the price of a visit to the dentist; the price of an apartment; or the price of a symphony orchestra concert.[1] The economic and customary terms are used interchangeably in this chapter. A review of the table serves other more useful purposes. It suggests the great variety of environments in which service pricing decisions are made, and related to this, the distinctively different variables which enter into the decisions. Also, the reader will be struck by conventional marketing's neglect of the pricing situations represented in the table. This suggests an unexplored area of research.

In general, service providers, unlike many goods sellers, do not use pricing as a direct, short-term strategy element to bring about favorable market reaction. Public regulation, strong ethical overtones, prominent areas of inelastic demand, lack of understanding of pricing strategy in

Table 5.1.

TYPICAL TERMS USED FOR PRICING IN THE SERVICE SECTOR

Nature of Service	Typical Price Terminology
Communications	Rate
Consulting and Business Facilitating	Fee, Commission, Retainer
Educational	Tuition
Financial	Interest
Health	Fee, Charge
Household Operations	Rate, Charge
Housing	Rent
Insurance	Premium*
Legal	Fee, Retainer
Personal	Charge
Recreational	Admission
Transportation	Tariff

*In the case of life insurance, premium must be adjusted for dividends and cash surrender (savings) to arrive at the true price.

numerous performance-oriented small service shops, and the presence of substantial nonprofit service operatives limit the adoption of pricing strategy to varying degrees.

The variety of settings and considerations in the service sector argues strongly against any general treatment of service pricing; exceptions would far outnumber the rule. Some type of discriminating classification is mandatory. The typical ultimate consumer-industrial classification is of little help; each group is so inclusive that it would suffer from the same defects as a service-wide approach. The private profit-nonprofit-public classification offers only modest clarification since it does not appear to be relevant to the pricing function in service marketing. (However, when there is competition between two or three elements, price issues become serious.[2]) The distinction between large and small service sellers not only suffers from the problems of distinguishing between large and small and absolute *versus* relative size issues, but also has little bearing on the pricing question in the service sector.

One meaningful differentiation for better understanding of service pricing is to utilize the human-centered and machine-centered classification shown in Table 1.1. Cost and productivity issues and problems are quite different in these two classes of services which result in distinctively different variables in price-making.

PRICE CLASSIFICATION OF SERVICES

Rather surprisingly, at least from a conventional marketing standpoint, it appears that the most meaningful price classification is between those services subject to public regulation; those which are subject to formal self-regulation; and those which are subject only to the regulation of the marketplace (or which appear to be above any kind of formal or market price regulation). While some reference is made to the man-machine (labor-capital) classification, the distinction by nature of regulation is the primary reference point in the discussion that follows.

The significance of this classification may be more apparent through illustration. Pricing by a regulated firm such as a public utility, a telephone company, or a railroad (as is aptly illustrated in the reading that follows) is quite different from anything found in the marketing of manufactured goods and in the marketing of services not subject to public regulatory agencies. In the case of many professional services, the notion of price competition is repugnant and, in fact, considered unethical. Sanctions carrying varying degrees of universality and effectiveness may be imposed upon sellers who are too eager to utilize pricing in their marketing strategy. Pricing of rented housing, hotels and motels, personal services, and household repair services is more likely to reflect market conditions even though those which are labor-intensive may be circumscribed by union-imposed wage uniformity. Finally, certain services, particularly in the private nonprofit category seem to be free of any form of regulation, formal or market. Tuition charges of private institutions of higher learning seem to the writer, at least, to be free of external constraints.

Pricing Theory Applied to Services

Economic theory identifies four market environments in which prices are set in a free economy: pure competition, monopolistic competition, oligopoly, and pure monopoly.[3] Conditions of *pure competition* are as unreal in the service sector as they are in the goods sector. Two defeating conditions in particular are present: (1) knowledge of conditions on the other side of the market are imperfect or unequally distributed with the buyer being especially disadvantaged and (2) the nonstandardized nature of most service products. The theory of *monopolistic competition* is the most appropriate theoretical explanation of market conditions under which the prices of services are set. There are typically many sellers and many buyers. However, the seller has a unique product to sell: the performance of his own mix of human labor, aptitudes, and skills. A reputation for superior performance enables the seller to charge a higher price, up to the point, of course, that the buyer chooses other service sellers of possibly lesser reputation, or makes a "do-it-yourself" decision. A monopoly element in the price of services can also be achieved through nonprice competition: location, amenities, image development, and, to some extent, personal selling and advertising.

Conditions of *oligopoly* are present in some services. Sellers are few in any given market and performance is substantially substitutable. Thus, pricing decisions of one are likely to be matched by others. Nothing much is gained through price reductions, and price increases are less risky. Broadcast advertising on both a national and a local level falls in this category; hospitals and multi-unit rental housing also tend to follow oligopolistic pricing practices.

Pure monopoly pricing is as unlikely as pure competitive pricing. However, the issue has been raised in several service industries. Through the process of acquisition, many trading areas are now served by only one newspaper; it is argued that this enables the owner to extract monopoly prices from advertisers. The argument is stronger if both print and broadcast media covering a single trading area are under one ownership. The charge of monopoly has also been raised in the area of professional sports where a particular region is represented by only one team in any given sport.

Finally, it should be noted that pricing theory assumes a profit motive. This assumption is appropriate in the United States if it applies to the production and marketing of goods. The assumption must be dropped when considering pricing theory for private nonprofit and public service providers.

PRICING POLICIES

In addition to the presence or absence of public regulation and ethical factors in a variety of services, several other differentiating characteristics of service marketing should be noted because of their relevance to service pricing policies. First, some services are standardized (units of electricity, space in a parking lot, or temporal measures of communication) whereas other services vary with each buyer (consulting services other than the "packaged" variety, the diagnostic services of physicians, and the services of lawyers in trials). Second, a distinction should be drawn between services which are purchased routinely (haircuts), contractually (leasing and insurance), and sporadically (repairs and recreational travel). Third, buyer knowledge of sources of supply, market conditions, and the very nature of the service product itself varies markedly among services.

The following paragraphs are an attempt to fit pricing in the service sector into the three traditional classes of pricing policy: a single price to all; one price to all under given conditions; and variable prices. Whether this attempt to adapt services to concepts which originated in the goods sector is appropriate can be questioned. More discriminating classifications of service pricing policies must be left to future marketing scholars. In the meantime, the conventional classification is a rough and sometimes awkward but still useful tool.

Single Price Policy

In this day of market segmentation, the policy of a single price to all is almost an anachronism in both the goods and service sectors. Higher education offers an example of a single price to all. Regardless of age, sex, income, or any other market characteristic and regardless of when the purchase and payment are made, the price is the same to all buyers: a tuition charge for one semester of work. Nor is the price changed if the buyer takes the minimum or maximum number of allowable hours of work. Neither does the course (product) mix have any bearing on the price. (Night school programs, scholarships, and exchange programs are exceptions.) Some personal services, such as barbering (the author, who is bald, does not support this policy) and dry cleaning, follow a single price policy, although in the case of the former, higher prices may be charged on Saturday. Among the professional services certain standardized procedures are priced the same to all buyers. In the case of medical services, schedules of allowances established by health insurance carriers often serve as a basis for a single price policy.

One Price to All Under Given Conditions

Classic examples of this pricing policy are found in the four service categories subject to public regulation of prices: communications; the utilities segment of household operation; transportation; and financial services. For example, everyone who makes a one minute phone call from New York to Chicago over a public telephone line at 7:55 A.M. pays one price; everyone who makes the same one minute phone call between the same points at 8:01 A.M. pays a different price. Prices for many utilities vary with the quantity of energy or water consumed. In the case of transatlantic air travel, the conditions under which one price is levied on all buyers have grown to fantastic levels: seasonal variations; differences in the length of stay; week-day vs. week-end travel. Of course, first-class vs. economy class, and group vs. independent travel fares are additional conditions. Financial institutions offer a variety of savings options, the principle conditions being minimum balances and varying minimum periods of time during which funds are on deposit.

Several major classes of services whose prices are not regulated also follow a policy of a single price to all under certain conditions. For example, the price of identical life insurance policies varies according to the age of the policyholder. Or, putting it another way, everyone who otherwise qualifies for life insurance falling within the same age bracket pays the same price. The major condition affecting the price of admission to theatrical, musical, and sporting events is the location of the seat. In the rental housing, hotel, and motel industries prices vary according to the length of time of use, season, and location of rented units. Postage rates vary according to weight, speed, and security.

Variable Prices

According to conventional marketing, a variable price policy authorizes charging different prices to different buyers of the same product under the same conditions depending upon the competitive situation and the bargaining ability of the buyer. It is particularly difficult to reconcile the characteristics of this policy with the service sector. It does apply where the service firm submits a bid. Financial institutions lend funds at varying rates, based in part on competitive conditions and in part on risk involved. Professional services may be priced according to the ability to pay. Finally, small household and personal service establishments follow an implicit variable price policy for lack of an explicit pricing policy of any kind. Perhaps it would be more appropriate to use the term "intuitive pricing."

Discount Policies

The various discounts which are so common in the marketing of goods are either nonexistent or of quite limited applicability in service marketing because of the intangible nature of the product, the predominance of direct marketing, or custom. Since services are not resold, there are no trade discounts. Agents' commissions are expenses of the seller in the case of insurance. They are an expense of the buyer, in the case of the employment agent. Cash discounts are seldom offered, although the advertising agency business is an exception. Utilities often submit a gross and a net price, the latter applying up to a specified date. Again, because of the direct nature of service marketing, there are no promotional discounts, although franchisers might grant them to service franchisees.

On the other hand, standardized services which permit the measurement of units of service purchased are commonly offered with quantity discount opportunities. In the case of utilities, increasing levels of consumption are charged decreasing rates; groups of passengers pay less per individual than independent passengers; carload rates are lower than less-than-carload rates. The purchase of season tickets to various forms of entertainment results in lower prices per event than prices charged for a single event.

Two other pricing policies which are common to goods marketing are not relevant in the service sector. First, a policy of resale price maintenance is not possible because of the direct nature of the marketing effort (see Chapter 3). Second, geographic pricing policies are largely inapplicable, although there are exceptions: it costs more to provide certain utility and local telephone services to distant customers, yet rates do not reflect distance; therefore, a modest form of "phantom freight" and "freight absorption" exists. The fee distinction between house and office calls made by physicians and "portal-to-portal" pricing of household repairmen are forms of geographic pricing policies.

PRICING METHODS

Attention is now directed to techniques of setting a specific price. Conventional marketing identifies two broad classes of pricing methods: cost-oriented and market-oriented, the latter containing both demand and competitive components. The former makes wide use of formulas and standards to account for variable and fixed costs, whereas the latter makes use of the market or competitive price, price lining, psychological pricing, and promotional pricing techniques. The two approaches are not mutually exclusive; ultimately, cost-oriented prices must take into account market conditions, and, ultimately, prices set according to the market must accommodate the necessity of covering costs.

Prices of some services are set using goods-sector methods whereas others appear to be set through techniques unique to services. On the other hand, some of the pricing methods found in the goods sector, particularly those which attempt to take into account demand conditions, find only limited application in the service sector.

Prices Based on the Cost of Service

The great majority of service prices are determined through some explicit or implicit cost-plus formula. This is true whether one is speaking of automobile repairs, business consulting, life insurance, or higher education. Services provided by public agencies and other nonprofit institutions use cost-oriented pricing methods.

Except for capital-intensive services, the major cost component is labor—skilled, technical, clerical, and managerial. As labor costs go up, prices go up. The resulting "cost-push factor" of services is a major reason for the generally higher inflationary rate in the service sector. Until recently, it has been assumed that capital substitution was unavailable as a means of increasing productivity and stabilizing service prices. The advent of programmed learning and the computer, and a trend toward standardization in a number of service areas suggest that the close relationship between labor cost and prices is not necessarily sacrosanct.

A modification of the cost-oriented pricing technique is one in which the price is set according to the difficulty of the assignment. This method is found in the professional services. For example, one transaction between a physician and patient or lawyer or consultant and client may call upon the ultimate expertise of the provider, either because it plumbs the depth of the professional's accumulated knowledge and skill or because it calls for the involvement of a more highly skilled mix of professionals. These cost-incurring inputs are reflected in higher prices and rightly so.

Rate-of-Return Pricing

Prices of services which are capital-intensive, whether regulated or unregulated, are typically set in order to achieve a desired rate of return. This is another manifestation of cost-oriented pricing. In the case of service industries whose prices are regulated, approval of the regulatory body is necessary before a price change can be made. A notice accompanying a recent utility invoice contained the following statement: "Revised electric and gas rates *to offset specific items of increased costs* were *permitted* by the Public Service Commission after four months of study and public hearings." (Italics added.) In effect, the regulators attempt to substitute for the competitive market. In the case of regulated monopolies (public utilities), their concern is with an adequate rate-of-return, but not an excessive one. In the case of regulated oligopolies (public transportation), the regulatory bodies attempt to balance the public interest and the need to maintain viable competition between specified points for specified commodities, if at all possible.[4] In its capacity as a representative of the public, the regulatory body is, in effect, introducing demand considerations in pricing. This is particularly evident if the regulated service industry applies for a rate increase to cover added costs while it is concurrently subject to widespread criticism from the public for deteriorating service.

Competitive Pricing

Examples of competitive pricing or, more appropriately, true price competition, are not common in the service sector. It does not occur in regulated services, nor is it practiced, overtly, in the self-regulated services. Among those services subject neither to public nor to self-regulation, such as household and automotive repairs and many forms of entertainment, labor costs (the major cost item) are common to competitors. Thus only limited flexibility for price competition is possible. On the demand side, the general inelasticity of prices for many services indicates that little would be gained through price competition. In addition, price-cutting would imply to many buyers a reduction in quality of service.

One classic exception in the status of pricing is transatlantic air travel, where price competition has taken on some of the characteristics of a price war. Why has it occurred? An increasing number of competing lines; more flights; larger planes; lack of regulatory jurisdiction; national interests; increasing leisure time; substitution of lower-priced charter flights for scheduled service; and the acknowledgment that pleasure travel, at some point, becomes quite price elastic. The airlines can justify price competition on the basis that any contribution to overhead after direct charges is better than nothing. However, their price lining is defective; first-class travelers cannot perceive the justification for the price they are charged and therefore opt for a lower-priced service.

Demand-Oriented Pricing

As a generalization, demand characteristics, like competition, play a lesser role than costs in the determination of service prices. Moreover, demand components are relatively less significant in the pricing of services relative to the pricing of goods. However, there are exceptions, and to simply stop with generalizations would be misleading.

When the price-setter incorporates demand in pricing decisions he is making a judgment that buyers are sensitive to price levels and price movements. Usually, lower prices and price reductions have a positive effect on demand if the buyer is sensitive. Of course, sensitivity to prices varies over time for the same product and in intensity for different products. For some products, and this is particularly true of certain services, sensitivity is inverse—lower prices have adverse effects on demand.[5]

A number of characteristics of services currently justify the price-setter's tendency to de-emphasize the significance of demand. (Exceptions are in parentheses.)

First, prices which must be authorized by regulatory bodies cannot be influenced directly by the buyer; his influence is limited to "hearings" before various state and federal commissions. Presumably his pricing interests are taken into consideration by the regulator.

Second, when negotiating with the provider of professional services, there is reluctance on the part of most consumers to display price sensitivity because of their perception of the professional-layman relationship.

Third, because services are invisible and typically nonstandardized, meaningful price comparisons are difficult to make. (Where there are standards and visibility, recognition of price sensitivity is occurring: economy motels and price appeals in the car rental industry, for example. Interestingly, trade names and brands in these two areas facilitate price comparison.)

Fourth, for many services, there is no substitute in the sense that if the price of meat is too high, patronage can be shifted to less expensive foods. (One most significant caveat must be entered: throughout the service sector there is usually the opportunity to substitute "do-it-yourself." The reader could produce a long list of examples of this form of substitution ranging from self-insurance and corporate staff consultants to home barbering, commuter travel, and self-treatment of illness.)

Fifth, demand of a crisis nature such as need for automobile repairs en route, problems requiring legal advice, and calling upon the services of funeral directors is not subject to postponement and is price insensitive.

Sixth, services such as education, recreation, and artistic activities serve higher-level needs; it could be argued that consumers are less likely to be price-sensitive at these levels even though they may be quite sensitive to the price of food, clothing, and shelter products.

Seventh, there appears to be a lower propensity to shop or bargain for attractive prices in the service sector. Today, a major tenet of consumerism is to stress the importance of shopping for insurance, housing repairs, and education opportunities, for example.

The preceding discussion of price sensitivity has a strong consumer bias. In general, industrial buyers are much more conscious of the price of service alternatives.

MARKETING ISSUES IN THE PRICING OF SERVICES

Pricing Flexibility

Implicit throughout this discussion is the view that prices play a rather passive role in marketing strategy; there are few examples of imaginative or innovative pricing in the service sector. Public regulation, ethical considerations, preeminence of cost over demand, and lack of understanding of the role of pricing have been cited.

There are at least five dimensions of service *output* which could provide criteria for a more effective pricing strategy in services. Two are objective and fairly widely used: (1) the time required to perform a particular service and (2) the extent to which capital goods are utilized in performance. Length of time, scheduling of performance time, and continuity of performance over time are only a few of the possibilities for strategic pricing related to time. Substituting capital for labor performance provides opportunities for service standardization and improved productivity, both of which enhance opportunities for greater pricing flexibility.

Pricing can take on a more dynamic character through consideration of three output criteria of a subjective nature, currently: (1) the quality of performance; (2) the specialization content of performance; and (3) the value of performance to the buyer or client. Assuming a correlation between quality and price of performance, the experience, reputation, prior knowledge, and skills necessary to properly perform a given service should be provided, not more or less. Law clerks and paramedics can substitute for law partners and physicians in the performance of many routine and relatively simple services. Moreover, it should be possible to break up a service assignment so that different quality levels can be assigned where appropriate.[6] In short, the more precise the application of quality in service performance, the greater the pricing flexibility. Similarly, adjusting the ratios of standardized to specialized components in terms of the needs of the buyer provides added opportunities for pricing flexibility.

Finally, the value criterion can be considered in pricing. The length of time during which the results of service performance will be felt by the buyer and the extent of buyer organization involvement are rough measures of value. Also, the relative dollar cost of the service output to the buyer is a measure of value. Although difficult to measure, the relative significance of the service to the buyer is another value criterion which could be reflected in price.

Price Regulation in Services

The regulation of service prices is another potential quagmire. Accordingly, it is essential that the total service sector be reduced to some degree of homogeneity. Excluded are service industries whose prices must be approved by regulatory agencies—utilities and common carriers, for example. Also excluded are services sold by government bodies—publicly-owned recreational facilities, parking garages, interest rates on government loans, and premiums charged for government insurance, for example. At present, it is probably appropriate to exclude nonprofit organizations which sell services—universities, symphony orchestras, and private hospitals, for example.

It is particularly difficult to generalize about price regulation in those service trades and professions characterized by a high degree of formal self-regulation. At one extreme, most state legislatures grant authority to local barber groups to establish minimum prices; various states have granted the same authority to cosmetologists, laundries, and dry cleaners.

(Public health was the original justification for government involvement.) At the other extreme is the increasing concern of consumer groups and antitrust agencies over pricing performance within the self-regulated professional services.

A society of professional engineers was prohibited by consent decree from limiting the submissions of price quotations for engineering services by its members. The order also prohibited the association from stating or implying in its publications that submission of price quotations was unethical, unprofessional or contrary to the society's policies.

A similar result was obtained against a society of architects. It should be noted that, as interpreted, the associations may lobby before legislative and administrative bodies for laws and regulations which would forbid price competition. Furthermore, they may advise that customers should select an engineer or an architect on a basis other than price. However, members of these professions may submit competitive price quotations without suffering professional harm. It would also appear that the traditional efforts of local bar associations to maintain minimum fee schedules may be subject to antitrust action if the Justice Department chooses to act.[7]

With regard to general laws designed to maintain competition, the reader is referred to Chapter 3 where the Sherman, Federal Trade Commission, and Robinson-Patman Acts are considered.

Two trends are evident. First, professional consumerists in their zeal to challenge "The Establishment" are questioning all service prices whether publicly-regulated, self-regulated, market-regulated, or non-regulated. The basis for the challenge is the general belief that prices of services have risen at an exorbitant rate. A second trend is a more inclusive conception of "business" and "commerce" and a broader application of antitrust laws. Professional sports have been defined as a business by the Supreme Court. Legal authorities are increasingly viewing professions as businesses, at least in their competitive characteristics. Eventually, nonprofit service institutions are likely to be included also, particularly as their performance takes on more and more the characteristics of a commercial enterprise.

Price Trends in Services

There is the commonly held and widely articulated belief that the level and trend of prices in the service sector have been detrimental to the interests of the consumer; typically, the high labor component, much of it unskilled, has been blamed.

A *cursory* survey of price data tends to support the generalization. In January, 1973, the Consumer Price Index for all items stood at 127.7 (1967 equals 100). Commodities stood at 123.4 and services at 135.[8]

However, as will be shown, there are extreme variations within the service sector. Some of the influencing factors include the extent to which the service purchase can be postponed or waived; degree of pricing freedom (regulated vs. unregulated); length of time during which the price is fixed (interest, rent, and insurance premiums, for example); extent to which capital can be substituted for labor; and the extent to which standard services can be substituted for custom services. In addition, the intensity and character of competition is not uniform throughout the service sector.

Table 5.2 provides more detail. Keep in mind: (1) only services to ultimate consumers are shown (unfortunately, the Wholesale Price Index covers commodities only, with the exception of electrical energy); (2) the Index is for a specific time period—1967 to January 1973; (3) there is no weighting—services vary in their impact on consumer expenditures; (4) the list is representative but not inclusive; and (5) changes in the quality of service purchased are not reflected, an important qualification yet a difficult one to determine.

Comparison of price performance of the various services shown in Table 5.2 permits some quite tentative observations. First, prices of the self-regulated or professional services have risen consistently at a greater rate than the overall Consumer Price Index. A hasty conclusion here could be an erroneous one. The professional services shown in Table 5.2 are not denied to those in need but without the ability to pay. Moreover, there is a difference between charges and payment. If services are rendered for which no charge is made or if the Index were based on the price of services for which payment is, in fact, received, the rate of rise might be quite different in view of the deeper involvement of these professionals in the social issues of our time. Second, with exceptions, the prices of labor-intensive services have risen faster than those of the capital-intensive services. In this regard, note the performance of shelter repair and maintenance services where trade unions are in control. Third, those services provided exclusively or substantially by government agencies have shown greater price increases than those in the private enterprise sector; note postal charges, local transit fares, hospitals, and parking fees. The greatest price rise has occurred for hospital services. (It is of some interest to note that 52 percent of American hospitals are controlled by private nonprofit bodies; 38 percent are controlled by government agencies at the federal, state, or local level, and only 10 percent of the hospitals are operated for profit.)[9]

Space does not permit more intensive analysis. Moreover, analysis should be made only by those with a thorough understanding of each service category. In any event, it is hoped that whenever pontifical, generalized statements regarding the price of services are made, the reader will ask: Which service?

Table 5.2

CONSUMER PRICE INDEXES (1967 = 100)

	January 1973
Publicly Regulated	
Gas and electricity	124.1
Residential telephone services	114.6
Postal charges*	146.6
Local transit fares	150.6
Taxicab fares	135.6
Railroad fares (coach)	122.2
Airplane fares (chiefly coach)	132.1
Bus fares (intercity)	144.0
Self-Regulated	
Physicians' fees	135.7
Dentists' fees	134.3
Hospitals (semi-private rooms)	177.6
Hospitals (operating room)	173.5
Hospitals (x-ray)	130.7
Legal services (short form will)	155.5
Insurance	
Property	124.5
Auto	138.4
Market-Regulated	
Rent, residential	136.9
Maintenance and repair (shelter)	151.9
Housekeeping:	
Domestic services	141.9
Babysitter	139.2
Laundry	142.1
Licensed day care	125.8
Washing machine repairs	144.1
Apparel services:	
Dry cleaning	119.0
Automatic laundry	115.8
Laundry, men's shirts	125.3
Tailoring charges	135.9
Shoe repairs	119.1
Auto repairs and maintenance	138.4
Parking fees	149.7
Personal care services	125.6
Recreation:	
Indoor movie admissions	142.7
Drive-in movie admissions	148.2
Bowling fees	122.2
TV repair (picture tube replacement)	98.7
Film developing, color	116.2
Piano lessons, beginner	125.2
Funeral services	123.0

*A special type of public regulation indeed: both the regulator and regulated are a government body.
Source: *The Consumer Price Index* (April 1973), pp. 16-19.

FOOTNOTES

1. Where payment is not made by the beneficiary of a specific service performed the word "price" should read "tax" or "donation."

2. See Stephen Grover, "Is a Cultural Center an Appropriate Setting for Lawrence Welk?" *The Wall Street Journal,* 7 May 1973, p. 1.

3. It is assumed that the reader is already familiar with broad outlines of economic theory discussed here.

4. See Robert A. Lynn, *Price Policies and Marketing Management* (Homewood, Illinois: Richard D. Irwin, Inc. 1967), pp. 279-293.

5. This discussion pertains to the price elasticity of demand. Thorough coverage is found in any standard marketing text. Sensitivity is considered a more precise word.

6. For a useful approach to costing people, see Howard E. McDonald and T. L. Stromberger, "Cost Control for the Professional Service Firm," *Harvard Business Review* 47 no. 1, (January-February 1969), pp. 109-121.

7. "Legal Developments in Marketing," *Journal of Marketing* 37 no. 1, (January 1973), p. 73.

8. *The Consumer Price Index* (April 1973), p. 8.

9. *Hospital Statistics, 1971* (Chicago: American Hospital Association, 1972), p. 32.

MARKETING AND PRICING IN REGULATED INDUSTRIES

John G. B. Hutchins

Freight transportation is a regulated service. Shippers are not so regulated. Price-making in this unusual market is quite unconventional when viewed from a marketing perspective.

The industries with which we are here concerned are those held to be public utilities by the courts and regulated by federal or state law or both. The leading decision here, Munn v. Illinois, 1877 (which cited ancient English law that those businesses peculiarly affected with a public interest, such as toll roads, bridges, and town docks, might be easily controlled by the authorities), held that regulation was not a violation of the Fourteenth Amendment concerning deprivation of property without due process of law. Thereafter a special class of regulated enterprise grew up. The United States leads the world in elaborate and sophisticated systems of regulation by commission.

The industries involved may be divided structurally into those which are essentially monopolistic, and usually economically stable, and those which are mixtures of monopoly, oligopoly, and competition, and are often very unstable, both with reference to demand and competitive relations. In the first group we find the electric utilities, each of which has its service territory, the retail gas systems, which are in the same position, the long distance gas pipelines, which sometimes compete for markets but are basically monopolistic, and the telephone companies. When one is selling products having few if any close substitutes to thousands of buyers, small and large, the problems of regulation concern mainly the allowable rate of return and the acquisition of sufficient new capital to sustain rates of expansion in the high range of 7 to 10 percent annually. In the second category the most prominent group consists

The author is Professor of Business History and Transportation at the Graduate School of Business and Public Administration, Cornell University.

of the transportation industries—rail, motor carrier, domestic water carrier, and airline. Within each mode the structure may range from monopoly through tight and loose oligopoly to competition, and among modes there is often intense competition. At the same time operators must cooperate intramodally and intermodally to provide through rates and service. We shall be concerned with this second group.

Also from the structural point of view it should be noted that there is much countervailing power in freight transportation in that the buyers are generally sophisticated freight traffic managers of great skill and knowledge. Furthermore, many buyers have the alternatives of operating their own trucks, barges, ships, and aircraft, and many do. Generally the buyer may be thought to have a strategic advantage over the carrier sales representative.

Another unusual feature of the transportation market is that it is highly organized through rate bureaus, rate conferences, traffic clubs, trade associations, and chambers of commerce. In 1947, as a result of major antitrust activity, Congress enacted the Reed-Bulwinkle Act, which gave antitrust immunity to rate bureaus and conferences whose articles of organization pass ICC approval. Most important is the right of unpenalized withdrawal for a carrier. The major function of the rate bureau or conference is to make rates for traffic subject to its jurisdiction and to publish these for the membership collectively. These organizations cover the carriers in defined territories, such as New England and the Middle Atlantic states for motor carriers and the transcontinental movements for railroads. There are also separate bureaus for important traffic such as coal. Still another role of the bureaus and conferences is to maintain a private tribunal to which shippers can appeal for adjustments. Shippers, especially the larger ones, are likely to be represented by their own expert traffic people or by traffic consultants. Others who may be affected by a decision may be asked to appear. Finally, the conferences and bureaus have the task of adjusting or equalizing rates over various routings, and of executing any ICC orders within their jurisdiction. Thus instead of having to maintain up to date a file of some 10,000 to 15,000 individual tariffs, a company with national distribution may need less than a hundred bureau or conference tariffs. This system has often been styled monopolistic, as it is, but it also provides for much rationalization.

Crucial to the problem of marketing in transportation is the economics of the business. As between rail, motor, water, and air transport the economics differ strikingly; hence a major problem facing the ICC has been to determine the desirable equilibrium adjustment in the market. It is desirable to start with railroad economics, which have created over the years the characteristic pricing system of all modes. To begin with, a rail line, once built, is subject to decreasing average costs as volume increases, up to capacity. Since little if any trackage is used to capacity, marginal cost is nearly always well below average cost. It would be especially low where excess cars and power are available. At the extreme, to put an extra 1,000 lbs. on a freight car lightly loaded at 10,000 lbs. and already in a scheduled train, would be almost costless. Various limitations may arise as volume increases, notably with respect to cars, power, and freight terminal capacity, but some are readily remedied in the short run. There are economies of scale in the loading of individual cars, in the size of car used, in the number of cars in the train, in the density of trains on the line, and in the distance run. Furthermore, the business is affected with joint cost on an enormous scale, primarily with respect to the backhaul problem, and occasionally in connection with fixed equipment consists in which the space available for passengers, freight, and mail in any vehicle is given. As is well known, where there are joint costs, total costs are apportioned according to demand. Finally there are common costs, such as for signals, drawbridges, and even maintenance of way, which are difficult to apportion between trains and shipments, especially where the costs are related mainly to time and weather. The result is that the rail rate system is an enormous mass of more or less rational discriminations in which the upper limit is ability to pay and the lower, hopefully, long run marginal cost.

The motor and water carriers have quite different economics. Beyond the volume involved in the double trailer load there are few economies of scale in the line haul in motor transport. The governments provide the roadbed, and carrier capacity can be quickly changed by buying, selling, or leasing vehicles. Normally operating costs are a high percentage (92-96) of revenues. But although fixed costs are minor, joint costs still prevail. With some exceptions the motor carriers have tended to follow the railroad rate pattern, but to endeavor to exclude traffic below motor marginal cost. Above this level motors and rails compete in a value of service pricing system. The governments, of course, carry the costs of the highway system which they meet out of registration fees, fuel taxes, and general revenues. In inland water transport, which handles mainly bulk and heavy loading cargoes, there are some economies related to size of tow or of ocean ship, but these have minor impacts on rates.

The result of these economic structures is a rate system of unusual complexity involving organized and more or less rational discrimination with respect to (1) commodities, (2) distance, and

(3) volume. It is necessary for a marketer or traffic man to be thoroughly familiar with these features.

In rail and motor carrier service, commodity discrimination occurs in two forms. The first is the classification system, in which all commodities moving are given a rating in terms of first-class or par, between 400 and 13. The vast majority of ratings are between 100 and 40. Ratings are based on value of service factors, principally market value per 100 lbs., and cost of service factors, such as cubic space per 100 lbs., liability to be damaged or to cause damage, and special equipment requirements. The higher rated products are usually finished manufactures. At the lower end of the scale are such things as sand and gravel. To develop the actual rate to be paid it is necessary to multiply the class 100 distance rate by the rating. Class rates move only a small proportion of the traffic by volume, but much more by value. The rest goes on commodity rates, which apply chiefly to foods, raw materials, and semi-finished manufactures. There are for each customer industry special adjustments which tend to maintain competitive marketing equilibria among customers and competitive stability among carriers. These may seriously disregard distance.

Distance discrimination is caused by (1) competitive pressures in customer markets, and (2) competition among routes, carriers, and gateways. The principal devices are groups, in which all points within the group take the same rate; blankets, which are much larger groups sometimes covering hundreds of miles, key point rates, which are low and influence rates to adjacent points; taper in the class rate distance scales such that the rate increase is increasingly less than proportional to the distance as the latter extends, and for rails the transit privilege, under which commodities can move over indirect routes to processing or storage points while paying the direct through rate. Crucial is the fact that in the United States one can often ship over alternate routings, some of which may have opposite compass bearings. For example, one can ship from Pittsburgh to California west by rail, or east via Atlantic ports and Panama. Groups and blankets develop because of rivalry among carriers and routes.

Volume discrimination is based mainly on the economies of heavier loads, and is chiefly a railroad phenomenon. It takes the form of incentive rates for heavier loading of cars, lower rates for larger cars, and especially, low trainload rates. The extreme is the full-sized coal or grain integrated shuttle train. Some of the reductions from the single car rate have been as high as 50 percent. Such rates are often made to compete with water service, or electric wire transmission, or to open up new business, such as the supply of Buffalo millers with grain from Kansas and Nebraska in competition with that from the Northwest via the Lakes.

A marketer in transportation must be particularly aware of the Interstate Commerce Act of 1887, which as amended is very much alive. The original statute required (1) that rates be just and reasonable, an issue usually settled by comparison; (2) that there be no personal discrimination, meaning like charges and service to all customers having like and contemporaneous requirements; (3) that there be no unreasonable preference given to persons, firms localities, and goods; and (4) that, except as allowed by the Commission, rates on a short haul could not be higher than those on a long haul on the same route. The Elkins Act of 1903 gave a published tariff the force of law, and imposed severe penalties on both carriers and shippers for violations. Hence one attempts to shave or discount published rates at his peril. There are many other features of the modern act, but these are not directly germane to our purpose.

One can thus ask what a sales representative of a common carrier can do, especially when he is dealing with highly sophisticated industrial traffic people, many of whom will have a wider horizon than he. Mostly he can be helpful, especially with respect to complex questions of classification, rate quotation and interpretation, advice regarding service and sometimes arrangements for service, tracing shipments, and handling mistakes in paper work. But he cannot cut the legitimate or proper rate for the traffic, and he cannot promise to give without charge special services, such as extra switching of plants, special trains for the benefit of particular shippers, and undue preference in car allocation in time of shortage. He can, however, report back the competitive pressures as he finds them and make proposals for new rates and schedules which might draw business.

In particular he must find a way to cooperate with the operating people. These often tend to favor holding freight cars to make up large trains, thus improving their operating records and lowering costs, but also diverting traffic to the ever-present trucks. At a time when prompt shipment is increasingly important as inventories are pared, the flexibility of the truck, particularly the unregulated private truck, presents great advantage to shippers.

There are some other matters of interest. Motor common carriers are by the amendments of 1935 restricted in their service to the routes, points, and commodities listed on their certificates. Routes may be inter-city, usually over numbered highways, or fixed base radial over irregular routes. A showing of fitness is required. However, motor carriers of products of agriculture and the fisheries, raw or nearly so, are exempt from regulation. Herein has been a source of argument over many years. A private carrier, which is a business whose primary activity is other than transportation, is also exempt from regulation. Some grocery chains and large industries operate fleets of hundreds of vehicles on regular schedules.

The transportation world is thus a maze of regulated and unregulated carriers, of economies of scale of different types, of complex pricing systems, of competition among carriers of various types, and of extensive regulation. Railroads endeavor to compete with barges by means of low rates on a marginal cost basis. In rail-truck competition the rails might well recover much business from trucks were they allowed to cut selectively. Forwarders, who now generally load trailers, compete with truckers by shipping them in rail trailer-on-flatcar service, a growing business. This piggyback operation may have rail-owned trailers at rail rates, motor common carrier trailers at motor rates, private trailers at per trailer all-freight rates, and forwarder trailers. Some middlemen offer a complete service consisting of trailers and rail cars ready to go. There are special boat trains of containers for the steamship lines. Thus, there is great diversity within which the experienced traffic man can find many opportunities to improve his firm's shipping operation despite the regulation.

The entire transportation structure is under intense criticism because of its complexities and alleged irrationalities. The collective system of rate-making is under attack as monopolistic. The ICC is accused of preventing carriers from competing for traffic which they could carry profitably while insisting on the continuation of loss operations. Should the present system, which was built up mainly in the twenties and thirties, be greatly changed there would undoubtedly be much more intense competition, much more discrimination, many mergers, many failures, many new service patterns, and drastic financial changes. Whatever else might happen, the role of the sales organization would change from service to promotion. On the other hand, it is also probable that many buyers prefer the stability, the protection against haggling, and the organized procedures both private and public of the present structure. In the long run, buyers are probably more concerned with relative than with absolute rates. Some major change appears to be likely because of the serious deficiencies which have developed and, in particular, the bankruptcies of many eastern rail systems.

6

PROMOTING SERVICES

In contemporary marketing, interpersonal communication theory provides a scientific basis for the promotion *process*. Similarly, the behavioral sciences of psychology, social psychology and sociology provide a scientific frame of reference for the *content* of promotion. In terms of these two foundations, no distinction need be made between the promotion of goods and the promotion of services; they are equally relevant to both. In view of the incremental approach of this book, detailed consideration of communication and behavioral theory would be redundant; conventional presentations of promotion with their typical goods orientation are adequate. Rather, emphasis is placed on how the promotion of services differs from the promotion of goods, in practice.

An overview of service promotion suggests that these differences fall into two categories: (1) concepts of the role of promotion in service marketing and (2) the execution of promotion.

Since differences in promotion are grounded in that which differentiates services from goods it is appropriate at this point to quickly review these distinguishing characteristics: (1) the intangibility of the product; (2) the high degree of buyer dependence on seller; (3) simultaneous production and consumption; (4) the in-being nature of the service facility; and (5) the nonuniformity of service performance, with limited exceptions. While the effect of these characteristics on service promotion is discussed subsequently, it would be a useful mental exercise for the reader to stop for a moment to make his own appraisal.

It is often observed that promotion plays a more modest role in the marketing of services than of goods and some data tend to support this notion. For example, only 10 of the top 100 advertisers in 1971 were service firms and several of these also manufactured industrial and consumer goods and, presumably, significant portions of their advertising dollars were expended to promote goods; moreover, these 10 service firms accounted for only 6.6 percent of advertising expenditures of the top 100 advertisers.[1] In addition, many service organizations do not employ people whose sole function is to promote their services; consider, for example, personal, legal, health care, educational, and recreational services.

There are several reasons why there is an *apparent* de-emphasis of conventional promotion. Services are relatively unconcentrated and there are only a few with the resources and market coverage to promote on a nationwide scale. Promotional practices are frowned upon in some services. Throughout the service sector there is a tendency to stress quality of performance and reputation as the most valuable form of promotion. Mass or impersonal selling can be awkward in those many services in which each transaction involves a unique service product.

As a matter of fact, promotion plays a very significant role in service marketing. It differs from conventional views of promotion more in terms of objectives and form than in significance and quantity.

Table 6.1 is a liberal interpretation of 1960 Census occupational data. The total shown represents less than 17 percent of all employed people designated as sales workers. It will be noted that only those services making extensive use of agent intermediaries are identified. It is quite unlikely that the residual classification at the end of the table encompasses all people engaged in personal selling in the communications, banking, utility, and transportation service industries. Aside from the relatively imprecise treatment of marketing occupations in Census classifications, the reasons for the rather small number of designated sales workers in the service sector include the following: (1) the prominence of single proprietorships in many services in which the proprietor both performs and sells his service (an automobile repair shop, for example); (2) the widespread beliefs that the performance and sale of a service are intertwined in practice and that every contact between service provider and customer or client is a selling contact (business facilitating services, for example); and (3) the perceived impropriety of a designated sales occupation and function in those services requiring a deep involvement on the part of the client in their performance (health care services, for example).

Table 6.1.

DESIGNATED SALES WORKERS IN SERVICE SECTOR

Advertising agents and salesmen	34,762
Insurance agents, brokers, and underwriters	369,230
Real estate agents and brokers*	195,742
Stock and bond salesmen	29,018
Salesmen and sales clerks; other industries**	185,591
Total	814,343

*Rental and leasing transactions only. The *sale* of real estate is the sale of a good.

**Residual after manufacturing, wholesale trade, and retail trade. Assumed to be services.

Source: U.S. Bureau of the Census. *U.S. Census of Population 1960. Detailed Characteristics. U.S. Summary.* Final Report PC(1)-1D. Table 201.

THE ROLE OF PROMOTION IN THE SERVICE SECTOR

For the layman, more often than not, promotion *is* marketing. Marketing literature places major stress on promotion. There have been many statements regarding the role or objectives of promotion. None is more succinct and precise than McCarthy's: the broad objectives of promotion are to inform, persuade, or remind.[2] However, treatment of promotion within the totality of marketing has not been balanced. Consumer goods have received more consideration than industrial goods. Within consumer goods, the promotion of nondurables has been stressed over durables. In terms of media, impersonal means of promotion have received much greater recognition than personal approaches. Among the various impersonal media, focus has been on mass selling through newspapers, magazines, and television at the expense of various forms of sales promotion, direct mail, and publicity. And, with reluctance, it must be noted once more that the service sector has been included in discussions of promotion only implicitly, for the most part. The essential strangeness in relating promotion and services can be illustrated by asking a question. How does a public accountant inform, persuade, or remind its active or potential clientele—a university, a barber, a television network, a trucking line, or a zoo?

Because of the heterogeneity of the service sector, some appropriate classification scheme is essential. First, there are services which are sold not for profit including those provided both by private and public enterprises and agencies. Second, in the case of some services which are sold, overt promotion techniques are not approved. Third, there are the majority of services in which promotion does, or could, make a substantial contribution to profitable service performance.

Service Promotion Not for Profit

Lacking the discipline of the need to make a profit, one might question the need for promoting services in this category. As a matter of fact, among public enterprises such as the Tennessee Valley Authority, the Postal Service, state park systems, toll roads, and publicly-owned transit systems and stadiums there is (or should be) the strong motive to expand and maintain demand so that the enterprise is self-supporting rather than the beneficiary of subsidy from general taxation. Moreover, public administrators (not political appointees) have the same enthusiasm for the service they provide as their counterparts in the private sector and therefore desire to improve the quality and expand the range of services under their jurisdiction. Promotion techniques are an appropriate mechanism. A major problem can arise, of course, if the public service competes directly or even semi-directly with private alternatives. Because of this possibility, hard-sell, persuasive promotion is unlikely; rather, public service promotion is designed to inform and remind.

In the same way, private nonprofit service providers have a stake in self-sufficiency and growth in order to avoid the need for *private* subsidy. Promotion, primarily to inform, is quite appropriate. Many readers are students at publicly supported or private institutions of higher learning. Consider for a moment how your school communicated with you before your decision to "buy" its educational services. What media did it use? What did it say? Did it inform you adequately? If it was persuasive, what form did the persuasion take? Announcements, bulletins, brochures, seminars, and publicity are typical. Increasingly, mass-selling media including newspapers, radio, and television are coming into use by colleges and universities and while the objective remains basically informational, as financial pressures mount, low-key or indirect persuasion is becoming evident.

While this text is concerned primarily with services which are sold in a variety of marketplaces, it should be noted that both highly persuasive and quite sophisticated promotion is transmitted through major media in the interest of nonprofit activities seeking moral and financial support. These include both charities such as the United Fund and foundations whose goals are to reduce or eradicate various diseases all of which have nearly universal approval or "causes" such as those of the environmentalist and consumerist whose goals may be more controversial. An informal calculation of commercial time devoted to these interests during any given evening will confirm the new importance of public service promotion.

Promotion in the Professional Services

As noted in Chapter 3, in a number of professional services competition through promotion is discouraged. As a result, the professional service provider communicates with his market through exposure or visibility. At the local level, the professional participates in community activities, serves on their committees, and on church and school boards. Since the professional is barred from promoting his services in a commercial manner, he must do something to provide visibility so that when his services are needed, which may be quite infrequently, his name will be recalled. Exposure by these means is quite appropriate and communities are the beneficiaries. At the national level, rather than overt promotion, professional service firms obtain exposure through professionally-oriented house organs, technical articles, and technical papers at conferences. Many professionals, on the other hand, take none of these steps, preferring to exclude communications from their marketing mix and to let performance "speak for itself."

Two exceptions to the proscription against overt promotion have emerged. Both local and national societies and associations of professionals are promoting the interests of their members through mass media and the use of a variety of themes; beneficiaries are *groups* of professionals, not individuals. And the Oregon State Bar Association permits law firms devoting at least half their time to public interest cases to advertise for clients. The purpose is to "ease client access to public interest lawyers."[3] This is a classic example of the application of marketing to a new marketplace.

Conventional Promotion of Services for Profit

Attention is now directed to those services which are performed for profit-making purposes and whose promotion does not fall under professional disapproval. Included in this category are most of the following: communications, business facilitating, banking, utilities, housing services, insurance, personal, recreational and transportation services.

Promoting an Intangible

It is difficult or meaningless to promote an intangible product as a tangible product. An intangible does not lend itself to visual presentation. In addition, either the visualization of a service being performed or a word description, whether written or spoken, offers only limited opportunity to inform, persuade, or remind the service customer or prospect. As a result, the intangibility of services leads to the adoption of what many believe to be a superior form of promotion: the sale of an idea.

Some services promote ideas indirectly through stress on surrogates. For example, facilitating goods rather than the service itself are emphasized. Both air and surface passenger transportation services and hotels often stress amenities; financial institutions dealing with the general public call attention to the convenience of their facilities and saving and borrowing options; and some consulting and business facilitating services describe how their work is performed (an attempt to visualize a service). The environment of a service is a second surrogate. Various recreational travel industries and rental housing often use this promotional theme with stress on status symbols.

For the most part, however, the intangibility of a service requires that it be promoted on the basis of a very simple idea—an idea which receives universal approbation—consumer, user, client benefits. This is at the heart of promotion in the insurance industry; utilities stress convenience; telephone advertising calls attention to the satisfaction in phoning home or phoning a loved one; consultants and business facilitating firms stress achieving objectives—cutting costs, for example—even though results are, of course, not guaranteed; the benefit idea is the major unifying theme of equipment leasing and automobile rentals; and freight transport promotion stresses speed and specialized service.

Service Product Differentiation

For a variety of reasons, services have been traditionally viewed as undifferentiated products. Or, at least, explicit steps to differentiate were seldom taken by the service provider. He was willing to allow the buyer to make his own differentiation on the basis of experience. Now this is changing. With the increasing acceptance and use of promotion in the service sector, the need to focus demand and not simply to generate primary demand is recognized.

Two practices in particular are evident. First, a major objective of the franchise system is to communicate differentiated uniform quality performance. Second, service firms are making increased use of trademarks and trade names and other differentiating characteristics. Consider for example: Citybank, Avis, Prudential's Rock, and Howard Johnson's orange-colored roofs. A casual review by the reader of business journals, national weeklies, or the telephone directory's Yellow Pages will disclose numerous illustrations of efforts to differentiate service products.

Conventional marketing distinguishes between "push" and "pull" promotion by the producer of goods or provider of services to gain channel support for its products. Among those services making use of an agency form of channel, a "pulling" role is assigned to promotion; in other words, the agent depends on the service firm to stimulate demand, whether he be a theater ticket agent, a travel agent, or a property insurance agent. One exception is life insurance where the agent represents but one company and a major effort is made to develop demand through the agency system.

Promoting "Undesired" Services

How does one promote the demand for services which merely correct defects or return the buyer to a condition of normalcy. As noted elsewhere, certain services such as health care, legal services in court actions, and household and automotive repairs are purchased only when conditions force their purchase. The idea of creating demand for them through promotional methods is somewhat ludicrous. However, two roles are evident. First, promotion can stress the in-being nature of repair services in particular; promotion enables the buyer to *recall* the existence of a service facility ready to perform. Second, service providers who are typically called upon only when a crisis forces demand are increasingly offering their services to prevent a crisis. For example, auto repair services are promoting the desirability of "tune-ups"; and professional services, through acceptable channels, are communicating the idea of legal review of contemplated actions to prevent legal difficulties and annual health check-ups to prevent disease.

Depromoting a Service

The service sector may soon be the scene of the first formal effort to depromote demand for a legitimate product. The American public may be called upon to reduce its demand for energy. In the recent past, during periods of peak demand, utilities have sporadically taken various steps to reduce demand for their product. In the future, they may be called upon to carry on this type of communication on a continuing and more intensive basis. How best to do this—what to say and what media to use—presents service marketing with an objective without precedent. Hopefully, efforts to depromote demand will be voluntary; however, several states are considering outright bans on utility advertising or excluding advertising expenses from costs of doing business for rate-making purposes. The implications are significant, for depromotion runs counter to the most basic and pervasive role of marketing: the expansion, not the contraction, of profitable demand. The present oil crisis may place marketers in the transportation and recreation services in an equally awkward predicament.

THE PROMOTION PROCESS IN THE SERVICE SECTOR

The process of service promotion differs from the promotion of goods primarily in terms of *relative importance* assigned in the total marketing program and in *media mix*. The process of *creating* effective promotional communications is common to goods and services.

For example, the process of promoting air freight would not differ materially from the process of promoting consumer durables or machine tools, and air freight marketing operations are organized along the lines found in manufacturing. Similarly, the process of promoting a small personal service proprietorship would parallel that of a local specialty retailer. With few exceptions, however (air freight is one, telecommunications, commercial banking, and insurance are others), promotional practices are non-existent or unorganized and unplanned.

Promotion Mix Variables

In a normative sense, a number of factors are at work in determining the promotion mix of both entire service industries and individual service firms or institutions. First, the distinction between profit and non-profit services is a factor, particularly with respect to the content of promotional messages. Second, the details of professional constraints and the extent of profession-wide support for these constraints have an overriding influence on professional promotion practice. Third, the extent of competition, if any, and its nature have a significant impact on the level and intensity of promotional communications. For example, compare promotion by a regulated electrical utility monopoly with that in the motel or banking industry where competition is strong. Fourth, as would be expected, promotional media vary according to the size of the geographical market served by the service firm. Fifth, in a number of service industries, entertainment, travel, and employment services, for example, custom appears to dictate promotional practice. Sixth, practice is greatly influenced by the degree of managerial sophistication in promotion input/output relations—the extent to which promotional media reinforce each other and the kinds of market behavior one can anticipate from the use of various media. Closely related to this factor of managerial understanding is the extent to which the service firm is cognizant of *any* contribution from promotion.

Advertising in Services

In general, advertising media are selected which are best suited to inform buyers of the availability of services and to describe their benefits. Because of the intermittent nature of demand for many services, media with "staying power" are particularly well suited. Most consumer services are provided by local or regional establishments; therefore media which are confined to local or regional markets are preferred. Accordingly, consumer services are heavy users of telephone directory advertising, direct mail, and newspapers. Broadcast media are less widely used because of the temporary nature of the communication and the lesser significance of color and motion in the promotion of intangibles. National media are not widely used. For example, in the June, 1973 issue of the *Ladies Home Journal,* only 6 percent of the advertising space was devoted to services (transportation, travel, and communications).

A greater proportion of service advertising to industry is found in national media, particularly business papers. The importance of service advertising varies with the managerial function and the level of management of the readership. For example, in a recent issue of *Sales Management,* 17 percent of the space was devoted to services (transportation, hotel, and business facilitating); in *Traffic World,* 58 percent of the space was devoted to services (transportation); in *Plant Operating Management* only 3 percent of the space was devoted to services; and in *Business Week,* a nonfunctionally oriented business paper, 35 percent of the space was devoted to service advertising (finance, transportation, insurance, and leasing, primarily).[4]

Advertising message content must relate to the prevailing characteristics of the buying process. Advertising services which are bought routinely and on a repeat basis should engender confidence through stress on dependability, as in the case of many personal services. Moreover, the message should be designed to hold present patrons and attract new ones. In the case of utilities and telephone services, where market coverage is total, advertising messages typically encourage more intensive consumption: advertising to expand long distance calling is an example.

The advertiser of services which are purchased only as needed seeks to keep the potential customer aware of his availability. The intention of the message is to implant a trade name or a location on the mind of the prospect so that, if and when the service is needed, the provider's identity will come to mind. Persuasive messages serve no purpose unless of course, the advertiser is encouraging preventive services.

Finally, the most challenging assignment for the creator of service advertising occurs where buyer attitudes and practices must be changed if a transaction is to occur. This is the situation facing service providers in such industries as transportation, recreation, insurance, and many business facilitating services. The message must attract the attention of latent users and develop a sufficiently strong interest to generate some initiative. Persuasive messages, whether in the form of copy or visual, are of paramount importance; benefits are stressed through testimonials of users, through before-and-after comparisons, and through stress on personal satisfaction derived from purchase of the service. In view of the intangibility of the product, this type of message is not easy to create; given the materialistic orientation of our society, with its emphasis on the acquisition of things, the creator of service advertising must somehow break through this obstacle to the purchase of experiences or the purchase of peace of mind. Moreover, particular care must be taken that persuasive messages are not misleading given the typical dependent relationship of the buyer to the seller.

The Importance of Publicity

Interestingly, certain segments of the service sector have developed publicity to a fine art. The travel industry, entertainment, including motion pictures, theater arts, concert music, museums, spectator sports, both professional and amateur, and higher education are notable for their sensitivity to the effectiveness of publicity. As a matter of fact, in many cases publicity is the important and senior communications medium, conventional advertising being a subsidiary activity. The editorial content of appropriate sections of daily and Sunday newspapers demonstrates that almost every item of "news" is a form of publicity. Also, the publicity generated by the professional critic should be noted. These people are a type of consumer "ombudsman" unique to the performing and artistic entertainment services. Their publicity can be either promotional or depromotional. In this age of consumerism, it is rather strange that the concept of critical review which is well nigh universal in the above noted services has not been expanded.

Personal Selling in Services

In order to obtain a proper perspective of the personal selling element in service promotion, certain service characteristics should be repeated: (1) Most services are labor-intensive, that is, the service is performed by people, not machines. (2) For many services there is a direct personal interaction between the provider and the customer of services; in many cases, performance requires the participation of the buyer. (3) It is difficult for the buyer to "see," literally, the service being performed; however, the customer can "see" the human element. (4) Many services are custom performed, not mass performed; the total selling process cannot be accomplished through mass marketing means alone.

All of this suggests that service flexibility must be achieved on a one-to-one basis; all personnel of the service establishment who are in contact with the market are engaged in personal selling (this observation is often treated as a cliché in marketing literature—it is very real in service promotion); and the consummation of a service transaction typically calls for a sensitivity and an ability to articulate the service's characteristics in a personalized manner.

There are three categories of salesmen in the service sector. First, as is shown in the succeeding chapter, numerous services are sold by independent agents who are compensated by service providers on the basis of business actually generated. Second, some services have their own sales force: communications, transportation, and public utilities, for example, as do many business facilitating services. Seldom do they have the title of "salesman." Business, customer, account, or traffic "representative" is a more common title. Typically, these sales personnel are responsible not only for acquiring new business but, of equal importance, maintaining a healthy seller-buyer relationship after the initial contract. The third type of salesman is any service firm's employee who is in personal contact with the customer, be he a passenger train conductor, a university registrar, an auditor, or an auto mechanic. As noted earlier these are the visible aspects of a service and, therefore, the major basis for differential advantage. The leverage in a good understanding of human relations is apparent.

MARKETING ISSUES IN SERVICE PROMOTION

A review of service promotion from a marketing perspective identifies several areas in a condition of transition. There is controversy; there are innovators and traditionalists; and there are unanswered questions.

In the first place, one is struck by the strength of custom or tradition in service promotion. The negative attitudes of professional services and many segments of the financial community are a case in point. The strong tradition of the agency system in insurance is another. A review of the Sunday edition of the *New York Times* discloses a strong custom-dictated uniformity in the advertising found in the business, entertainment, and travel sections. Yet the reader can identify departures from tradition: the establishment of sales training programs in commercial banks; the use of television to advertise educational institutions; the substitution of direct mail for agents in insurance; and the addition of more imaginative copy and illustration to supplement the traditional "who, when, and how much" type of information in travel and recreation advertising. Whether these trends are good or bad for the various services or for society cannot be established here. The fact is, as recognition of marketing within the service sector grows, new and imaginative forms of promotion are likely to emerge. Services are sufficiently different from goods to warrant new promotional concepts and practices; moreover, the newness of promotion in services relative to goods offers an unencumbered point of departure for innovative promotion. In the second place, a marketing approach also underscores the need to develop a demand sensitivity among the many service providers who have a personal contact with the buyer. While it is desirable, it is not so essential to have this same sensitivity among production workers in the goods sector. It is mandatory in services, not only because marketplace success is more likely but also because the "social responsibility" of the service sector is more likely to be met. One of the major criticisms of services by consumers is the perceived cavalier, impersonal, and disinterested attitude of service providers toward their customers.

Third, with some exceptions, there is little evidence that service firms view promotion as an integrated activity. What is lacking is a planned promotional program in which each element is assigned goals which are appropriate for it and which are reinforcing in terms of the total program. The exceptions, air transportation and commercial banking, for example, illustrate the transition to comprehensive service promotion.

Finally, two segments of the service sector offer opportunities for *group* promotion. First, professional services can enhance their image, expand demand for their services, and achieve professional goals (legal aid for the poor, early cancer detection, or tooth decay reduction, for example) through appropriate communications sponsored by professional societies. Second, local, regional, and national trade associations of specialized service providers whose members are typically small, inexperienced, and limited in working capital, have an opportunity to expand demand for the services of their membership through group promotion programs of a quality equal to that of the large firm.

FOOTNOTES

1.   *Advertising Age,* 24 July 1972, pp. 55-56.

2.   E. Jerome McCarthy, *Basic Marketing,* 4th ed. (Homewood, Illinois: Richard D. Irwin, Inc., 1971), p. 514.

3.   "Commentary/Social Issues," *Business Week,* 28 July 1973, p. 71.

4.   By contrast, in the equivalent dated issue of *Business Week* in 1948, twenty-five years earlier, less than 11 percent of the advertising space promoted services (transportation, business facilitating, insurance, finance, and communications). Note: space percentages are approximate.

7

DISTRIBUTION AND DELIVERY OF
SERVICES

The fourth major element in the marketing mix is variously characterized as place or location, channel, distribution, and structure. Two of these terms are particularly relevant to services. *Location* refers to the distribution of people and facilities prepared to perform services; *channel* refers to a network designed to deliver services to the ultimate consumer or industrial user. To facilitate integration with conventional thought, location and distribution, and channel and delivery are used interchangeably. The term "delivery" is new to marketing but should gain wider currency. In the area of public services, health care, and other social services it is widely used and, in fact, refers to the marketing of services. It is a particularly apt descriptive term for a service channel network.

The distribution of service facilities and the length and breadth of delivery or channel networks reflect the differentiating characteristics of services. Consider: the repair of household electrical appliances and the delivery of electrical energy to a household; a general practitioner and a specialist in the field of medicine; and recreation travel and theatrical entertainment. Obviously, the diversity of services forestalls easy generalizations. It is often stated that services are marketed through short channels. This may be true relative to the marketing of goods but length and complexity vary from service to service. Also, new institutions and combinations are appearing to facilitate the flow of services from seller/provider to buyer.

Conventional marketing teaches that the marketing channel contributes time and place utility to the tangible or intangible product—the appropriate availability of the product at the right time and place. For services, the relative importance of time and place utility is greater than in the case of goods. The inability to store or ship intangibles and the need to have service facilities in being to meet intermittent or random demand over time suggest that the price paid reflects a substantial portion of time and place utility in the total value of the service product. Consider, for example, the time and place utility in a telephone; a stock exchange;

emergency medical care; electricity; automobile repair services; a motel; and a metropolitan airport.

Parenthetically, in the recreation-tourism-hotel and motel-transportation complex of services, time and place utility appear to be the essence of the product itself. That is, any attempt to distinguish between the performance utility, as discussed in Chapter 4, and the time and place utility of these services is futile and meaningless.

LOCATION CONSIDERATIONS

Probably you have needed a service of one kind or another without having any idea of where or how to obtain it or when it might be feasible. Where does one find a public telephone? Where would a marketing executive seek outside advice on a sales training program? How does a household or a business obtain financial assistance? How does one find a family physician or obtain legal counsel? How does one find lodging while traveling on the interstate highway system? Even more importantly, how often have you given up the search and either foregone the service or performed it yourself? On the other hand, have you ever noticed how convenient some services are: utilities and private telephones; drive-in banks; and one-stop service systems? These are predominantly questions of location or distribution and they are becoming increasingly critical as services assume a more important component of supply in the marketplace.

Location Classification of Services

Services are classified by location in three ways: they may be concentrated, dispersed, or location may be irrelevant. (See Figure 7.1.) This classification is based on where the service is performed and not necessarily on the postal address of the service institution. For example, Hartford, Connecticut is the location of a large number of insurance home offices, but that does not make it a geographically concentrated industry; insurance services are performed by dispersed sub-offices throughout the country.

Those services for which location is an irrelevant factor can be considered briefly. They include many household operations services and communications. Utilities, the telephone, and television are ubiquitous, neither dispersed nor concentrated but performed wherever the consumer is. (Illustration "d" in Figure 7.1.)

Where dispersion or concentration options are open to the service marketer, supply and demand forces and custom or inertia are determining factors. Dispersed services have acknowledged the preeminence of demand whereas the concentrated services find supply considerations to be overriding along with custom.

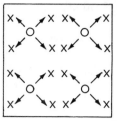

a. Dispersed: Institutionally
and Operationally

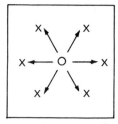

b. Dispersed: Operationally
Concentrated: Institutionally

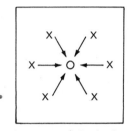

c. Concentrated: Institutionally
and Operationally

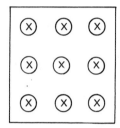

d. Location Irrelevant

Figure 7.1   *SERVICE LOCATION PATTERNS (CURRENTLY PREVAILING)*

Personal and housing services (that is, rental housing) are probably the best examples of dispersed services. Both must locate in terms of market potential. A survey of any shopping center will uncover personal service facilities which have followed the market to the suburbs. Also consider the decline of the downtown hotel and the success of the outlying motel. (Illustration "a" in Figure 7.1.)

Another group of services may be institutionally centralized but go to the consumer or user in order to perform their services. For example, business consulting and facilitating services may be headquartered in New York or Chicago yet the performance of their services demands that they go to the customer, not the reverse. The same thing is true of freight transportation and insurance, as noted earlier. In other words, both the nature of the service and the characteristics of demand reward the service seller who positions his facilities in terms of the needs of the buyer. (Illustration "b" in Figure 7.1.)

For many services, however, conditions of supply and custom act as centripetal forces. In cities of all sizes, banks tend to be concentrated in financial districts. Madison Avenue is synonymous with the advertising agency. Physicians have tended to move out of residential neighborhoods to centralized professional buildings located near hospitals. Law offices cluster around the court house. New York has its theater district. Because of space, pollution, and congestion problems, the transportation of people has become increasingly supply- rather than demand-oriented in regard to location. (The heliport is designed to bring transportation to the consumer.) While primary and secondary education have located in terms of demand, higher education has not. (Illustration "c" in Figure 7.1.)

Various reasons can be cited for spatial concentration of services. Concentration of professional and technical manpower may be more attractive than dispersion into the market. Specialization within services encourages concentration so that the specialist can turn quickly to complementary assistance. The mobility of consumers has permitted the service marketer to sit back and wait for the consumer to come to him. Services whose demand is sporadic are not under pressure to be quickly accessible. Some locations have become symbols of status, particularly in the area of recreation. In some cases, growth has been so rapid that the need for a demand orientation has not yet been apparent.

Trends in Location

The trend is unmistakable from concentration to dispersion. Increased purchasing power, higher educational attainment, new tastes and changing life styles with their emphasis on individuality and self-actualization favor a dispersion of services. Health clinics are established in outlying areas and in poorer sections of urban centers. "Store-front" law offices are bringing legal services from the courthouse to the poor. Branch banking is a classic example of service dispersion. Community colleges and "universities without walls" are bringing higher education to the consumer. Increasingly, theatrical groups, ballet companies, and symphony orchestras travel to the market.

Services provided by public bodies should be accessible in the public interest. The federal government is establishing information centers throughout the country; the Internal Revenue Service is much more of a network of facilities than ever before; the Consumer Protection Agency has established offices in a number of cities throughout the country.

The trend toward dispersion in services will be encouraged through diversification into the service sector by manufacturers and retailers of goods who have already accepted the marketing concept with its mandate for accessibility and convenience.

Buyer Classifications of Services Related to Location

As noted in Chapter 1, services, like goods, may be of the convenience, shopping, and specialty variety.[1] Which category a particular service falls in is determined by the buyer and the same service may be classified in all three categories by various buyers. For example, one firm may seek out a particular advertising agency, another may request several agencies to submit proposals, and still a third may go to the "convenient" local agency. Similarly, one patient may select a distant clinic for treatment, a second may shop the "Yellow Pages," whereas a third may search out the most convenient physician. Of course, the physical condition of the patient and the objective for seeking health care are controlling factors. One visit may be for diagnostic purposes, another for prevention of illness, and a third may be of an emergency nature. This leads to another point: over time, a consumer classification of particular services can change as age, life style, and income change. That which was once viewed as a shopping service becomes a convenience service and that which was a convenience may become a specialty service.

Nevertheless, there are typical classifications of services which represent the prevailing attitudes of buyers. These attitudes are the key to success in locating where a service is to be performed. (Of course, there is an opportunity for the unusual service firm to appeal to the nontypical service buyer, for example, some travelers will go out of their way to stay at a particular hotel.)

The following characteristics of service marketing in general and of particular classes of services which, typically, are not associated with goods marketing tend to accentuate the application of this type of classification (convenience, shopping, specialty) to the location of service performance. First, services which are not appropriately located may not be performed at all—it is easier to postpone the purchase of a service, excepting emergency services, or discard the planned purchase completely; in addition, a poorly located service facility invites a "do-it-yourself" decision. Second, human-centered services are more easily shifted, spatially, than machine-centered services to meet the market's changing perceptions of the service product. Athletic and theatrical performances and legal and insurance services are more mobile than communications and transportation services. Third, as noted in Chapter 3, competition through either price or promotion is considered unethical in a number of service areas. This makes location a more critically important marketing element. Fourth, a number of important services are regulated monopolies or oligopolies, an institutional arrangement unknown in the manufacturing and marketing of goods. In exchange for the relatively low risk of a monopoly position, the regulated service agency must take extra pains to assure that its services are available to the maximum number of potential customers. Thus, utilities and telephone companies do not have the luxury of distinguishing between intensive and thin markets: each must receive the same quality of service.

There will be an increasing tendency to view services as convenience or specialty products. In a complex, fast-moving affluent society and industrial system, self-contained household units and industrial and business enterprises will give way to the practice of calling upon outside service specialists so that both the household's and the firm's resources are not utilized for peripheral and sub-optimal purposes. Thus, a firm asks an outside executive search organization to find top management candidates rather than do it itself; a university contracts with a private enterprise to manage its housing and dining rather than do it itself; and a household hires a caterer rather than prepare party food itself. A major factor in the expansion of this propensity to buy services rather than self-performance is the location or accessibility of the service firm.

Another trend which is likely to develop is the spatial concentration of *complementary* services which together make up *systems* of services. Rather than *like* services concentrating in certain areas, the future will see unlike but mutually-reinforcing services in close proximity. This is already occurring in health care; in outdoor recreation; in travel and entertainment. Concentration of manufacturing is a focal point for a complex of satellite industrial services.

CHANNEL (DELIVERY) CONSIDERATIONS

As already noted, product characteristics of services limit channel options. However, there are a variety of rather unusual intermediaries in the service sector. Continuing growth and competition are likely to encourage more innovations in the use of middlemen as a mechanism for closing the gap between the service-performer and the consumer.

Channel Components

At the beginning of the service marketing channel is the creator or performer and at the end is the consumer or industrial user. (See Figure 7.2.) A service channel confined to these two components is equivalent to direct marketing of goods. However, in the case of services it is much more common and, in fact, mandatory in many instances, for example: household operations, legal services, and communications.

The two intermediaries in service marketing channels are the agent and the broker. While the two forms of operation are distinguished in conventional marketing, the terms are used interchangeably in the case of services. Regardless of label, their essential function is to bring performer and consumer or user together. They represent either of the primary channel components and the longest service channel results where agents and brokers representing both seller and buyer intervene.

Examples include the following. Rental agents represent the owners

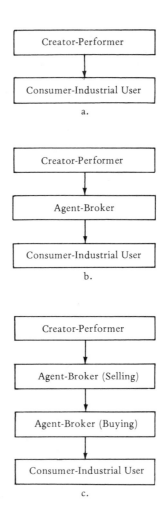

Figure 7.2 *SERVICE CHANNEL PATTERNS (CURRENTLY PREVAILING)*

of rental housing and office space. (Real estate agents and brokers sell a tangible good, not a service.) Travel agents represent all types of travel services: surface and air transportation, hotels and motels, and packaged tours. (See the reading that follows.) Insurance agents and brokers are probably the most widely known service intermediaries. The former typically represents one insurer whereas the latter represents two or more. Artistic performers and entertainers are represented by agents. There appears to be a universal reluctance on the part of performers in artistic categories to enter the marketplace.

In several service industries there is a trend toward group buying. When this occurs, another intermediary representing the buyer joins the channel. Civic music associations are one example. Composers, the orchestra director, and the individual artists making up a symphony orchestra are represented in the marketplace by an agent when it is on the road. The agent in turn negotiates for the purchase of the orchestra's services with a local civic association acting as a representative of the consumer. An increasingly common intermediary representing the buyer is loosely termed an affinity group. Probably every reader has been exposed to the opportunity to buy insurance or travel by reason of his membership in professional associations or because he is a student or alumnus of a particular school.

There is no uniformity in the functions performed by intermediaries. For example, the insurance agent sells whereas the creator of a packaged tour develops a product system. Agents representing artistic performers generally have much wider functional responsibilities somewhat akin to the sales agent in conventional marketing. Others, such as rental agents are simply processors of transactions rather than decision-makers.

In addition to the trend toward dispersion through branching discussed in the earlier section on location, franchising is a growing phenomenon in the following service industries: automobile and truck repairing; automobile, truck, and trailer rentals; carpet and upholstery cleaning; coin operated and regular laundry and dry cleaning; motels; moving companies; temporary help services; tool and equipment rentals; and water conditioning systems and services. In fact, any *standardized* service is an appropriate candidate for franchising. Probably because opportunities for quantity discounts in buying services are limited, chain organizations are not common. However, in order to compete with franchise operations and branches, local independent service firms are forming cooperative networks in order to provide broader geographical opportunities for services consumers and users.

Channel Concepts in Public Services

Until recently the political philosophy of this country has favored the centralization of public services in Washington; today, decentralization is in the ascendancy. Agencies are contracting with private firms to facilitate or even execute public services. In addition, through the revenue-sharing mechanism, the national government is turning over more and more public services to state and local government agencies. In essence, the national government *develops the social product* through legislation and compensates decentralized governmental bodies for performing the *other elements* in the social marketing mix.

Conventional Channel Concepts and the Service Sector

Because of the rather restricted nature of marketing channels for services, the concept of *channel captain* has limited application. In general, the creator or performer of the service directs the marketing channel and program rather than the agent. However, as a generalization, the more removed the creator or performer of the service is from the world of commerce, the more likely the agent or broker will assume leadership of the marketing channel.

Similarly, the concept of *dual distribution* has limited applicability in services. One example is in the field of health insurance wherein the insurer may utilize the following: company representatives; direct mail; vending machines; and blanket and franchise insurance largely underwritten on a group basis and with or without agent representative participation. Travel and transportation services may be sold directly to the ultimate consumer or corporate user or through the travel agent. Otherwise, single channels of distribution seem to prevail.

On the other hand, *channel conflicts* are increasing as diversification in the service sector expands. Television networks create as well as transmit programs; accounting firms perform business consulting services; manufacturers are establishing educational programs in competition with colleges and universities; commercial banks have expanded into insurance, credit cards, stock and bond underwriting, and computer services, to name but a few; airlines operate hotels and offer their own tours; and advertising agencies advise in product development and conduct marketing research. "Scrambled merchandising" is an apt description of trends in a number of service industries today; undoubtedly, a reassessment will be in order.

Extensive, selective, and *exclusive* distribution policies are inapplicable or unformulated in the great majority of services. The one significant exception is found in franchising where selective or exclusive distribution policies are probably universal. Otherwise, if any discretion is possible in the use of agent intermediaries, an implicit policy of intensive distribution is in effect.

In summary, the nature of service marketing to date has permitted relatively little creativity in the use of location and channels for developing an effective marketing program. At the same time, the limited penetration of marketing practices and the marketing concept in the service sector leads to the conclusion that there are numerous opportunities for improving the means of bringing the creator or performer of services closer to the consumer and industrial user. In general, those service industries showing the greatest recognition for marketing—insurance and financial—have also shown the greatest interest in experimentation and development of improved location and utilization of channel alternatives.

Because the buyer of services is, in many cases, inexperienced or incapable of judging alternative services, there is an opportunity for new intermediaries who are truly representatives—agents or brokers—of the buyer. The tests would be: Whose interests are represented in the service marketplace? Who pays the intermediary? As the reading in Chapter 10 shows, the physician is the patient's agent in selecting health care services (hospitals) and health care goods (drugs). The stock broker represents the buyer and is compensated by the buyer. Whatever the other merits are of the fee system over the commission plan of compensation for advertising agencies, one is the clear understanding that the agency represents the buyer of advertising services and is paid by the buyer (i.e., the advertiser).

FOOTNOTES

1. E. Jerome McCarthy. *Basic Marketing,* 4th ed. (Homewood, Illinois: Richard D. Irwin, Inc., 1971), pp. 303-312.

CHANNELS OF DISTRIBUTION IN THE HOTEL INDUSTRY

William H. Kaven

A fragmented service industry dependent upon a dispersed market develops a channel structure to link supply and demand efficiently.

The hotel industry must be widely defined to include the broad spectrum of lodging establishments other than hotels, such as motels, motor inns, tourist courts, and in some instances, rental condominiums. If we are to gain the perspective necessary to define and describe the hotel industry's channels of distribution, we must adopt an even broader view and see hotels as they function within the whole travel industry. No longer are the various travel vendors neatly separated, for example, into hotel companies, transportation companies, travel agents, tour operators, and caterers. Instead there has been movement toward the development of what Kotler calls vertical marketing systems (VMS) in which hotel and transportation companies, especially airlines, work within the same corporate systems and perhaps even engage in catering operations and travel tour operations.

This paper will define the marketing channels found in the hotel industry and relate them to that larger framework of the travel industry.

The Customer's Need for Information

The endless combinations and permutations of alternative routes, transportation modes, times, and lodging accommodations make many travel decisions difficult even for the initiated. When the seasonal changes in rates and schedules are added to the confusion, the need for good information and promotion becomes necessary so that the industry can function.

We must consider in addition to travel complications, the sur-

The author is Associate Professor in Hotel Administration, School of Hotel Administration, Cornell University.

prising lack of consumer knowledge regarding lodging and transportation. Even in the United States almost 50 percent of the people have never stayed in a hotel, travelled more than 200 miles from home, nor travelled by plane or train. The heavy users of U.S. travel and lodging facilities are those business, government, and organization personnel who spend 60-90 days a year away from home conducting business. Only 8 percent of the U.S. business population accounts for 80 percent of the business dollars spent for travel and lodging domestically. For the totally uninitiated traveler, a flight to Akron and a night in a local motel is a complicated experience. At the same time, even a sophisticated U.S. business traveler who is accustomed to jetting frequently all over this country might find a trip to Africa, Japan, or India very complicated.

However, with disposable income growing around the globe and with the increased speed and frequency of jet flights, the growth of travel, both domestic and foreign, appears assured. New travel destinations are developing and people now collect lists of countries visited as symbols of their worldliness and affluence. Further, the business world has moved to multi-national firms operating on virtually every continent, so overseas business travel is now common.

The speedy dissemination of reliable travel information is therefore necessary to accommodate both the growing demand for, and the increasing complexity of, lodging and transportation arrangements.

The Seller's Need to Be Identified in the Marketplace

With the emergence of increasing demand, new travelers, and new destinations, there arises a complicating problem from the supply side of the travel industry—mainly the supply of lodging accommodations. Hotels generally throughout the world tend to be both small and independent, averaging in the U.S. barely 40 rooms per establishment. Over 40 percent of U.S. hotels and motels are too small to even have one paid employee, and account for less than 5 percent of total room nights sold domestically. The problem is universal: *hundreds of thousands of lodging establishments are seeking to gain identity with untold millions of potential customers covering the whole spectrum of incomes, interests, knowledge, sophistication, and needs;* but few single establishments can afford the marketing costs.

The solution of this fundamental problem leads us to the development of the current channels of distribution in the travel industry.

Channels of Distribution: Direct and Indirect

Accepting the premise of the basic industry problem, scattered and little-known establishments seeking identity among a world of potential customers, it quickly becomes apparent that hotels have a need to be represented to customers. Since cost limitations obviously prohibit every hotel from being represented personally, apparently the most economical channel for selling of rooms is to follow (a) the informational flow giving location, price, room availability and reservation verification, and (b) the promotional flow which consists of personal selling by agents who also provide a platform for distribution of promotional literature.

Essentially, the distribution channels between hotel and customer can be categorized simply as either direct or indirect. Regardless of whether the hotel is independent or affiliated, the direct channel between a given hotel and the consumer, while absolutely vital, is concerned chiefly with the sales function. More specifically the individual hotel's salesmen concentrate upon (a) maintaining sales contact with channel intermediaries such as tour operators, travel agents, representatives and transportation companies; (b) maintaining sales contact with community firms and organizations in an attempt to obtain lodging and function business; (c) following leads furnished by other sources, for example, the headquarters marketing department if it is part of a chain organization. It is a common practice for the local hotel salesman to travel considerable distance across the country seeking to close a major sale such as a business meeting or convention. The hotel cannot survive without its own sales force regardless of the power of the headquarters sales and marketing force.

But of increasing importance now to the lodging industry is the growth of indirect channels of distributing through such intermediaries as the travel agents, hotel representatives, tour operators, space brokers, airlines, and the centralized reservation and sales operations of franchised or chain hotels to help make the room sales for the hotels.

While travel agents may contract on the customer's behalf directly with a hotel, frequently they deal through other intermediaries who hold blocks of rooms or otherwise act as agents for the hotels. Thus there are frequently two or more agent intermediaries involved in consummating the sale of a room. The functions and activities of these intermediaries can be described as follows:

Hotel Representatives act as sales and reservation agents for a number of noncompeting hotels such as resorts, but the hotel representative concept is more frequently used by foreign hotels selling to the U.S. market.

Tour Operators reserve wholesale blocks of rooms in anticipation of selling group tours through their retailers, the travel agents.

Automated Reservation Service such as American Express Space Bank, maintains for a fee in their computers an inventory of available hotel rooms from around the world so that travel agents can buy rooms for their customers.

Airlines, chiefly for overseas destinations, maintain an inventory of room availability to accommodate customers and travel agents who prefer to make complete arrangements with but one phone call for flight and room reservations.

Centralized Reservation and Sales Operation of associated, franchised, or chain hotels/motels facilitate the flow of room availability information to potential consumers, and, of course, promote, sell, and accept reservations for space. While it has proven helpful to utilize travel agents and other sorts of intermediaries as listed above to sell hotel rooms, there have been several significant changes recently. As a result of movement of independents to affiliate with each other, the development of large groups of franchised establishments, and the surge in industry corporate chain growth there have come (a) greater economies of scale in promotion, (b) increased speed and economy in the flow of information in both directions in the channels between hotels and clients, and (c) a moving of the point-of-sale closer to the customer's point-of-decision to travel. This latter has been accomplished chiefly through the development of the 24-hour per day single-number, nationwide, toll-free reservation system, for example, the 1-800 telephone number. This one device makes it possible to buy a hotel room almost anywhere in the world at the moment of the decision, wherever the customer may be.

The consumer need for simplified travel decisions, built-in companionship and sociability, and low retail prices have made package tours popular and strengthened the role of the channel intermediaries. What is important to recognize here is that the marketing strength of some of these intermediate channel members has grown to the point that many hotel operators are no longer captains of their channels. Thus not only do the hotels face horizontal competition with each other for the customer's patronage, but they face vertical competition with their channel intermediaries for a share of the consumer dollar. Various intermediaries are able to develop their own consumer loyalty or franchise, "We always take XYZ tours and they pick out the hotels for us," or "My airline agent put us into the ABC hotel in London," have become common statements. While the market power developed by such intermediaries may have no effect on the customer's hotel rate, it may be manifested sharply in the hotel's net rate after commissions. The potential threat to the hotel that a strong channel intermediary may begin

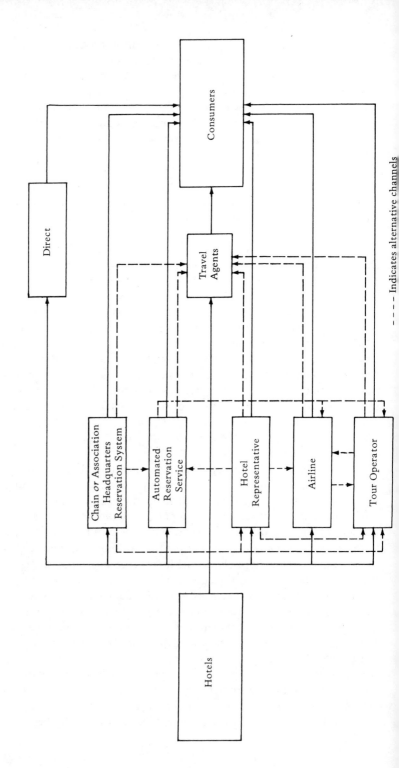

- - - - Indicates alternative channels

booking with another hotel is a constant depressant to the hotel's net price of the rooms.

A further shift in market power has resulted from the growth of the toll-free nationwide hotel telephone reservation number. Many customers tend to book domestic reservations in this simplified fashion and a lot of desirable independent hotels are bypassed; travel agents also are hurt. Travel agents and hotels are further upset by the agreement of some domestic airlines to sell rooms for a commission or a fee, to customers booking flights to cities where a particular hotel company operates.

Trends and Conclusions

All of the channels illustrated and described above are functioning now because they are economically necessary to make a market between hoteliers and consumers. Because hotel space is a service, its distribution channels are relatively fluid and responsive to change—unlike the distribution channels for goods which are subject to the time and cost limitations of physical distribution.

Thus, so long as competitive innovations occur and entrepreneurs seek to implement them in search of survival, growth, and profit, these channels of distribution are subject to change.

The several discernible trends described below are likely to shape future channels of distribution for the hotel industry.

Increasing Horizontal Economic Concentration. An increasing percentage and absolute number of hotel rooms are coming under the management, control, or ownership of name-brand hotel organizations. While some establishments are only voluntary members of such organizations and other establishments are franchisees, many are owned outright by corporate chains. This trend to concentration is the result of a number of factors, not the least of which is the restructuring of our city patterns and the new Interstate Highway System which have brought new location opportunities to the industry. Regardless of the type of affiliation, the purposes of the affiliation are: (a) to present to the public the image of a national company of high standards with whom customers can deal in confidence; (b) to obtain economies of scale in promotion; (c) to establish and maintain an ongoing reservation system that will help promote and perpetuate the organization—and serve the customers; and (d) in some instances, to obtain economies of scale in purchasing and operations.

The net result is that an increasing number of rooms are controlled or owned by a relatively small number of organizations or firms.

Increasing Vertical Economic Concentration. The financial, power, synergic, and ego benefits of a well-managed, large-scale, fully-integrated, system are irresistible to the entrepreneur, and the travel industry is no exception. Certainly, there is much economic sense in developing a one-management system that can take care of all of the customer's travel needs.

There are already strong beginnings of vertical marketing systems. The two basic ingredients are the major sales generators, hotels and airlines, which are natural allies. Examples abound: TWA-Hilton International, American-Americana, Pan American-Intercontinental, United-Western International, and others. Not all ties are so direct; one hotel chain operates with an airline by agreement just to handle reservations.

Vertical ancillary services or functions then follow easily into the overall VMS as together the hotel and airline can often generate sufficient patronage to virtually support these services. Included are the functions performed by the other intermediaries in the hotels' channels of distribution—travel agents, tour operators, automated reservation services, and hotel representatives—as well as other services such as auto rentals, credit cards, travel insurance, in-flight feeding, airport restaurants, and other shops.

Increasing Competition Among the Separate Vertical Marketing Systems. Competition is not yet extremely vigorous among the separate VMS because they are still interdependent. Airlines do not yet have their own hotels in all of their ports-of-call, nor do they necessarily have landing rights everywhere they have acquired hotels. Thus they are still dependent on each other as well as on other channel intermediaries for patronage. In addition, corporate decentralization practices and antitrust considerations may frequently separate hotel and airline operations within a given corporate VMS.

Probably as each vertical marketing system becomes more developed and complete, its major channels of distribution to the consumer will be contained internally. This is similar to a large supermarket chain that not only maintains its own retail outlets, but is integrated vertically into ancillary functions such as wholesaling, manufacturing, brokerage, storage, and transportation.

One cannot assume, however, that the consumer will eventually be forced to choose among separate and mutually exclusive total travel systems; there is too much need to service the specific wishes and travel needs of many travelers. But the most economical travel packages will probably come entirely from a given corporate VMS. Competition between systems will be more vigorous and prices low, the travel decisions and options will be simplified and perhaps even one-step, so that even the slow adapters to the idea of travel will be attracted. Such added business should further push the industry into economic concentration.

One final note. Faster movement toward trends described here appears to be retarded mainly by (a) the continuing adherence of some sellers, such as tour operators and travel agents, and consumers to traditional trading methods and (b) the fact that growing vertical marketing systems are not yet fully developed.

MARKETING IN
SPECIFIC SERVICES

Reality: the need for circumspection when relating marketing and services far removed from the conventional marketplace

MARKETING SPECTATOR SPORTS

The awkwardness of the term "services" is most evident when applied to the intangible product considered in this chapter. Viewing a sporting event as a service performed requires a return to basic marketing concepts. While connotations inherent in the term lead to additional difficulty, one must accept the fact that sporting events contain utilities of value to segments of demand. They have been intentionally selected because they do stretch the conventional concept of goods and services to a new nonutilitarian and nonfunctional boundary.

The subject has also been selected because it is a true growth industry, at least on the demand side. Increases in attendance shown in Table 8.1 should be compared with a general population growth of 34.8 percent during the decades of the '50's and '60's. In addition to the sports shown, major league hockey attendance increased 171 percent in the five year period, 1966-1971.

While attendance at sporting events dates at least from the Olympics of ancient time, the emergence of sports as an organized "industry" is quite recent. In this country (beginning with baseball, for years our

Table 8.1

ATTENDANCE FIGURES: SELECTED SPECTATOR SPORTS

(Thousands)

	1950	1971	Percent Increase
Baseball	17,659	29,544	67.3
Basketball, professional*	3,317	8,425	154.0
Football, collegiate	18,962	30,455	60.6
Football, professional**	2,966	10,560	256.0
Horseracing	29,291	73,619	151.3

*NBA beginning in 1960; ABA in 1966.
**AFL beginning in 1960.

Note: Team sports: major leagues only.

Source: U.S. Bureau of the Census, *Statistical Abstract of the United States: 1972.* (93rd edition.) Washington, D.C., 1972, p. 207.

"national pastime"), its recent rapid growth results from the confluence of a number of developments in the social environment. First, the shorter work day and work week opened up time to be filled. Second, the dispersion of discretionary purchasing power broadens consumption options. Third, viewing sporting events acts as an antidote or outlet for the tensions and pressures of both production and conventional consumption. Finally, the constraints of urbanization require that the sporting or competitive instinct be satisfied by observation rather than by participation.

SPECTATOR SPORTS DEMAND CHARACTERISTICS

Both the macro and micro characteristics of demand for spectator sports are presented in fascinating detail in the reading that follows. Discussion here would be redundant. However, segmentation of the market for spectator sports is based on characteristics which are unique and therefore warrant consideration.

One segment, the core market, consists of people who *attend* a sporting event in person. A second market segment, the intermediate market, is made up of people who *follow* particular sports and particular teams through television and radio. A third segment, the fringe market, are those who are *interested* in various sports but limit their participation to the sporting pages of the daily newspaper. Allocation of consumers to these three market segments is in part a function of the relative intensity of interest and in part a function of location. In any event, the first segment consists of the brand-loyal regular customers of a particular sport. These are the "paying" customers. The second segment is of value to the marketer of spectator sports because its size is the major determinant of the value of broadcast rights, a significant source of income. The third segment is of importance because it is open to conversion to either of the other more meaningful segments of the market: Attention and interest are already present and achieving this segment's active involvement is a major marketing challenge.

The relative size of the three segments could best be determined by using a measure of exposure—time either in terms of a percentage of potential exposure or in terms of a division of time among the three segments. Actual attendance figures are misleading measures of the extent of the market because they represent attendees ranging from those who "buy" every event to those who may "buy" only once in a lifetime.

The marketing significance of segmentation is clear. Growth for the organized seller of spectator sports be it a high school or university on the one hand or a professional major league on the other must be achieved by moving followers through the segments from the fringe to the core and by increasing the rate of consumption.

SPECTATOR SPORTS SUPPLY CHARACTERISTICS

Whenever a major component of any service product is of an artistic and noncommercial nature as contrasted with services which are technical and functional and largely governed by market forces, a discussion of supply characteristics becomes quite complex. In the case of spectator sports, a service which does not fit neatly into the conventional mold of marketed services, there is an additional complicating factor: two forms of competition are involved—the more conventional economic competition and the artistic competition if one accepts the view that playing football or baseball is an art. For most sports, success in artistic competition is reflected in the win-loss columns. In Olympics competition, success is determined by performance against standards, officially. Unofficially, competition between national teams is quite evident.

The first major supply resource is team *owners* whose typical contribution is financial support. Reasons for ownership include: a search for profits, a "liking for the game," benefits from ownership which may contribute to the success of other ventures, and for some, ownership may be in the nature of an avocation or a source of some personal satisfaction whose definition may be best left to the owner himself.

Traditionally owners have consisted of single individuals or small groups in which ownership of the team or club was one of many business ventures or individuals who were full-time promoters. In a few cases, teams were owned by the facility in which they played. More recently, as spectator sports have taken on more of the characteristics of large-scale enterprises, ownership has shifted to corporations, and syndicates of owners.[1] The *management* of a team, as in other enterprises, is delegated to professional managers, many of whom have come up through the ranks of the sport, particularly those in line management. The *team* itself is somewhat equivalent to a manufacturing firm in conventional marketing with a horizontal organizational structure, both line and staff responsibilities, and a specialization of labor.

Another major supply component consists of the *facilities*. For the core market these are the arenas and stadiums in which sporting events occur. While formerly privately owned and limited to one form of sport, ownership of facilities is shifting to local government bodies and new construction is designed for multiple sporting use. There is evidence of a growing sense of local pride in these edifices which may have little or no relationship to the economics of the matter.[2] Of course, for intermediate and peripheral markets, those who view sporting events through television or simply "follow" teams in print media, such facilities would be unnecessary. The stadium, in some respects is similar to the retailer in conventional marketing—particularly as a provider of time and place utility.

An obvious resource is the *individual performer*—the nonmanagerial employee in the conventional firm. Each performer, be he a quarterback, a forward, or a right fielder, seeks to excel and each team, manager, and owner wishes to acquire or develop superior performance at every position. But here, the two parallel forms of competition must be considered. Were a team to be successful in acquiring the very best performers in each position and so become the strongest competitor in terms of skill and artistry, economic competition would suffer. This raises a significant marketing issue. Certainly many consumers are interested in seeing superlative skill in their own team, however few would pay to see a contest or take time to view it at home were the result to be a foregone conclusion because of a total imbalance in the quality of performance. The marketplace rules-of-the-road cannot be wholly transferred to the gridiron or diamond.[3]

Competition between performers is another important and unique resource in the service identified as spectator sports. Here again, the disparity between the two forms of competition is evident. In economic competition, the greater the competitive superiority of one firm over the other, the more it will be viewed as successful in the marketplace. On the other hand, a 6-5 victory on the baseball diamond is as successful as a 10-0 victory and much more likely to sustain demand.[4] For, above all, a major value in spectator sports in all three market segments is excitement.

MARKETING ISSUES IN SPECTATOR SPORTS

While the distinction cannot be made throughout this chapter, the reader should be reminded of another unique characteristic of spectator sports: its performance at both the amateur and professional level. In fact, the amateur sporting event may be the only product, tangible or intangible, for which there is a market price where the performer, or seller, receives no compensation for his efforts and, in fact, the amateur nature of his participation is held in esteem. Actually, the two forms— professional and amateur—are two different industries with different variables on both the demand and supply side. Economic competition between amateur and professional spectator sports is another unusual characteristic of this service.

The Sports Product

The basic transaction in spectator sports is the sale of a sporting event by the owner-employers of professional contestants or the sponsors of amateur contestants to ultimate consumers. In many instances, there is also an industrial type of transaction in which the same sellers promote the same sporting event to television media.

In the retail transaction, the sporting event or performance is consumed personally and directly. In the industrial transaction, the event is a resource purchased by a radio or television network or station, quite similar to the manufacturer's purchase of materials and parts.[5]

In both transactions, the key questions are: What is purchased? Why does demand decline and grow? Why do individuals buy one form of sport and not another? Answers are suggested by the nature of the product.

Consumers pay to attend a particular event for the following reasons. (For each buyer, their relative importance will vary.) (1) Skill in execution even at the amateur level attracts the *aficionado*. (2) Fairly evenly balanced competition is another. (3) For those who have participated in a particular sport in the past, attendance at an event is almost akin to attendance at professional meetings. (4) There is the potential elation following victory where team affinity is strong. (5) Undoubtedly, the excitement and stimulation of the crowd is a product characteristic. (6) There is the hope of a closely fought contest. To the extent that these factors are present and grow, demand is likely to increase; where they are absent or are declining, demand falters. (7) Brand loyalty exists at both the professional and amateur levels but probably has a longer life in the latter instance.

As spectator sports in total have become more formalized and commercialized and in greater demand according to every measure of growth, investment requirements and the risk element have grown correspondingly. As a result, owners of professional teams and sponsors of amateur teams attempt to maintain demand at adequate levels by supplementing the sporting event with other intangible products ranging from fireworks to style shows and marching bands—a process of enriching the product offer.

The television or radio vehicle is looking for other product characteristics: skills, glamour, reputation, and popularity, for example. These are economic considerations. The nature of the sporting event is a matter of indifference. The medium is interested in the size and character of the arm-chair audience, for this determines his revenue from advertisers. The financial aspects are clear: time revenue must cover the purchase price of the event (broadcasting rights) and expenses incurred in producing it for a profit to result. Risks are high. Rights are purchased before time is sold and the appeal of contestants is determined in sport competition, not economic competition.

Pricing Spectator Sports

Pricing appears to be demand-oriented and generally inelastic. Sporting events which meet the product criteria noted earlier achieve capacity demand regardless of prices (note the presence of scalpers). On the other hand, events which fail to meet the criteria do not attract demand regardless of the bargain nature of the admission price. Some elasticity occurs, of course, at extreme price premiums or discounts.

Several forms of differential pricing occur. Prices per event are lower if bought for the season rather than singly. Better locations within the stadium command higher prices. Higher prices are also charged for events which occur during the time of day or week when potential demand is greater. Little is known regarding the pricing of broadcast rights. Apparently the right goes to the highest bidder.

Promoting Spectator Sports

Conventional advertising is limited and primarily informative at both the professional and amateur levels. Time, place, and price of event are the principal copy elements. More persuasive advertising is appearing and is likely to expand substantially. One reason for the relatively modest use of advertising is the exceptionally heavy dependence on publicity. Almost every action leading up to a sporting event is the subject of a press release. The publicity director is a key member of the management staff in the world of spectator sports. Both teams and individual participants communicate with their markets through promotional tie-ins ranging from testimonial advertising to picture collecting.

In view of the unusual relationships existing between the buyer and seller of spectator sports, word-of-mouth advertising is probably the key promotional or communication medium. Conversation in neighborhood, local, and work groups invariably centers around sporting events at one time or another. The effects are felt in decisions to watch an event and thereby increase the viewing audience (intermediate market) or attend an event and thereby increase the gate receipts (core market).

Distribution of Spectator Sports: Channel and Location

A form of dual distribution exists: Either the consumer can go directly to the event or allow it to come to him via radio or television. In conventional marketing, where the consumer has a choice of chain store vs. independent, quite pragmatic variables as convenience, economy, and likelihood of availability are overriding. The manufacturer typically sells both directly to the chain and through the wholesaler to the independent for volume, turnover, and profit reasons. In the case of spectator sports, a fairly successful practice has prevented these options from being available to buyer and seller—the process of "blacking out" the indirect channel of distribution in order to protect the direct channel. Congress has recently ended the blackout if admission sales equal seating capacity by a specified time in advance of the event.

Sites of sporting events are faced with the same location problems of other retailers. Accessibility, congestion, safety, and an attractive environment are important considerations. Another factor of a location nature is the low occupancy rate for the typical spectator sport facility. They are productive only for a short period of the year and for only a few times during a season. To correct this, newer facilities are constructed to accommodate a variety of activities so that fixed costs can be divided over a broader base.[6]

Regulation of Spectator Sports

Traditionally, sporting events have been subjected to no external regulations. As they grew in popularity and became more formally organized, forms of self-regulation emerged ranging from the Olympics Committees to the provisos of a local high school football league. Now, regulations of the sporting activity itself and economic regulations are becoming intermixed and problems are resulting.

In 1922 the Supreme Court held that baseball is not subject to the antitrust laws because among other things it did not manufacture anything. This view is now being challenged in two respects—one having to do with the "ownership" of players and the other with allocation of franchises. The former is much too complex for consideration here and is somewhat peripheral to marketing. The latter holds significant marketing considerations. (The discussion applies to professional spectator sports only; apparently the antitrust laws are not an issue in amateur events—at least not yet.)

In team sports, self-regulation is administered by the various leagues. Apparently, franchises have been granted in the past by league members in terms of their own interests and not in free and open competition; there was not freedom of entry. However, to define this as a form of "market sharing" confuses the economic and the noneconomic issues. A team in Chicago competes with a team in San Francisco in *noneconomic* terms. To apply economic concepts is illogical.

It has also been argued that a metropolitan area should not be limited to one team as was the case in former years. Today as two or more leagues emerge in any given sport this type of locational monopoly is less likely to exist. Inter-league competition is limited to end-of-year season championships and it might be in the best (sporting) interests of the buyer and (economic) interests of the seller if there were more competition between teams in the same area, even though members of different leagues. In any event, some form of quasi-public regulatory body may be established to control this very unusual service product wherein physical, behavioral, and economic elements are interrelated.[7]

Marketing Concepts in Spectator Sports

Of particular interest is the marketing concept of the life cycle. Spectator sports appear to have the same cycle of growth and decline as other goods and services and the same steps can be taken to expand growth, hold a high plateau, and postpone decline. It has been observed that soccer, professional volleyball, and track and field are in a pioneering stage, that hockey and basketball are in a period of intense growth, that football is on a plateau and that baseball and boxing are on the downslope of the life-cycle curve.

Life-cycle concepts should be adopted with caution, however. Changes in the environment may revive or deflate demand; sellers can take the initiative in reversing the trend toward maturity and decline. Of particular importance in spectator sports, the development of an attachment for a particular sport can begin at a very early age and continue through a lifetime. Consider the impact of the Little League on the demand for baseball. Here again, the difficulty of generalizing from conventional marketing is apparent.

The marketing concepts of "triers" and "users" are applicable to spectator sports. Obviously, the need to convert triers into users is apparent whether in terms of attendance or viewing. The season ticket is a step in this direction. Closer relations between professional and amateurs are desirable in this regard. More imaginative advertising is in order. Communicating the color and excitement and the appeal of performance skills can be particularly effective.

Behaviorally-oriented marketing research should be of great value in advancing the field. Major decisions now are made on the basis of experience and intuition. Without in any way diminishing the importance of these two inputs, spectator sports could benefit from research directed to the consumer, for it is only through this marketing process that the real reasons why people attend or view sporting events are determined.

FOOTNOTES

1. *The New York Times,* 9 January 1972, sec. 3, p. 1.

2. Charles G. Burck, "The Superstadium Game," *Fortune* 87 no. 2 (March 1973), pp. 105-107.

3. Simon Rottenberg, "The Baseball Players' Labor Market," *Journal of Political Economy,* no. 3 (June 1956), pp. 242-258.

4. *Ibid.*

5. For an informative discussion of the economics of spectator sports see Judson Gooding, "The Tennis Industry," *Fortune* 87 no. 6 (June 1973), pp. 125-133.

6. In this discussion of the marketing mix, the author is indebted to Messrs. Greenland and Healy who wrote the paper that follows.

7. *The New York Times,* 9 January 1972, sec. 3, p. 1.

A MARKETING APPROACH TO SPECTATOR SPORTS

Frederick A. Greenland and Timothy J. Healy

An intensive appraisal of spectator sports from a marketing perspective.

Spectator sports are considered to be formal contests requiring varying degrees of demonstrable physical and/or mental expertise by human and/or animal which noncontestants witness either in person or through media ostensibly for the purpose of entertainment.

The focus on "formal contests" is necessary in order to facilitate a marketing approach to the subject. Therefore, "formal contests" are meant to preclude activities like spur-of-the-moment neighborhood games, while encompassing the range of formal sports from amateur events like Little League Baseball to all types of professional sports. The contest element of the definition may be divided into four categories: individual vs. measure (19-foot pole vault or 4-minute mile); individual vs. individual (match play in golf); team vs. measure (the 3-minute mile relay); and team vs. team (football). This is not to say that each category is mutually exclusive in a given sports event.

The constraint "demonstrable . . . expertise" is the most flexible element of the definition. Whether an activity is demonstrable or not is a function of the potential spectators' perceptual skills. For example, in a bridge tournament the degree of "demonstrable . . . expertise" past the actual win or loss is directly proportional to the degree to which the spectator can perceive the skill of the contestant; or, in football the demonstrability of the defensive captain's calls are only existent, for all practical purposes, to the extent that spectators can perceive and identify their execution in the overall activity of the event. This seems to suggest that there is a continual educational role for spectator sports marketers to fulfill.

The authors are graduates of the Graduate School of Business and Public administration, Cornell University. Mr. Greenland is Brand Assistant, Procter & Gamble Company and Mr. Healy is Assistant Business Manager, Tennis, Wilson Sporting Goods Company.

No spectator sport, within the above definition, is solely physical or mental. It is, however, either physical exertion (woodchopping contests) or intensive mental exertion (chess tournaments), and such explication may be helpful in formulating promotional strategies.

The "human and/or animal" stipulation is included so as to encompass canine and equitation sports within the definition. Also, the intent is to tie the "nonparticipant" element of the definition, used to identify the spectator, to the "entertainment" aspect so as to preclude facilitating personnel (vendors, announcers, managers, family, etc.) being considered as nonparticipants.

"Media" include television and radio only since it is through attendance of these two media that nonparticipants "witness" sporting activities in the sense that there is a dollar exchange involved in the consumption of the contest. That is, dollars flow from attending spectators and from the media by way of broadcast rights. These are the primary means by which these activities generate income.

SPECTATOR SPORTS MODEL

The model for the marketing of spectator sports is divided into two major parts. The first consists of the supply generating elements: endogenous factors that produce the service, exogenous factors that play a supportive role, and legitimation agencies. The second major part includes the demand elements consisting of exogenous factors characterized by formal socialization units as they interact with the general public.

Supply Generation

Figure 8.1 is a diagrammatic presentation of the endogenous factors which produce the "pure service" (the sporting activity itself void of exogenous factors and legitimation agency involvement). The constituent parts of the endogenous factors are divided into human and physical elements with the subset of the human elements being arranged in a hierarchical manner.

The involvement of the owner in the contest generation may be extensive (the professional team owner) or virtually nonexistent (public high school or state university sporting events where the public is a passive owner). In situations of the latter type administrative personnel assume the role of the owner in the hierarchy of human elements. The interactions of the owner with the other factors in supply generation are principally financial and directive in nature.

Technical personnel, who directly facilitate the "pure service,"

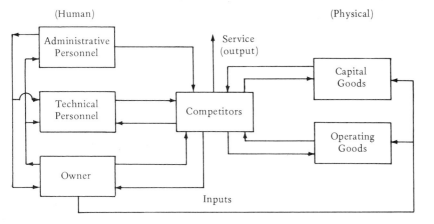

(Human)   (Physical)

Figure 8.1 *ENDOGENOUS FACTORS IN SPECTATOR SPORTS*

are coaches, trainers, etc., whereas the administrative personnel fulfill a relatively more indirect role. The facilitating flows between the technical and administrative personnel and the other endogenous factors are mainly those of expertise and information.

The physical inputs have been divided into capital and operating goods. Capital goods include immobile facilities within which or upon which the contest occurs. They are the "place" of the contest. Operating goods are necessary to the performance of the "pure service" irrespective of place (protective equipment, balls, training equipment, etc.).

The human and physical inputs combine with competitor(s) to produce the "pure service." However, the structure among the endogenous factors may not be as extensive as depicted in Figure 8.1 for each spectator sport. While it may be representative of professional baseball, the touring professional golfer may be the only human input element among the endogenous factors in production of the "pure service." The competitor is the factor upon which all endogenous elements focus. One rather inconsistent fact with respect to the competitor is that in situations like tournaments he pays money in the form of entry fees in order to compete whereas in most other sports the opposite is true.

If one were to substitute workers for competitors, the model at this point would look quite similar to an economic model for the production of any product. However, the similarity between spectator sports production and goods production—or even the production of other services—ends here.

Legitimation agencies are unique to the marketing of spectator sports. It is their function to endow the service generated by the endogenous factors with a favorable aura thereby making the activities "legitimate" and "acceptable" for consumption. For instance, the Milwaukee Bucks organization legitimizes the basketball played by a certain set of players. The Milwaukee Bucks name causes expectations among potential spectators as to the type of event that will occur when the Bucks play basketball.

The intangible nature of spectator sports makes this legitimation role crucial. Admittedly, there is also an element of expectation which arises when associating a producer's name with a product in the goods sector. But even without the producer's name the tangible aspect of goods facilitates exchange since goods can often be inspected and tried before purchase. This is not true of spectator sports, hence legitimation agencies differentiate this service to some extent. What is being consumed is not just basketball but rather the Milwaukee Bucks basketball. Sponsors (for the Soap Box Derby, tournaments, etc.) are also legitimation agencies.

The distinctions between legitimation agencies become clearer when one considers their full range as shown in Figure 8.2. Private nonprofit and public enterprise legitimation agencies are quite similar if one thinks of private universities as examples of the private nonprofit and state universities as examples of public legitimation agencies. Both legitimize spectator sports which are but one of the many outputs of their operations. It is by way of a "spillover" effect that colleges and universities legitimize sports. There is an implicit assumption that educational institutions tend to excellence in acceptable activities. Therefore, the respectability of, for instance, the University of Southern California as an educational institution lends respectability to its sports programs.

Figure 8.2 includes a survival continuum evident among legitimation agencies. If we accept a professional team as an example of a private profit-oriented legitimation agency, it is analogous to the single product firm. That is, survival is dependent on continued demand for the contest it is legitimizing. However, private nonprofit and public enterprise legitimation agencies are analogous to multi-product firms since they are less dependent upon the spectator sports they legitimize for survival. Notice that the continuum is presented in such a manner that the private nonprofit type agency occupies a middle position. This indicates their greater dependency on the revenue or promotional value of their sports programs for survival than is common among public enterprises.

Demand Facilitators

This segment of the model constitutes the exogenous factors

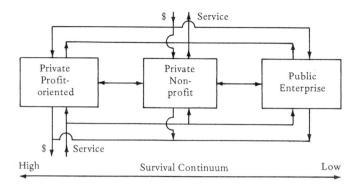

Figure 8.2   *LEGITIMATION AGENCIES IN SPECTATOR SPORTS*

which exist in the production and marketing of spectator sports. These factors consist of the three types of organizations depicted in Figure 8.3. They characteristically play a dual role. They are supportive of the supply creation activities among the endogenous factors and are also socialization units in that they are constantly prescribing sports norms and keeping sporting activities before the general public. Examples of self-regulatory agencies are the NCAA, NBA, and the NFL. A supportive role is performed by them when they prescribe standards and procedures in their respective sports. This results in standardization of the form of the contest and also tends to standardize the quality (by way of player drafts, etc.) within given sports. The endogenous factors subscribe to the regula-

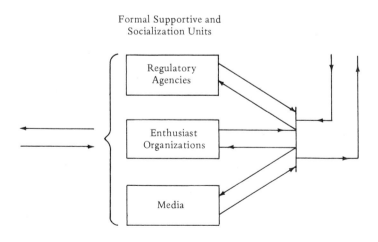

Figure 8.3   *EXOGENOUS FACTORS IN SPECTATOR SPORTS*

tory agencies since standardization eradicates some of the uncertainties which might otherwise exist (what is "fair," proper conduct, etc.) in the sport. The regulatory agencies secondly function in a socializing manner by suggesting to potential spectators sports norms and concepts. Also, their sanction of events lends form and credence to the acceptability of the sports.

The enthusiast organizations play a strong supportive role. They are unique to spectator sports. Examples of such organizations are quarterback clubs, booster clubs of various sports, and alumni associations to some extent. These groups may lend support of an intangible nature or may be involved in the actual production and marketing of the service. This latter phenomenon is common in enthusiast organizations like the Sports Car Club of America (SCCA) which provides personnel to run events like the United States Grand Prix at Watkins Glen. The return received by enthusiast organizations is typically intangible. It may be the chance to be near exotic machinery and big-name drivers as in the case of the Grand Prix or else a means of facilitating the vicarious extension element to be discussed in the determinants of demand section.

Whatever the reasons for the enthusiast organizations to fulfill the supportive role, they also perform a socialization function. This occurs through interplay of enthusiast organization members with potential spectators. The enthusiast organizations socialize a particular sport by relating to potential spectators specific sports concepts, enthusiasm, and information and by serving as an example that the sport is an "acceptable," fulfilling, and entertaining entity with which to identify. Enthusiast organizations could be utilized more extensively in spectator sport production and marketing.

The media are the third major exogenous factor in the spectator sports model. As used in the model they consist of television, radio, and sports publications. The media are supportive by reason of the large sums paid to the legitimation agencies for broadcast rights. The socialization role of media also quite clearly exists, though it is not an explicit goal of the media. Rather it seems to occur almost subliminally since an underlying assumption of the constant reporting of sports events is that they are "acceptable" or "moral" activities. The media may convey questions about the propriety of some sports (the violence of football) but such urgings are soon buried in the flood of sports information to which we are exposed daily.

Figure 8.4 is the integrated spectator sports model. Several points should be reaffirmed with respect to it. First, the model is limited to those common to the United States. Second, the model should not be construed to suggest that every spectator sport has all elements functioning in production and marketing of the sport. Even whole blocks of the model may not be applicable to certain spectator sports. Third, the attempt is to present an economic and behavioral model in order to identify functions and interactions which are or may be present in the production and marketing of spectator sports.

COMPONENTS OF DEMAND

The components of demand for spectator sports can be grouped into three broad categories: conventional, social-psychological (normal), and social-psychological (abnormal). The interaction of these components defines the wants and needs of the individual consumer of spectator sports. They facilitate an explanation of why one individual is an avid follower of professional sports, while his neighbor is content to limit his consumption to an occasional amateur tennis match.

Conventional: Demographic

Age. The significance of age as a determinant of demand is reflected in the relationship between participant and spectator. Participation, either past or present, is a direct stimulus to the consumption of a specific spectator sport. Therefore, if the average age of golf participants is greater than the average age of participants in baseball, the average age of the golf spectator would be greater than that of a baseball spectator. This relationship is, of course, conjectural; yet we do feel that there is a measurable difference in the mean age of spectators among various sports. Until data are available, we assume that this assumption is tenable.

Leisure Time. As stated earlier, Americans are gaining increasing free time. There may be a direct causal relationship between that increase and the increase in consumption of spectator sports. During the past decade, the amount of leisure time increased by almost 35 percent, while attendance at American spectator sports increased by an equal percentage in the same period.[1]

Socio-economic. The class-income distinction is possibly the most significant demographic factor in demand determination. A study of metropolitan residents by Gregory P. Stone indicates that while upper-class individuals preferred participation to spectator roles, 64.4 percent to 35.6 percent, lower-class people preferred the spec-

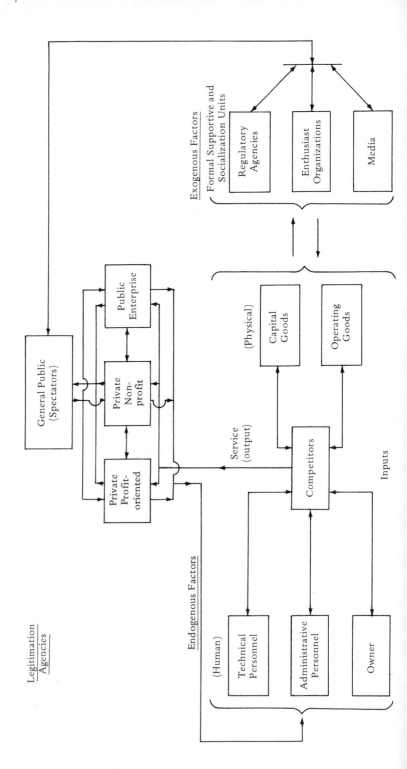

tator role 54.7 percent of the time and the participant role only 45.3 percent of the time.[2]

In the same study, Stone also found that while lower-class metropolitan residents designated baseball, boxing, and bowling more frequently than other classes as their favorite sports, upper-class people had the same tendency toward golf and tennis.[3] These findings imply that different social classes have preferences for different types of sports.

For example, it appears that certain sports are indigenous to the upper classes—polo, in particular, must be viewed as a one-class sport. We would therefore speculate that the exclusivity of participation leads to a predominant upper-class following. The antithesis is, however, not true; a lower-class participant sport does not necessarily have a predominantly lower-class following. Boxing is a case in point. It is indeed possible that television, by exposing the public to all types of sports, as mentioned below, will reduce class barriers for sports such as polo and eventually eliminate class as a significant demand variable.

Sex. Does the American male have a greater demand for certain spectator sports than his female counterpart? Certainly the recent development of "pro-footballitis" which is contracted during every weekend from late August until mid-January is an indication of a distinctive preference pattern. If indeed, males and females have different preferences for specific sports, then the marketing policies of spectator sports could be adjusted for this distinction. In the Stone study mentioned above, it was found that males exhibited a statistically significant preference for boxing, baseball, and hockey while females opted for non-contact sports.[4]

Climate. This variable is proscriptive in nature, due to the constraint it places upon the actual performance of certain sports. A primary example is auto racing. Throughout the late winter and spring months when racing is impossible on northern tracks, the major southern racing events take place (such as the Daytona 24-hour race, Southern 500, Permatex 200). In a classical economic context, the sponsorship of a major auto racing event in the north during colder seasons, given the elastic demand, could be a profitable venture.

Population Density. Again, we are faced with a lack of statistical information to compare with our inferences. However, in our opinion, those individuals with rural backgrounds, who are accustomed to rigorous physical activity, would be more inclined to participate in and become spectators of outdoor sports such as hunting, fishing, and track and field. Conversely, the urban child who plays those sports for which physical facilities are available—basketball, boxing, billiards, and baseball—become spectators of these sports.

These distinctions are indeed tenuous because of the significant relationship between population density and income. However, they remain a possibility to be proven or disproven.

Geographical Region. While closely related to climate, the geographical region of the spectator serves as a socialization agent. A primary example is ice hockey in the Northeast. Interscholastic and intercollegiate hockey are played almost exclusively within this region. As a result, the major professional hockey teams have located in this area. With the recent expansion of the NHL to Los Angeles, it was found that the attendance figures were significantly lower than those of other equally mediocre expansion teams. The fact that Californians had not been exposed to ice hockey during their childhood—they had not been socialized toward acceptance— must be viewed as a significant factor. It can be said that geographical socialization shapes the individual's set of acceptable spectator sports. Geography is another example of a proscriptive demand variable.

Conventional: Other

Media Exposure. Television has had a greater impact upon the incredible growth of spectator popularity than any other demand variable. It has exposed individuals of all classes to the "thrill of victory and the agony of defeat" through such programs as the Wide World of Sports. It has been a movement toward equilibrium in demand and supply of spectator sports. With up to 50 hours per week of sports programming, even the most avid fan has been satiated.

How, specifically, does exposure to the media affect individual demand? Let's look at Mr. Buff, B(TV) (before television) and A(TV) (after television). B(TV) Mr. Buff went to as many major league baseball games as he could. He went to an occasional pro football game. Other professional sports were of passing interest to Mr. Buff, who had come from an urban area and had actually participated only in baseball and football as a child. Now we see Mr. Buff A(TV). He is not only an avid pro ice hockey fan since the team came to his town A(TV), but he is also an enthusiastic pro basketball fan—the team also came to his town a few years A(TV). He always watches the CBS golf classic. Mr. Buff gives us an example of the two-fold impact of television. First, it has broadened the knowledge of spectators to a myriad of sports and made them aware of the exciting characteristics of each. Secondly, and possibly of greater importance, TV revenues have allowed for expansion of major American spectator sports to many new cities, so that the millions of Mr. Buffs, whose interest has been stimulated, can now view the events in their own city.

Contest Significance. The American spectator, much like his Greek and Roman predecessors, has a great desire to view the spectacle. For this reason, the Super Bowl and the NCAA Basketball Championships, the Kentucky Derby and Indianapolis 500, the Masters and the Stanley Cup, etc., are events which are generally characterized by excessive demand. With very few exceptions the importance of the contest will dictate the demand for tickets and also their price. Conversely, regular season major league baseball games will be predictably characterized by excess supply, as represented in the many empty seats. Although the same level of expertise is displayed throughout the season, the contest does not possess the obvious significance of the World Series.

Team or Competitors' Level of Expertise. What causes the typical high school football game to draw 2,000 spectators, while professional football averaged over 50,000 per game per team last year? One distinctive characteristic is the degree of physical superiority exemplified by colorful running backs, spectacular 60-yard pass plays, and 50-yard field goals. The demand for professional expertise is greater because the probability of exciting individual performances and the "big" play is much greater at the professional level. For this reason, there is greater demand.

Team or Competitors' Historical Success. Another demand variable is the relative success of the team. This concept does not apply, of course, to certain sports such as pro football which are presently characterized by near capacity attendance. Why has the University of Nebraska filled its football stadium for the past 11 years while Cornell University has not once reached capacity? A probable explanation is the fact that the University of Nebraska has gone to nine post-season bowl games in 10 years while Cornell has only once had a winning season.

Place Utility. The final demographic variable affecting demand is the physical availability and attractiveness of the facility in which the event is to take place. The migration of many professional sports arenas from the inner city is a primary example. Transportation difficulties encountered in a venture to an inner-city stadium, plus the fear of robbery have diminished the attendance appeal. The concerns caused by these potential difficulties may be greater than the utility of the event and thus turn potential spectators away.

Social-Psychological: Normal

Peer Group Pressure. To what extent do the activities and need for acceptance within a peer group affect an individual's demand for spectator sports? It is our belief that the sports selected and viewed by the individual are not independently determined. A primary example might be the weekend football clique. Characteristically, groups of 4 or 5 travel to the nearest football stadium for an afternoon of beer drinking and companionship. The individual who wishes to retain or gain membership in this group must conform to the group norm of football avidity. This formation of small groups on the basis of sports enthusiasm is a phenomenon which has not been considered in social-psychological literature. It is possible that this type of group formulation may supplant church, work, and neighborhood groups as the amount of leisure time and spectator attendance increases.

Past or Present Participation. Possibly the most significant of the (normal) social-psychological determinants of demand is the relationship between present or past participation and spectator attendance.

The assumption that participation facilitates either a simultaneous or future spectator role is pivotal to our discussions of age and vicarious extension as demand determinants. However, television may tend to lessen the need for participation as a prerequisite to continuous demand for a sport in the future.

Participation provides the individual with immediate knowledge of the rules and records of the game, the skill level involved, the physical demands of the sport, and most important, a recognition of the potential excitement of the activity. Without this experience, the potential spectator has a greater difficulty following the game, recognizing key plays and extraordinary individual performances, and in anticipating a thrilling occurrence.

The individual is also unable to project himself into the game, the concept which we call vicarious extension. Participation facilitates anticipation of a rewarding experience, and stimulates demand. Without it, or its surrogate, television, we feel there is a low potential for continuous demand.

Spectatorization. This term refers to socialization processes directly related to the development of a felt need to view spectator sports. The family plays a primary role in this developmental process. Through the sports which the family as a whole views, either in person or on television, the child begins to formulate a set of acceptable sports. This set may be broadened or narrowed during the educational process, based upon those activities in which he participates. Finally, the set may again be broadened by his exposure to both printed and visual media. The spectatorization process is continuous. We are to some degree spectatorized every day—in our conversations, our reading, our viewing. The predominant place sports hold in the American way of life makes it virtually impossible to escape some degree of spectatorization. The greater the exposure, the more likely the individual will regularly demand some form of spectator recreation.

Social-Psychological: Abnormal

Gladiator Syndrome. Within the past decade, there has been a large increase in demand for professional football and ice hockey, while baseball has suffered a relative decline in attendance. Both football and ice hockey are characterized by physical violence. It is our contention that this rise in demand is in part due to a cultural priority—the acceptability of violence. Dr. Joyce Brothers has stated, "Today, there is more demand for violence and speed. Violence breeds a tolerance of violence and a desire for violence."[5] Again, this syndrome—the gladiator syndrome—may have been precipitated by the proliferation of television. Whatever the source, however, it must be viewed as a potential pervasive social phenomenon—the desire to view humans doing heavy physical combat in an arena— which was previously exemplified by boxing. Based on this trend, it may be possible that games such as lacrosse and jai alai may soon gain widespread following. If this is the case, and leaving value judgments aside, if latent demand does exist for violent sports, then greater marketing potential lies in the promotion of these sports in the future.

Vicarious Extension. Americans are becoming an increasingly inactive nation, due, in part, to the growth of white collar occupations, and the shortening of the work week. Consistent with these changes is the need for physical expression. However, to many individuals, the thought of overt physical exertion is frightening. The American male has found a method of physical expression which involves only the ordinary task of sitting. By extending himself into the role of the professional athlete, the individual fantasizes a participation which he is physically incapable of performing. This vicarious extension of self satiates the need for exertion and is remarkably painless in nature. If the hypothesis is true, spectator sports have been aided in their growth by a pseudo-participant, and it appears that this potential market can only grow in the future.

FOOTNOTES

1. "1969 Survey on Sports Attendance," *The Morning Telegraph and Daily Racing Form,* (April 1970), various paging.

2. Gregory P. Stone, "Some Meanings of American Sport—An Extended View," *Proceedings of CIC Symposium on the Sociology of Sport,* Gerald S. Kenyon, ed., p. 10.

3. Ibid.

4. Ibid.

5. "Who Says Baseball is Like a Ballet?", *Forbes,* 1 April 1971, p. 26.

9

MARKETING IN COMMERCIAL BANKING

Until recently, neither banker nor layman associated marketing with commercial banking. To the former, a bank performed clearly defined services for a limited market. The layman took the initiative when in need of banking services. Marketing, because of its association with overt competition, was viewed as unethical by the former and invited the skepticism and suspicion of the latter.

Now, commercial banks face new forms of competition in their traditional market, borrowers, and for their basic raw material resource, deposits. In short, marketplace realities now face commercial banking just as they have faced manufacturing and trade in the not too distant past. The response pattern has been the same: (1) reluctant and piecemeal interest in the *forms* of marketing; (2) acceptance of marketing *practice* as a result of a better understanding of its inclusive meaning and increasing external pressures; and (3) the emergence of marketing organizations, marketing professionals, and a body of marketing literature in the commercial banking field.

Unlike other service industries, the transition to a marketing orientation and adoption of the marketing concept have been rapid and real. In a 1970 study of banks with deposits of 10 million dollars and more, the percentage of banks having formal marketing departments ranged from 31 percent in the group of smallest banks to 82 percent in the group representing the largest banks.[1] Of the banks with formal marketing departments, only 12 percent of the smallest banks and 15 percent of the largest banks reported marketing departments in existence over ten years.[2]

Another index of the adoption of marketing in commercial banking is its evolution in the American Bankers Association. From 1959 through 1962 there was a subcommittee on market research in the Association's Economics Department. In 1963 market research was teamed with the Automation Department. In 1965, market research and public relations were combined and in 1966 marketing became a separate department. In 1967 the Association held the first of its annual national meetings on marketing and today it has a substantial library on marketing ranging from advertising to bank location and market analysis.

Commercial banks have not adopted marketing practices merely because others have. As noted, new forms of competition are encroaching on their traditional markets: mutual savings banks, savings and loan associations, mutual funds, pension funds, credit unions, insurance companies, employee benefit programs, and special annuity plans. In addition, increasingly sophisticated financial officers in industry are turning to other sources of credit. The real-time nature of business information systems has lowered the level of deposit balances, a major source of loanable funds. Accordingly, marketing has become commercial banking's cutting edge for meeting new forms of competition and for searching out new opportunities.

It should be apparent to the reader that bank marketing offers a career opportunity currently not being met by traditional business school curricula. Banking courses still emphasize money and investment, and marketing courses are still engrossed with tangibles. The purpose of this chapter is to broaden the concept of marketing to include commercial banking and to introduce the field as a growth opportunity for business school graduates.

Before proceeding, the functions of a commercial bank should be identified. First, is the safe-keeping function. In effect, firms and individuals store their funds. Lending funds is the second major function. The third major function is to provide a variety of services not directly or only indirectly related to the other two. Computer services and safety deposit boxes, for example. The balance of this chapter is concerned with the interaction of marketing and these three basic functions.

DEMAND COMPONENTS IN COMMERCIAL BANKING

In the language of the industry, banks service two markets: wholesale and retail customers. In marketing language, banks serve industrial markets and ultimate consumer markets.

With the advent of marketing, banks now segment their markets. Rather than looking at their wholesale customers as a homogeneous group, they identify significant classes of customers within their trading area and study their specific financial needs. One bank may find agricultural producers and processors making up two segments. Another may identify steel mills or furniture manufacturers. Government or trade centers may be important for still a third.[3]

Similarly, ultimate consumer markets can be identified. In addition to the traditional "ideal" retail customer, the white-collar executive and professional, the commercial bank may find entirely new market opportunities by identifying and measuring such appropriate segments as:

blue-collar workers, young marrieds, senior citizens, and college students.

As the banking industry shifts from a supply or "production" orientation to one which recognizes the significance of the market in determining institutional success, two implications for bank management become apparent. First, bank planning must be built around market needs—not market needs in general—but the identified needs of the bank's own trading area. No longer will plans built around bank organization or functions exclusive of the market environment be adequate. Moreover, planning must reflect not only the economic and demographic character of its market segments but also their attitudes and values regarding money, saving, spending, and security. Second, incorporation of market variables in bank planning makes possible a balancing of market opportunities, bank resources, and competitive position in the interests of growth and profitability.

SUPPLY COMPONENTS IN COMMERCIAL BANKING

Typical of all services, a commercial bank's basic resources are skilled manpower and specialized facilities ranging from bank vaults and computers to record keeping systems which must be in being before services are performed. In addition, the lending function of the bank requires a third resource: an inventory of lendable funds. The analogy of deposits as a type of raw material inventory (resource) is only partial in that title to the inventory rests with the depositor. It is a type of leased inventory somewhat akin to leased capital goods.

The structure of supply has changed markedly since World War II. Between 1952 and 1971 the number of commercial banks declined from 14,693 to 14,294. During the same period the number of branches increased from 5,158 to 24,566.[4] It should be kept in mind that this growth in the number of branches occurred even though approximately one-third of the states prohibit branch banking and another one-third permit it under limited conditions only. Branch banking is similar to the center-city department store establishing branches in the suburbs. In addition to advantages of a financial nature, two benefits of branch banking reflect marketing influence. First, banking facilities are brought physically closer to the consumer or industrial user and second, the product mix of the branch is adapted to the particular needs of the market in which it is located.

The multi-bank holding company is quite similar to the department store chain in that formerly independent banks have been acquired through the acquisition of stock. A subsidiary bank may continue to operate largely as an independent bank or approach the characteristics of a branch.[5]

From a marketing standpoint, two other structural arrangements of supply are worth noting. First, the one-bank holding company is a mechanism allowing banks to diversify their product line: each subsidiary offers a different set of product services. Second, while the system of correspondent banking was instituted to facilitate the transfer of funds, increasingly central-city correspondents provide services to their affiliates in the hinterland leading to higher operating efficiency and new service products.

Finally, the nature of the relationship between depositor and bank is quite unlike that existing between merchant and customer. The depositor has a stake in the continuity of the bank. Hence, expansion and contraction of supply is not a function of market forces alone. The bank operates under a charter which is only granted where: (1) there is a demonstrated need; (2) there is the likelihood of profitable operations; and (3) existing banks will not be harmed. In other words, stability in banking supply is not sacrificed for greater competition.

MARKETING ISSUES: COMMERCIAL BANKING

Product Development

Assume a bank has limited its operations to the performance of the two traditional services: lending and accepting deposits. More precisely, it lends funds to local merchants and manufacturers which it has obtained from local merchants and manufacturers in the form of demand deposits. In addition, the bank accepts the deposits of individuals in accounts whose funds are available on demand (checking accounts) and in savings accounts. The major sources of bank income are interest earned on loans and investments and fees received from demand deposits. (Investments and investment income are not considered in this chapter.) Out of this income it must pay for the operation of the bank and interest on savings.

Now assume that competition begins to erode the leadership of the bank in its community. Competition may come from new banks or established banks which have launched an aggressive expansion campaign. Or it may come from new institutions and mechanisms for lending and saving. In response, the bank can take several steps, one of which is the development of new service products based on a thorough analysis of its market.

First, it can follow a policy of market extension through the development of new lending and savings programs designed to meet more precisely the needs of various segments of its market. It may establish Christmas and vacation savings clubs, launch a program of mortgage lending, and offer installment loans and collaborate with local retailers to provide for installment purchases. It could offer certificates of deposit, automatic lines of credit, and a plan for borrowing against savings accounts. Finally, it might participate in a credit card plan. Note that all of these new products are modifications of the traditional lending and deposit services of the bank.

Second, bank management recognizes that its facilities in being open opportunities for implementing a policy of product extension. It could provide commercial billing services for local utilities and handle company payrolls. (In Pennsylvania, banks distribute welfare checks for a fee paid by the state government.) The bank's computer can be made available to customers for electronic data processing, and cash dispensing machines might be installed.

Third, product extension policies are implemented through utilization of the bank's repository of financial acumen. Investment plans and financial counseling could be offered to existing customers and as a means of attracting new accounts. Likewise, the bank may offer a tax counseling service and prepare tax returns. Or it may seek subscriptions to monthly economic newsletters.

Fourth, the bank may follow a policy of conglomerate growth by establishing services, where regulations permit, which are clearly outside of the normal scope of commercial bank operations but which are complementary and are likely to further the use of other bank services. Factoring, equipment leasing, travel agency operations, insurance, and real estate services offered by commercial banks reflect a policy of conglomerate growth, both horizontal and vertical. Often these services are performed by subsidiaries of one-bank holding companies.

Before adding any of these services to its product line, the bank in the illustration needs to answer some very hard questions. What is the market potential for a proposed service and the bank's likely share of that potential? At what price should the service be offered? How much will it cost to perform the service? To what extent will the purchase of the proposed service lead to the purchase of other bank services? With answers to these questions and a knowledge of the bank's financial, facilities, and human resources available, management can select those services which are the most promising.

The bank credit card is an interesting example of product development in commercial banking. Approximately 9,000 commercial banks are included in the two national systems—Bank Americard and Master Charge. There are now more than twenty million active card holders and more than one million participating merchants and businesses.[6]

Nonexclusive franchises or licenses are granted to individual banks for which a fee is paid plus some form of annual compensation. The participating bank then markets the service to merchants and individual users. Merchants, of course, actively promote their affiliation with one or both of the national systems. Banks are compensated in two ways: Merchants are charged discounts on the volume of their bank card sales ranging from one to six percent, the higher the merchant's average sale the lower the discount rate. Card holders are assessed a finance charge for debts which are outstanding beyond the grace period, usually twenty-five days from the billing date.

The system is a costly one for a bank. The paperwork is substantial; credit losses have resulted through the aggressive promotion of free credit cards; and card holders who pay bills during the grace period generate no income to the bank. To reduce clerical costs, experiments are being conducted with point of sale authorization systems in which the merchant's clerks insert bank cards into a device that communicates with the card-issuing bank's computer; all transactions are added immediately to the card holder's outstanding debt. To generate additional income and reduce credit losses, some banks are initiating an annual fee for the right to use its credit card.

If the much-heralded system of cashless and checkless banking becomes a reality, the commercial bank will be required to develop many new services. For example, Californians can now have their paycheck credited to their bank account and routine bills paid from their account through electronic transfer of funds among the state's commercial banks. Bank income generated from this partial checkless system will be about the same as that resulting from conventional checking accounts plus fees paid by employers and billing companies. The service is optional and will require a marketing effort on the part of the bank to obtain the participation of the various parties.

The Role of Pricing in Commercial Bank Marketing

In general, commercial banks have not viewed pricing as an innovative and strategic marketing tool in the manner of the manufacturer of appliances or the food supermarket. First, federal and state regulations limit pricing freedom in order to protect the financial strength of banks. (The closing of a bank has more serious repercussions than the closing of a supermarket.) Second, there is a professional reluctance to compete on the basis of price even within the rather narrow bands of discretion which regulations allow. Third, pricing moves by one bank can be, and are, promptly duplicated by others.

Another factor which tends to diminish the use of pricing is the historical and widely-held view that lending is the prime function of a commercial bank and the prime source of its profits. All other services tend to be viewed as auxiliary or contributors to the lending function, that is, they are viewed as means. As a result, the pricing of these secondary or supplemental services has received relatively little consideration.

This leads to an anomaly in bank marketing: free services. Consider, for example, the rather simple act of cashing a check. This is an act of value to the bank customer; it certainly incurs costs for the bank. In any other enterprise a price would be set for the service. In the bank it is viewed more as a means of building goodwill or even as a form of sales promotion of the ultimate goal of expanding loans. Similarly, if one views the provision for saving money as a true service product of the bank, presumably the saver should pay a price for the service rendered; however, if one views savings as a raw material resource of the bank, then paying interest to savers is logical. The pricing anomaly persists in another major service of the bank: the provision of demand deposits, that is, checking accounts. For most banks, if demand deposits average above a certain minimum or do not fall at any time below the minimum during a specified period, there is no charge for this service. Otherwise, a price is charged. Again, the free service is justified because account balances are available for lending. A substantial number of banks, and the number appears to be growing, levy no charge for demand deposits— another "free" service; in this case, justification for this nonprice practice rests on its promotional value leading to profitable business where prices *are* charged for services rendered: lending and trust operations, for example. On the other hand, if demand deposits are viewed as bank resources rather than services rendered there is no reason why they should not be purchased as time deposits are, at least when viewed from a marketing perspective. For some decades, this practice has been prohibited by law (Regulation Q).

Marketing Communications in Commercial Banking

As banks adopt the concepts and practices of marketing, the quantity of promotional communications to the market increases, media base expands, message content changes, and responsibility for bank communications tends to rest with specialists.

Between 1946 and 1968, bank expenditures for advertising increased tenfold.[7] Part of this increase reflects growth in the cost of advertising; nevertheless, increasing use of advertising in commercial banking far exceeds the growth of advertising in general.

The traditional medium for communicating with the market has been publicity and public relations. Participation in community affairs, speeches, and press releases geared to inform rather than sell were deemed adequate. The atmosphere of the personal contact was that of counselor and client, not of seller and buyer of banking services. At both the personal and institutional level the objective of the communications program was to project an image of strength, confidence, and security. Even the architecture and the decor of the bank contributed to this image.

Today, commercial banks utilize practically all forms of communication. Table 9.1 shows a significant parallel between media preferences of all advertisers and commercial banks. Differences are largely accounted for by the local or regional nature of banking and a reluctance on the part

Table 9.1

RANK OF MEDIA EXPENDITURES

	All Advertisers*	Commercial Banks**
Newspapers	1	1
Miscellaneous	2	2
Television	3	4
Direct mail	4	5
Magazines (including business)	5	7
Radio	6	3
Outdoor	7	6

*Advertising Age, 7 August 1972, p. 66.
**Advertising and Promotion (Washington, D.C.: American Bankers Association, 1970), p. 39.

of bank managements to advertise in more costly media. Were the data for bank advertising to be more recent, television would be a more important medium because of growth in the use of spot commercials.

One unusual feature of bank promotion is the recent widespread adoption of premiums in an effort to expand the demand for services at the ultimate consumer level. They have been effective in establishing new savings accounts and introducing new branches. In the former case, the reason for the success of premiums lies in the otherwise undifferentiated nature of the service: Excluding a more convenient location, there is no reason why a consumer should transfer a savings account from one bank to another or start a new savings account. The premium becomes the differentiating feature. In the latter case, the new branch is, in effect, starting from scratch and must provide some inducement. The premium seems to be one answer.

Personal selling does not come easy to many bankers. Very few banks have sales forces, as such, and perhaps a better term should be used, such as account development. Nevertheless, as the commercial bank becomes a "full-service bank" and caters increasingly to various consumer market segments, some form of personal promotional effort is necessary. Sales training programs have been established for public contact personnel and a more organized effort is being made to encourage bank officers to go to the market rather than remain back of the desk.

Similarly, message content has shifted from simply stressing the bank's name and projecting an image, to more promotional appeals designed to increase deposits, loans, and other services, to increase traffic, and to some extent, to compete directly with other commercial banks and alternative institutions.

Typically, one or two officers are involved in performing bank advertising functions. However, the final decisions regarding the advertising budget, media selection, and message content are still made by the chief executive officer in most banks. The larger banks have decentralized the media and message decisions to advertising officers.[8]

Channel Considerations in Commercial Banking

A direct channel of distribution is universal. There are no agent middlemen. Time and place utility have advanced in commercial banking through several developments. The first is the growth of branch banking to which reference has already been made. The second is the provision of a variety of facilities for "after-hours" banking. Third is the provision for banking by mail which transfers the depositing process from the bank to the residence or place of business of the depositor. Automatic lines of credit also have the effect of bringing the lending service product of the bank to the point of decision. The resulting added utilities make it easier to do business with the bank and so expand demand for its services.

COMMERCIAL BANKING FROM A MARKETING PERSPECTIVE

New Perspectives from Marketing

In order to implement a formal marketing effort both bank philosophy and managerial decisions must grant precedence to demand: a bank is not in existence to perform banking activities but to satisfy market needs. The objectives of banking derive from the minds and attitudes of the consumer or industrial user. Thus, a bank does not lend money—it makes a college education possible; it builds a home; it expands employment opportunities in a community.

Lip service to marketing is meaningless; it must be given reality both in terms of organization and staffing. It should appear on the bank's organization chart and position descriptions for marketing personnel should be formulated.

In industry, marketing is one of the two major line activities; in trade it is the only significant activity. In banking, marketing is typically viewed as a staff function. In this regard it is quite similar to the role of a home office marketing group in a divisionalized company: marketing personnel are primarily advisory, consultative, and educational in their relations with other departments of the bank. It would be reasonable to assign line responsibility, that is, decision-making authority, in advertising, sales promotion, and premiums. It should have authority to conduct marketing research and establish training programs for those who contact the public. The marketing group should take an advocacy position on market factors bearing on decisions to inaugurate or terminate services and should participate in pricing decisions.

If marketing personnel come from the outside they should be educated in banking procedures and financial constraints to avoid a "bull-in-a-china-shop syndrome." On the other hand, if they come from within banking, executive development in marketing is most important. They should be selected for their ability to understand and work with other people, not necessarily because of demonstrated financial acumen. Marketing responsibility should not be merely an "add-on" charge for bank personnel already fully occupied.

Training for bank people responsible for obtaining and keeping customers should include: (1) the significance of marketing in commercial banking; (2) the value of the various services of the bank from the customer's standpoint; (3) an understanding of the economic, demographic, and behavioral characteristics of the bank's market; (4) experience in interpersonal contact where the goal is the sale of the bank's services; and (5) an understanding of the bank's administrative procedures and practices.

Formal acceptance of marketing requires that executives reassess the bank's financial statements. Initially, marketing expenditures may be viewed as additions to the bank's operating expenses and no more. But the real impact of marketing expenditures is at the top of the income statement—expanded revenue. Turning to the balance sheet, the marketing executive would argue that the bank's most important asset does not appear: its market. These observations suggest a change in approach and attitude. While many people in marketing would argue that expenditures for market development are investments rather than expenses, it is unlikely that this viewpoint will be reflected in financial statements. For present purposes, the function of marketing should be recognized; demand creation, revenue expansion, and market development at a profit, even though accounting practice dictates that expenditures be recorded as expenses.

Marketing's Impact on Banking Practice

First, marketing requires more attention to account profitability. Responsibility for its determination should rest with marketing personnel for the following reasons: (1) they are impartial; (2) marketing has the necessary skills; (3) marketing people need the information for planning and product development; and (4) profitable volume is the objective of marketing.[9] Account profitability is a function of interest paid by the borrower and the value of his compensating balances on the one hand, and the cost of funds used and checking account activity, loan-processing costs, and a risk-taking cost, on the other.[10]

Second, marketing research should be a major contribution to bank operations. A bank can: (1) determine the attitudes of people in its market toward the bank, toward saving and indebtedness; (2) make cost analyses of various bank services and establish profitability measures; (3) determine in advance the likely reception of new banking services; (4) identify prospects for services; (5) measure performance against that of competition; and (6) aid in determining the best location for branch sites. Much of this information can be obtained from a marketing-oriented analysis of internal records. Useful statistics can be generated by recording the results of customer contacts. Special studies making use of field or mail surveys can be used.

For example, conversion to a checkless or less-check financial system is costly. Moves in this direction *assume* that check users want it. Marketing research should verify this assumption. Are corporations and individuals willing to delegate control over outgo and income to electronic equipment? Which market segments are willing, which are not? Which transactions are least likely to meet resistance, which are most likely? Answers to questions such as these before commitment enable banks to pace their adoption of this new approach in accord with the market's acceptance of it.

Third, one of the most important contributions of marketing to commercial banking is the view that a bank offers a *system* of financial services, not simply a "menu" of services. As the bank's product line grows, the more feasible it becomes for it to satisfy all financial needs. Conceptually, a "full-service bank" is a system of services. In practice it could mean a complete reorganization of the bank in terms of markets rather than functions. Thus, one department would satisfy all the financial needs of retailers; or all the financial needs of manufacturers; or all the financial needs of households. Banking personnel could be account representatives, responsible for meeting all the financial needs of assigned accounts—both active acounts and prospects.

Problem Areas in Bank Marketing

Bank marketing literature is replete with references to "services." There is a tendency to identify every change or improvement as a new service. Some are *facilitating* efforts: improved statements and teller performance; more convenient banking hours; more convenient location and parking facilities. Some new "services" are really *communications* efforts: more attractive checks; providing facilities for community activities. Consistency and clarity suggest that the term "services" be limited to the bank's product line—services which the bank sells. Service products which could be sold but for which no charge is made, such as demand deposit balances above a specified minimum and financial counseling, probably should be viewed as a form of promotion, although, as noted earlier, the presence of these "free" services is a unique characteristic of bank marketing. Figure 9.1 depicts the unusual nature of bank marketing: the bank as a seller; as a buyer (of time deposits), and as a performer of "free" services. (Throughout this chapter "free" refers to explicit services rendered for which no charge is made. Someone pays, of course.)

As the bank becomes more marketing-oriented, the tendency to convert from soft to hard competition must be anticipated. In an earlier day, competition was more indirect: reputation, friendship, and image were the ingredients; competitive efforts were not overt. Now, bank marketers solicit business from new businesses and residents in its trading area and from the customers of competitors. These deliberate efforts, however, should concentrate on the quality of the bank's service products and

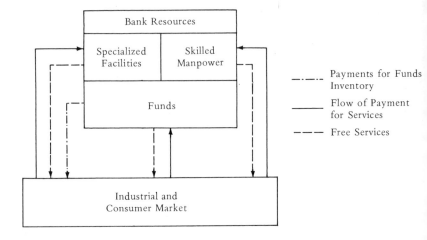

Figure 9.1 *MARKETING MODEL OF A COMMERCIAL BANK*

should be communicated in a professional manner. Strident advertising invites strident advertising with the result that nothing is gained and much is lost: the image of an institution of substance and dependability.

On the other hand, as banks diversify into new service products such as insurance, real estate, and data processing, they must be prepared to compete according to the patterns of competition. A third situation in which the nature of competition must be considered occurs when others perform services traditionally the responsibility of the commercial bank. Here the temptation to adopt hard competition is strongest.

Finally, the impact of regulation on bank marketing must be considered. State regulatory agencies, the Federal Deposit Insurance Corporation, the Federal Reserve System, and the Comptroller of the Currency in the Treasury Department have an interest in bank regulation. All are concerned with a reliable, orderly, and continuing financial system. Anyone who has lived through the Depression can appreciate their concern. However, it may be that the extent of regulation designed to protect the public has also stifled innovation in the development of bank marketing services. It is true that the public benefits from the maintenance of a sound banking system; but the public also benefits from a competitive system.

In this regard, the widespread and enthusiastic commitment to marketing that has characterized commercial banking has resulted in a problem which may be repeated in other regulated industries in the future as they adopt marketing practices. For commercial banking is partially regulated by agency and partially regulated by the marketplace. Governmental controls restrict product development, pricing, and channel policies in varying degrees depending on various state jurisdictions. Only promotion seems to be relatively free of regulation. As a result, the efficient application of a fully integrated marketing program is not possible.

If governmental regulation is to be relaxed in favor of more competition, more attention must be given to the need for clearly delineating the jurisdiction of the government agency and the jurisdiction of the marketplace. For example, from a marketing perspective it makes no sense to argue for more competition in banking and at the same time (1) control the prices at which banks are permitted to buy deposits and sell loans and (2) mandate price differentials between competing banking institutions.

When the commercial bank formally incorporates the marketing concept of its commercial customers into its own operations, three principles should underlie its activities: (1) the character of its market should be the starting point for marketing activities; (2) marketing should be consistent with the philosophy and abilities of bank management, its facilities, and financial resources; and (3) marketing should never compromise the bank's position in the community. After all, the bank's stock in trade, like that of the health care agency, is most basic: the well-being of the individual and of society.

FOOTNOTES

1. *Status of Bank Marketing* (Washington, D.C.: American Bankers Association, 1970), pp. 28-29.

2. Ibid., p. 30.

3. Gary H. Raddon, "Market Segmentation: a Successful Case in Wholesale Banking" in *Response and Responsibility: Customer Needs and Wants* (Washington, D.C.: American Bankers Association, 1970), pp. 205-210.

4. U.S. Bureau of the Census, *Statistical Abstract of the United States: 1972* (93rd edition.) Washington, D.C., 1972, p. 444.

5. Paul M. Horvitz, *Monetary Policy and the Financial System*, 2nd edition (Englewood Cliffs, N.J.: Prentice-Hall, Inc., 1969), p. 486.

6. "Bank Credit Cards," *Business Conditions* (Chicago, Illinois: Federal Reserve Bank of Chicago, July 1972), p. 8.

7. *Advertising and Promotion* (Washington, D.C.: American Bankers Association, 1970), p. 30-31.

8. Ibid., pp. 6-9.

9. John F. Falkenberg, "Pricing: Application of Profitability Analysis" in *Response and Responsibility: Customer Needs and Wants* op. cit., p. 326.

10. Ibid., p. 325.

BANK MARKETING

L. A. Capaldini

A review of the current status of bank marketing and how a student can consider a career calling for competence in marketing and banking.

There is much evidence that commercial banking is becoming marketing minded: news stories report instances of innovations by banks to serve customers better, bank stock evaluations by brokers include references to marketing effectiveness, more and more mass media advertising is by banks. Also, research and consulting firms are getting more business from banks.

The fact that this book contains this chapter is another piece of evidence. So is the fact that banking trade associations are receiving an increasing number of marketing-related inquiries from faculty and students of business schools.

This is surface evidence. What does the evidence show if one digs deeper? What's the future outlook on bank marketing? In addition to answering those two questions, this paper will attempt to guide the interested student toward useful sources for bank marketing.

NATURE OF COMMERCIAL BANKING

To understand the nature of commercial banking, let's examine its role:

> Two types of institutions channel the public's savings into loans and investments—commercial banks and financial intermediaries. What distinguishes the intermediaries from commercial banks is that they are basically just what they are called, intermediaries, conduits that channel the savings of the economy into debt instruments of various types. They can lend only the amount they have received from savers, and unlike the commercial banks, they cannot create new deposit money.[1]

The author is Director, Corporate Planning Division and formerly Director of Marketing, American Bankers Association.

The major forms of financial intermediaries are mutual savings banks, savings and loan associations, credit unions, life insurance companies, pension funds, mortgage companies and finance companies.

Table 9.2 gives some basic statistics on assets/liabilities and number of banking offices of commercial banks, mutual savings banks (MSBs) and savings and loan associations (S&Ls).

Commercial banking is a highly regulated industry. In the United States there are 53 governmental agencies with commercial bank chartering and/or regulation authority—three at the federal level (Comptroller of the Currency, Federal Reserve and Federal Deposit Insurance Corporation) and 50 at the state level (one in each state).

As an example of regulatory complexity, note the McFadden Act of 1927. The act permits national banks (those chartered by the Comptroller of the Currency) to branch in each state only to the extent state-chartered banks, by state law, can branch. State laws have liberalized since 1927. The branching situation in each of the 50 states and District of Columbia at year end 1972 is shown in Table 9.3.

Business Week noted that the 53 agencies ". . . (are) a monument to duplication" and went on to say, "The current structure of regulators—built up in layers by successive waves dating back into the 19th century—is a political fact of life."[2]

Both state and federal regulators have up to now regarded their jobs primarily as protecting depositors. This is somewhat understandable when one considers that in the 1930's over 9,000 banks failed with dire consequences for their depositors. Yet, as David Rockefeller, Chairman of Chase Manhattan Bank, New York City, pointed out, ". . . Congress and changing conditions in U.S. society are inexorably imposing new demands on banks."[3]

ROLES AND CHANGES

At one time the simplified definition of a commercial bank was a bank that accepted demand deposits (checking accounts) in addition to time and savings deposits and made all types of loans (business loans, consumer loans and mortgage loans to individuals). On the other hand, the MSBs and S&Ls, have historically specialized in serving individuals through savings and housing loans.

These lines of demarcation are blurring. As of this writing several states permit either or both of the MSBs or S&Ls in their borders to offer checking accounts, also to engage in loans other than mortgage or construction loans.

Impetus to the graying of previous distinctions is given when a

Table 9.2

BANKING COMPARISONS AT YEAR END - 1972

Category	Commercial Banks	Mutual Savings Banks*	Savings and Loan Associations
Assets/Liabilities ($-Million)	739.6	100.6	243.6
Number of Offices			
Main	13,950	486	5,448
Branches	24,872	1,354	5,793
	38,822	1,840	11,241

*Exist in only 18 states, mainly in the Northeast.

Source: Federal Deposit Insurance Corporation, United Savings and Loan League.

Table 9.3

BRANCHING LAWS FOR COMMERCIAL BANKS

Type Branching	Number of States
Statewide branching permitted	20
Limited area branching permitted	16
No branching (or limited service offices only)	15

Presidential Commission, popularly known as the Hunt Commission, in 1971 reported:

> The Commission's objective, then, is to move as far as possible toward freedom of financial markets and equip all institutions with the powers necessary to compete in such markets. Once these powers and services have been authorized, and a suitable time allowed for implementation, *each institution will be free to determine its own course.*[4] (Emphasis added.)

After study and much input from public interest and industry groups, the President forwarded the Hunt Commission recommendations pretty much intact to Congress. In his message to Congress the President contended, "Flexibility and efficiency will be enhanced by *placing competing institutions on a roughly equal footing* with regard to three essential considerations: deposit powers, lending powers, and tax burdens."[5] (Emphasis added.)

SOME IMPORTANT CURRENT TRENDS

Other factors contributing to the impetus of rapid change in commercial banking include:

1. Lowered margins of profit

2. Increased competition both within and without
3. Bank holding company movement
4. Technology making new products possible
5. Quest for new consumer markets
6. Crumbling barriers to branching
7. National and international expansion
8. Consumerism and social responsibility

Among the factors some would cite as obviating expanded and more competitive commercial banking are:

1. Natural resistance to change by banks
2. Natural resistance to change by bank customers
3. Fear of bigness and economic concentration
4. Populism
5. Puritan ethic, Protestant ethic
6. Dislike of depersonalization
7. Fear of invasion of privacy

IMPLICATIONS FOR MARKETING

While these trends had their beginning decades ago, they have a profound meaning for the marketing concept as applied to banking. Yet, it was not until 1960 that one began to see the term *marketing* in banking periodicals and other literature. As in other industries, the early stages of marketing were characterized by a "selling" approach—one that emphasized seller benefits in preference to buyer benefits.

That is not to say that certain alert bankers were not practicing the art at all. It is interesting to read in a book devoted to the history of marketing in this country that "Another fiber in marketing thought was spun by men concerned with credit."[6]

This writer noted in an address to bankers that "...consumer lending is a good example of an early and sound marketing response"[7] and that at year end 1972, commercial banks held $60 billion of $127 billion consumer installment credit outstanding, $7 billion of that being in a new form the Federal Reserve classifies as "bank card and check-credit plans."[8]

It would be fanciful to believe that commercial bankers have fully adopted and are committed to the marketing concept. The social sciences have taught us how to differentiate between support of a value as an attitude, that is, "I believe in marketing" and the actual realization of the value in behavioral terms (practice by policy making and other levels of management of marketing on an ongoing daily basis.)

Several small-scale studies have employed this approach. Brien and Stafford charged banks, "It is time to change the marketing concept in banking from myth to reality."[9] Donnelly and Ivancevich used a four-point criterion and concluded ". . . members of the banking community have been rather sluggish in embracing the marketing concept . . . and exhibited both a misunderstanding of the major principles of the concept and a failure to reflect these in their day-to-day marketing operations."[10] White used ten topics as criteria in his survey and stated there was a significant lack of marketing orientation in commercial banks.[11]

A large-scale study conducted in 1970 by Lester B. Knight & Associates, Inc., for the American Bankers Association, stated two major conclusions:

1. Marketing is broadly recognized and considered important in over 90 percent of the banks with deposits over $10 million. Chief executive officers and marketing management report the function of marketing is firmly established in banks throughout the country. There is a formal marketing department in 55 percent of the banks with deposits over $10 million. By contrast, the 1965 ABA survey showed that only one-third of the larger banks had established marketing departments.
2. Most bankers consider marketing as essentially an advertising and public relations job. Of the reporting banks, 73 percent said advertising and public relations is the most important function; 44 percent named sales promotion as next most important.[12]

This dichotomy should not be surprising, for a similar ambivalence has existed in industries which embraced the marketing concept earlier but experienced similar problems in operationalizing the concept into concrete management practices. As one reads Bartels[13] or Vizza, et al.,[14] one is left with the impression that in both consumer and industrial goods firms marketing progression and development is almost always somewhat disjointed and discontinuous. Even the popular Keith[15] and Borch[16] pieces suggest the difficulty firms encounter in achieving the understanding and successful practice of marketing.

Commercial banking, as an industry, is going through that very process. A good, recent example is a feature article by Jelliffe with a title straight from college marketing texts and a subtitle explaining "Marketing doesn't start with the ice box. It starts with the Eskimo."[17]

Does bank marketing offer a challenging career? This writer believes so, but suggests it will require a thorough grounding in *both* marketing and banking. Presently one can get a good college education in marketing but the tie-in to banking is lacking. Conversely, one can get a good college education in banking and finance but little tie-in to marketing. This will probably change as curricula change. In the meantime, should one's education lack the required dimension, on-the-job management training can, as it has, fill the void.

OUTLOOK

Admitting a strong bias, this writer offers an optimistic outlook for the student considering a career in bank marketing. There are simply not enough bank officers with the education, experience, and overall know-how to implement marketing strategies in dynamic and creative ways.

For example, almost all the factors referred to earlier are marketing "guides" to the banker able to perceive them as opportunities instead of problems and implement strategies such as these, which are cited as *examples only:*

1. National expansion—promote "we're with you" wherever your business or personal travels take you.
2. Natural resistance to change by bank customers—research and cite what is *not* being changed because they are inherently good; in presenting new ideas explain the roots from the past.
3. Protestant ethic—save for your needs and don't borrow unless you have to, and when you borrow let us show you how to save.
4. Dislike of depersonalization—we use computers so more of our skilled bankers can give you personal counseling when you want it.

How does a bank evaluate and test these strategies? By what process would it formulate other strategies? What specific marketing plans would be employed to implement these strategies?

Kotler, citing the consumer movement as an opportunity instead of a threat to banking, stated "Instead of future shock, the industry might well experience future confidence."[18]

The answers are complex and will require capable, dedicated bankers. Part of the great satisfaction for the student entering the marketing career path in banking is that he/she would be "pioneering." In addition, banks are paying better salaries than they used to, and there is the intellectual challenge of a business that is ". . . so terribly complex," according to Drucker.[19]

USEFUL SOURCES

Where does the interested marketing student turn for information and materials on bank marketing? Here are suggestions:

1. *Trade Associations.* Write for materials you can borrow or buy. Frequently a college library will, upon expression of interest by students or faculty, purchase scholarly items from trade associations. Inquire about the possibility of attending marketing conferences as an observer. Ask for leads as to bankers and American Institute of Banking Chapters and Bank Marketing Association Chapters in your town. Your best bet is to start with your own state's commercial banking trade association. After all, you're a voting citizen and they relate to you well. Each state and the District of Columbia has such a state-level association, usually headquartered in the state's capital city. There are also the commercial banking trade associations operating at the national level, for example: American Bankers Association, Bank Marketing Association, Bank Administration Institute and others. Check one of the trade association directories in your college library for complete addresses. Also, it is a good idea to know a little about the association before you write, phone or visit.

2. *Periodicals and Publications.* More and more banking periodicals are carrying marketing and marketing-related articles, and more and more college libraries are subscribing to such periodicals. Among the ones you should consider are: *Bank Marketing, Bankers Monthly, Banking, Burroughs Clearing House* (all monthly) and *The Bankers Magazine* (quarterly). Also, general business periodicals such as *Business Horizons, Fortune* and *Harvard Business Review* are useful to follow. Publications are produced by the ABA, BMA and BAI mentioned above. Textbook type materials are available from ABA's American Institute of Banking. On all these, check with your library.

3. *Bankers Schools.* The AIB offers courses at the local level, and is some instances the effort is a joint one with the local college. There are also intermediate-level schools generally a week in length sponsored by state bankers associations, and you might be allowed to audit a given school. It won't hurt to ask. Also there are graduate-level schools (generally two weeks in length). Check through your state bankers association.

4. *Bankers.* Call on your bankers, especially the personnel officers or marketing officers for information. You might be

invited in for a personal visit and look behind the scenes on how marketing works in a given bank. Also, if you are doing a research paper, ask for advice (almost everyone likes to help aspiring young people). If you've done a really good paper, offer to share it with your banker and trade associations.

CONCLUSION

The assessment of the current state of bank marketing given in *Business Week* is believed to be valid: ". . . some pluses, some minuses, but plenty of expectations."[20]

FOOTNOTES

1. Paul S. Nadler, *Commercial Banking in the Economy* (New York: Random House, 1968), pp. 12-13.

2. "The Drive to Thin the Regulatory Thicket," *Business Week,* 15 September 1973, p. 145.

3. Ibid.

4. *The Report of the President's Commission on Financial Structure & Regulation,* (Washington, D.C.: United States Government Printing Office, 1971), p. 9.

5. *Recommendations for Change in the U.S. Financial System,* (Washington, D.C.: United States Government Printing Office, 1973), p. 3.

6. Robert Bartels, *The Development of Marketing Thought* (Homewood, Illinois: Richard D. Irwin, Inc., 1962), p. 66.

7. L. A. Capaldini, "Will the Real Marketer Please Stand?", speech delivered at Consumer Credit Conference, North Carolina Bankers Association, Southern Pines, North Carolina, 21 February 1973 (unpublished).

8. Ibid.

9. Richard H. Brien and James E. Stafford, "The Myth of Marketing in Banking," *Business Horizons* (Spring 1967), p. 78.

10. James H. Donnelly and John M. Ivancevich, "How Marketing-Oriented Are Commercial Banks?", *Banking* (February 1969), p. 60.

11. S. Douglass White, "Marketing in Banking: Philosophies and Actions," *Journal of Bank Research* (Winter 1973), p. 268.

12. *Status of Bank Marketing* (Washington, D.C.: American Bankers Association, 1970), p. 111.

13. Bartels, op. cit., pp. 157-192.

14. Robert F. Vizza, Thomas E. Chambers, and Edward J. Cook, *Adoption of the Marketing Concept—Fact or Fiction?* (New York: Sales Executives Club of New York, Inc., 1967), pp. 117-119.

15. Robert J. Keith, "The Marketing Revolution," *Journal of Marketing* (January 1960), p. 35.

16. F. J. Borch, "The Marketing Philosophy As a Way of Business Life," Address to the American Management Association, February 1957, p. 1.

17.   C. Gordon Jelliffe, "It's Not Making Customers Buy Your Product. It's Making Products Your Customers Will Buy," *Banking* (August 1973), pp. 20-21.

18.   Philip Kotler, "Marketing's Role in the Age of the Consumer," in *Banking in the Age of Consumerism,* Proceedings of the ABA 1973 National Marketing Conference, The American Bankers Association, Washington, D.C., 1973, p. 24.

19.   Peter F. Drucker, "The Banker As a Marketer," *Response and Responsibility: Customer Needs and Wants,* Proceedings of the ABA 1970 National Marketing Conference, New York, 1970, pp. 39-46.

20.   "Tyros in the Marketing Game," *Business Week,* 15 September 1973, p. 80.

10

MARKETING HEALTH CARE SERVICES

This chapter is concerned with the service product responsible for the maintenance of the individual's physical well-being and, even more fundamentally, his continuing existence. Health care is estimated to be our third largest industry in terms of sales and number of employees, due in part to the extraordinary increase in quantity and improvement in quality of procedures, treatment, and facilities that have occurred during this century.

The health care industry is at a watershed point: tradition is being challenged by innovation in the *marketing* of health care because of two conditions. The first is inflation. While drugs and prescriptions have been relatively stable since 1960, physicians' fees have increased nearly 50 percent and hospital charges have more than tripled.

> The medical care system, for the most part, is shielded from [the market-oriented economy] and market forces are severely crippled. Despite the fact that about 60 percent of the funds paid out for health and medical care are private expenditures made in a market situation, the market signals yielded are confused and often go unheeded. Little *information* is generated on the most economically productive combinations of medical resources (doctors, nurses, and hospitals). For example, since neither doctors nor hospitals openly compete on price, charges vary for similar services. Among other things, this lack of competition hides information about the most efficient methods, hospitals, and doctors.[1]

The second condition has to do with the unequal availability of health care in this country. In part, this is a function of geography. Rural areas and smaller communities are often totally lacking in both physicians and hospitals. Clearly this is a marketing location problem. Also, many low-income market segments are inadequately served. While Americans accept the proposition that some can afford only a table model television whereas others can purchase an elaborate console model, when we regard health care we are reluctant to accept the idea that access to health care depends on the purchasing power of the market area. As a result, we, in this country, are faced with an anomaly. While it is unquestionably possible to obtain here the very best health care in the world, in fact, this country, relative to other developed nations, stands well down on the list of most statistical measures of physical well-being and health. Possibly, a marketing approach to the delivery of health care can assist in the resolution of these two conditions. Certainly it would help to close the current information gap between provider and client.

HEALTH CARE DEMAND CHARACTERISTICS

Macro Demand Factors

From birth to death all are included in the market potential for health care—some more, some less by choice or necessity. One estimate places expenditures at $90 billion for 1973, including services, goods, research, and medical facilities construction.[2] The incidence of health care consumption tends to correlate with income as noted earlier. Unfortunately, those least able to maintain good health because of their standard and style of living, the poor and the elderly, have been less likely to receive appropriate health care services because of ignorance, inaccessibility, or limited purchasing power. These conditions have resulted in a substantial growth of third-party financial participation in the purchase of health care services: private insurance, nonprofit agencies such as Blue Cross, and government, particularly the third. In 1970 it was estimated that direct payments by consumers were under 40 percent of total payments, public payments amounted to 35 percent, and the balance was made through private profit and nonprofit insurance systems.[3]

Micro Demand Factors

The goal of the individual consumer is to maintain or regain health—normatively, the former, and realistically, the latter—and postpone death. Without sounding morbid, one must stress an underlying, if unspoken, characteristic of individual demand for health care: ultimately these services must fail to satisfy the goals of the consumer. Parenthetically, in this affluent, complex, and tension-ridden society of ours, the terms "health" and "well-being" apply to both body and mind.

Even though health care providers stress prevention of illness through periodic, routine transactions between patient and physician, the demand for health care is for most people, postponable or of an emergency nature. Health care is viewed by the consumer as a means, not an end, except for those few who gain some satisfaction from medical attention per se. Moreover, it is viewed as a means to merely maintain or regain normal health; suppliers of health care services appear to offer no more than normalcy; this nondynamic view may have a depressing effect on desirable levels of demand. A marketing view would suggest that the benefits of normal health be made attractive.

Many consumers are caught on the horns of a dilemma: fear of the consequences of illness or fear of the means of attaining freedom from illness. This dilemma is even more acute if the treatment includes surgery. Here again, marketing would suggest the use of appropriate messages and media which tend to resolve this conflict.

Another characteristic of the demand for health care is the usual inability of the consumer to determine when services are needed or to know what is wrong; many illnesses "creep up" and discomfort signals do not necessarily disclose their source. For many, there seems to be a "critical mass" of symptoms before the need for health care propels the consumer into the marketplace.

There is also the strong temptation to "make" rather than "buy," that is, to try self-treatment rather than professional treatment. Undoubtedly, economic factors are at work here, but in addition, for males, self-treatment may be viewed as more manly. Beyond that, there is a more fundamental question. Some illnesses do not require professional treatment and the supply side of health care is limited. While data are not available, it can be surmised that the dividing line between self-treatment and professional treatment if the services are purchased by the consumer will differ from the dividing line where payment is made by a third-party intermediary, particularly if the third party is a government agency (that is, the services are "free").

The consumer is a client, not a customer, of the provider of health care. The distinction is profound. A customer takes title to a good upon purchase and the seller has no control over the consumption of the product—he can only advise. The client, on the other hand, places himself in the hands of the provider or seller. The buying decision is joint, not unilateral; the buyer is not free to pick and choose. In effect, the decision to buy is made by the buyer but the decision on what is purchased is made by the seller or provider.

Because of the intangible nature of the service, the client relationship, and the more common gradual nature of physical response to health care services, the consumer has very little objective basis for judging or comparing their quality. Trying one provider then another in order to find the "best buy" as one would try one brand and another of a product is difficult and inadvisable, if not dangerous. At the same time, beyond questions of malpractice, the buyer cannot expect any warranty or "money-back" guarantees. Yet, in measures of trust, physicians are held in the highest respect by their patients. This expression of confidence by most health care consumers has no counterpart in other buyer-seller relationships. As a result, the sensitivity of demand to price is quite inelastic.

HEALTH CARE SUPPLY CHARACTERISTICS

Until recently, supply of health services has been fragmented. The independence of the physician together with the trend toward specialization have provided formidable obstacles to efficient supply. As will be noted, the advent of health maintenance systems is a response to fragmentation.

Another characteristic of supply is the key role of the physician. Unless the consumer is treating himself, all health care services are determined by the primary physician. Drugs, nursing care, x-rays, hospitalization, and specialized medical practice, for example, are selected by the primary physician. He is the point of contact between the consumer and the supply side of health care.

Disequilibrium in the health care marketplace cannot be corrected through the forces of a competitive free market. For many segments of health care supply, the "profit motive" is lacking and alternative incentives are less direct in their effect. Health care facilities are costly and it is more difficult to marshal capital resources. Some argue that the supply of medical practitioners is held back for economic reasons. More likely, the profession refuses to dilute the quality of its practice through inappropriate short-cuts to catch up with demand. Those who are cynical on this score lose their cynicism on the operating table. It might be noted also that data of the American Association of Medical Colleges show that accepted applicants at medical schools grew from 9,123 in 1966-67 to an estimated 13,500 in 1972-73, an increase of 48 percent. While the absolute number may be too small in terms of market requirements, the trend hardly suggests an attempt to restrict the supply.[4]

Finally, it should be noted that health care supply is becoming increasingly machine centered. In addition to improving the quality of health care, growth in instrumentation both at the physician's office and in the hospital expands supply in partial response to the imbalance that presently exists. At the same time, health care becomes more impersonal with unfortunate effects on the behavioral aspects of the supply-demand relationship.

MARKETING ISSUES: PROFESSIONAL SERVICES

An initial issue from a marketing perspective and a major one in health care, is the relative shift from general to specialized practice. Perhaps greater prestige attaches to specialization. Possibly the proliferation of medical knowledge justifies a narrower approach to medical practice. Perhaps a smaller supply of more proficient specialists commands a higher price in the health care marketplace.

Granting that this trend toward specialization may improve the quality of medical practice, the search for appropriate professional care is made more difficult for the consumer. His inability to obtain access to the supply of professional services encourages postponement of treatment. In addition, the need to make appointments for months in advance is hardly in keeping with the stress on preventive medicine. The strongly entrenched negative view of market competition held by the medical profession is a constraining factor. Corrective steps which are professionally acceptable should be taken—enhancing the role of the general practitioner and redirecting medical education, for example.

Closely related to the above is the shift from "door-to-door" to "shopping center" practice, to use marketing terms. The supply of medical practice is thereby expanded since more time is devoted to practice and less to travel. The consumer must decide whether the service is worth the time and strain of going to the service rather than having it brought to him. Presumably, this tradeoff reduces the demand for unnecessary treatment yet it may also result in postponement where treatment is appropriate.

As noted earlier, it is argued that licensure is either a means of restricting supply or of controlling the quality of medical care. It would appear to be mandatory if quality is to be maintained in this basic service. As a matter of fact, examination and licensing are being recommended in other service areas where the buyer is subjected to wide ranges of service performance with no mechanism for evaluating them: repair, research, and tax services, for example.

In addition to increasing the supply of physicians, disequilibrium in the professional medical care marketplace is being met by expanding the number and increasing the responsibilities of paramedics, registered nurses, nurses aides, and other specialists. In marketing terms, the product line is being restructured to more adequately and efficiently meet consumer needs.

The pricing of professional medical services reflects a major departure from conventional marketing. Professional services rendered are in part a reflection of the degree of standardization in treatment and in part the condition of the patient. That is, a patient who is critically ill from a rare disease places quite different demands on the professional than one suffering from arthritis, for example. In addition, the price (or fee) may reflect ability to pay even though physicians are no "respecter of persons" in terms of services rendered. This practice of price differentiation is not so prevalent with the advent of third-party financial intermediaries; their schedule of payments for specified treatments becomes a type of price list.

Demand creation or the shifting of demand through promotion is unethical in the health care field. However, there is universal support among professionals for the use of advertising media to promote good health. Examples include counteradvertising of cigarettes, the campaign to educate the public of the warning signs of cancer, and the promotional efforts of dental groups to reduce the incidence of cavities. It should be noted that all of these efforts contribute to the objectives of the medical practitioner even though they reduce the demand for his services. Voluntary efforts by sellers to contract demand through depromotion is heresy in the marketing of goods in normal times. (During wartime and under crisis conditions of scarcity a quite different view can prevail, of course.)

MARKETING ISSUES: SERVICE FACILITIES

Product Line

To the layman, the distinction between a large and a small hospital is measured by the number of beds; a more meaningful distinction lies in the variety of services offered. The product line of a large, modern, and self-sufficient hospital includes the following: (basic services) post-operative recovery, emergency department, blood bank, physical therapy, pharmacy, histopathology, premature nursery, inhalation therapy, intensive care, electroencephalography, psychiatric emergency service, rehabilitation services; (clinical service) outpatient department, dental service, social work, occupational therapy, family planning, psychiatric outpatient department, rehabilitation services; and (special services) x-ray therapy, radio-isotope facility, radium therapy, intensive cardiac care, cobalt therapy, renal dialysis, self-care unit, open-heart surgery facility, extended care, and organ bank. These services both supplement and complement the customary hospital service products: surgery and bed care.

Among general hospitals, the principal form of competition, whether so expressed or not, seems to be in the extent of the service product line. The more extensive the services, the greater the likelihood the patient's "agent," his physician, will select the hospital.

In addition to the full-line hospital there are specialty hospitals in metropolitan markets. Some are limited to portions of the body (eye-ear-nose-and-throat); others focus on a particular disease (cancer); and others have a market orientation (infants). Other specialized hospitals include those associated with medical schools. As would be expected, many new health care products are developed and field or market tested, to use marketing terms, at these university-related institutions. Although most hospitals serve localized geographical markets, some have earned a national reputation for the quality of their services. Reflecting greater longevity and changing attitudes toward family structure, the nursing home is one of the fastest growing health care facilities. Whereas over 90 percent of hospitals are publicly owned or are operated as private, non-profit institutions, the majority of nursing homes are private enterprises operated for profit.

Pricing

Cost-plus pricing is the prevailing policy in the operation of health care facilities. Based on experience with cost-plus pricing in the private enterprise, goods sector, the marketing practitioner would immediately call attention to two issues. Are there incentives to control costs, lacking a competitive marketplace? Are there adequate controls to prevent over-treatment? In many areas, hospitals have locational monopolies; where two or more serve the same market, there is evidence of price leadership. With professional pressure to expand hospital services, cost-plus pricing and price leadership, and monopoly or oligopoly positions, the nearly perpendicular rise in hospital prices can be understood. As a result, the federal government and various states are tending to look at hospitals as public utilities requiring an increasing level of regulation.

Given the conditions of supply and the growth in demand, and pricing practices described here, the marketer would quickly identify an inevitable development; the advent of hospitals operated for profit. This has occurred. Some fifty companies are now operating chains of hospitals. Their appearance is a controversial issue in the health care field. It is charged that because of the profit motive they offer fewer services and are more selective in their admissions policies. Their future is not yet clear. However, from the standpoint of the consumer, they serve the useful purpose of acting as a yardstick against which nonprofit facilities can be measured.[5]

Promotion

As might be expected, health care facilities do not promote their services in the usual way. Publicity and public relations are acknowledged tools in view of the hospital's many diverse publics: patients, nurses and other employees, physicians, boards of directors or managers, political bodies if it is a public facility, and the community at large. Health care facilities do implicitly recognize the promotional value of amenities and the courtesy and thoughtfulness of employees in their relations with patients. Aside from publicity communicated through conventional media, the principal medium for promotion of health care facilities is word-of-mouth.

Channels

The channel of distribution consists of the health care facility, the doctor, and the patient. While compensation for health care services passes from the patient or his insurer to the hospital, he cannot "buy" hospital services in the usual meaning of the word but is dependent upon the physician for determining where he will go, what services will be performed, and for how long.

The newest institution in the health care field is the health maintenance organization (HMO). Hospitals, physicians, and other health care resources are incorporated in a single system which provides services to members for a premium paid in advance. Physicians are employees and are paid on a per capita basis rather than through a fee for service. As a result, emphasis is on prevention since the healthier the subscriber the lower the costs of the organization and the greater the reward for the physician. A major issue raised by opponents of the systems approach is their concern for too much cost-cutting. In short, are savings the result of decreased services and less care or from less costly arrangements for supplying adequate care?[6]

In addition to health care facilities for profit and health maintenance organizations, market opportunities encourage diversification into this area by business enterprises with the resources and skills necessary to provide health care efficiently and profitably at prices which are not confiscatory. Among others, firms in the following industries could enter the health care field: insurance, drug manufacturing, operators of hotel and motel chains, chemical firms, and computer manufacturers. Innovative retailers such as Sears, Roebuck are possibilities.[7]

HEALTH CARE FROM A MARKETING PERSPECTIVE

Marketing is capable of improving health care services in four ways: (1) enhancing or reasserting the position of the consumer; (2) providing means for maintaining good health; (3) contributing techniques for improving the efficiency of health care delivery; and (4) introducing market forces as a preferred alternative to government regulation.

Marketing asserts the supremacy of the consumer; in health care, supply is preeminent. Bigger and better facilities and greater competence in practice are stressed. The consumer is viewed less as the object of health care and more as a part of the process. Marketing would say to the health care profession: break down the economic and psychological barriers between demand and supply; reestablish the rapport that once existed between patient and physician. Marketing would state that demand for health care is universal and uniform; therefore supply should be universal and uniform. The marketing concept decries the lack of universal availability and applauds the uniformity of performance quality. For the great majority of practitioners there is no such thing as "Cadillac" treatment for some and "Vega" treatment for others.

Through the use of exhibits, various advertising media, publicity, seminars, educational and closed circuit television, and cassettes, the communication element in the marketing mix can contribute to the efforts of health care professionals towards shifting emphasis from cure to prevention. Total health care costs could thereby be reduced and professional skills allocated to more complex and critical needs. Much has already been done on this score but greater use can still be made of the techniques and professional skills of marketing communications.

Marketing techniques of research and quantitative analysis can provide factual guidance for allocating health care resources most appropriately. Geographical areas where supply may be too great or too small can be identified; attitudes of consumers can be ascertained; through sales analysis techniques, demand for various facilities can be measured and standards of performance established.

Finally, through the joint efforts of professionals in health care and marketing, the judicious introduction of market forces may be accomplished. New institutions or market-oriented rewards and a greater recognition of efficient use of resources can result without any diminution of quality or dilution of the professional nature of health care. It should be reiterated that this can be accomplished only through the *joint* efforts of professional people in both health care and marketing. While a shift of health care toward the marketplace may be distasteful to most in the field, the alternative is more regulation. The pervasive nature of health care and trends in its pricing no longer allow it to be immune from either the discipline of the marketplace or the discipline of regulation. The former should be tried first.

FOOTNOTES

1. W. Lee Hoskins, "Medical Care Policy: a Dose of Competition," *Business Review,* Federal Reserve Bank of Philadelphia (September 1971), p. 6.

2. "Changing the System of Health Care," *The Morgan Guaranty Survey* (December 1972), p. 7.

3. "Footing the Medical Care Bill," *Business Review,* Federal Reserve Bank of Philadelphia (September 1971), p. 15.

4. Arnold Eisen, "So You Want to Be a Doctor," *Pennsylvania Gazette* 71 no. 5 (March 1973), p. 35.

5. On the day this was written, the local evening paper announced plans for a health facility for profit. It will include a "Medi-Inn," an indoor recreation facility (tennis, squash, exercise room, and steam bath) for staff and "residents" [not "patients"], restaurant, and self-care apartments. A system of progressive stages of health care is envisioned. Obviously, marketing concepts are at work here.

6. "Changing the System of Health Care," op. cit., p. 9.

7. Edmund K. Faltermayer, "Better Care at Less Cost Without Miracles," *Fortune* 81 (January 1970), p. 127; Paul M. Ellwood, Jr. and Michael E. Herbert, "Health Care: Should Industry Buy It or Sell It?", *Harvard Business Review* 51 (July-August 1973), pp. 99-107.

THE MARKETING OF MEDICAL CARE SERVICES

Robert M. Crane, Spencer C. Johnson, Henry G. Lobl, and Corte J. Spencer

An imaginative integration of health care practice and marketing concepts.

Medical care is perhaps this nation's most important, if not most controversial, service industry. It accounts for seven percent of the gross national product (GNP) and it is the third largest industry in terms of the number of persons employed. Health care expenditures have grown over 500 percent during the last 20 years (from $12.9 billion in 1950 to $67.2 billion in 1970), with more than half due to inflation.[1]

The traditional medical care system has evolved with little deliberate planning, resulting in stresses between old methods and new technology. While sophisticated heart and kidney transplant procedures have been developed as a result of intensive medical research, over 40 million disadvantaged persons are denied basic medical treatment because of an ineffectual delivery system. Comprehensive (preventative, diagnostic, therapeutic, and rehabilitative) medical care was established as an individual right by national policy in the mid-1960's—yet there is no proposed delivery system that can honor that commitment.

Although we spend a greater percentage of our GNP on medical care than any other industrialized nation, by comparison we rank poorly by any standard measure of quality: 14th in infant mortality, 18th in male life expectancy, 11th in female life expectancy, and

The authors are graduates of the Graduate School of Business and Public Administration, Cornell University. Mr. Crane is Acting Chief, Technical Assistance Branch, Comprehensive Health Planning Service, Health Resources Administration, HEW. Mr. Johnson is Administrative Assistant to James F. Hastings, Representative from the 39th District, New York. Mr. Lobl is Assistant Executive Director, St. Mary's Hospital, Division of Catholic Medical Center of Brooklyn and Queens, Inc. Mr. Spencer is Assistant Administrator, Geneva General Hospital, Geneva, New York.

dropping in maternal mortality from first in the early 1950's to seventh in 1966.[2]

As a result of uneven growth and fragmentation, restricted markets affecting both supply and demand, and little or no ability on the part of the consumer to evaluate the quality and efficacy of the services he purchases, the medical care system is in stark contrast to the conventional marketing model.

MEDICAL CARE MARKET MODEL

Needs

A need is defined as an existing gap between a current state of being and a desired state.[3] In the case of health care the ultimate, or desired state of being, is freedom from illness or disease that would prevent an individual from performing his social role.

Needs may be of two types: that quantity of medical services an individual feels is necessary based on his own psychic perception of the seriousness of his illness and that quantity of medical services that the health professional believes is necessary based on his diagnosis of the illness.[4]

According to the proposed medical care marketing model, (see Figure 10.1) needs may arise from social requirements, perceived illness, or validation, (the general desire to be positive that one is free from unperceived illness).

Needs arising from social requirements include such things as insurance and employment physicals, routine premarital serologies, and public health immunization requirements. In such cases specific guidance is usually provided for the individual seeking such services.

An example of validation would be the annual physical or cancer check.

An individual may perceive symptoms of ill health and because of uncertainty seek a medical diagnosis and a prescribed course of treatment. Even if the consumer is certain of the causes of his ill health, many times he must seek access to the medical care system for the prescribed treatment by health professionals. In addition, minor health problems such as the common cold may be solved by the simple purchase of patent medicine from a drug store.

Finally, an ill individual, who may or may not have knowledge of the cause of his malady, can choose to defer the implementation of diagnosis and treatment because of emotional, social, cultural, educational, religious, and financial reasons. This deferral may be temporary or permanent, depending upon the risk of deferred treatment and the strength of the overriding factors.

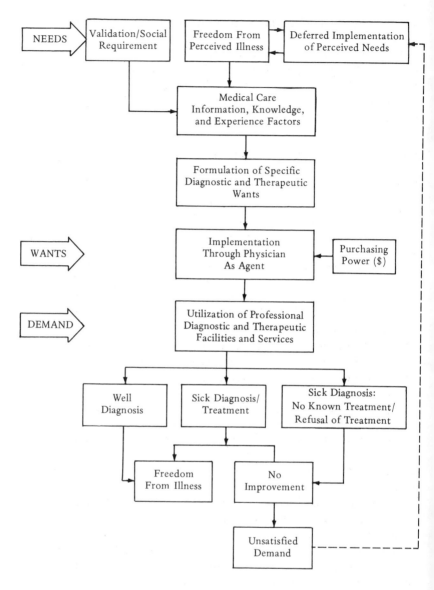

Figure 10.1   *MEDICAL CARE MARKET MODEL*

Wants

A want is a good or service that is desired to meet the particular needs of a buyer.[5] In the case of medical care, many options may be available depending upon consumer information, knowledge of the health system, and prior experience. Because the consumer has little knowledge of the health system and the science of medicine, a doctor will most likely be consulted.

Perhaps the two most important factors are the risk of deferred treatment, which is equal to the sum of the social, economic and physical costs, and the ability to pay, first for the physician's diagnosis and secondly for the recommended course of treatment. Seeking medical care is unique because of the aversion factor associated with the receipt of treatment. A consumer may have to go through pain and other physical/psychological trauma in order to be free of illness. In the minds of many, the treatment is worse than the disease and thus there is a tendency to defer implementation of a particular want.

The heart of the medical care delivery system is the physician. He is involved with the patient from the initial interview to the final discharge from the system. He is the key element in the organization and delivery of diagnostic and therapeutic services. When the consumer enters the medical care system, he surrenders his sovereignty to the doctor who acts as his agent by determining needs by diagnosis and implementing wants by the selection and purchase of available services on behalf of his client.

Based on his perceived needs of the patient, the doctor implements specific wants through the utilization of professional diagnostic and therapeutic facilities and services.

Payment for services is usually made by one or a combination of financing mechanisms: personal consumer expenditures and third-party payers. Payments by third parties may include Blue Cross/Blue Shield, Medicare, Medicaid, and private insurance plans. In fiscal year 1968-1969, for example, the consumer paid 40 percent of all personal health care expenditures, insurance companies 24 percent, and the government 36 percent.[6]

The ability and the means utilized to purchase health care are determining factors when choosing the type and mix of diagnostic and therapeutic services for any patient.

Diagnostic laboratory testing is a common example. Often a patient is admitted to the hospital for diagnostic testing which could be easily handled on an outpatient basis merely because his health insurance will pay for care only if he is hospitalized. Thus, because of inadequate benefits, most insurance plans are inflationary both to the level of facilities utilization and, ultimately, cost of medical care.

Demand

A market demand is the actual purchase of goods or services to satisfy specific wants.[7] Unlike conventional marketing procedure, the demand for medical care, diagnostic and therapeutic goods and services is implemented by the health professional rather than the consumer.

Demand for medical care services can result in a well diagnosis; that is, following complete diagnostic testing, an individual is judged to be free of any illness. A patient may be diagnosed as ill and treatment prescribed which could result in recovery or possibly no improvement. In the latter case the demand is unsatisfied and the consumer must pass through the diagnostic and therapeutic system again, or defer reentry until a later date. Finally, a patient may receive an illness diagnosis for which there is no known treatment or decide to refuse the treatment if it is too costly or of limited benefit (for example, terminal cancer patients). Again, as in the previous case, no improvement is possible, the demand is unsatisfied, and reentry is deferred.

MEDICAL CARE AND MARKETING CONCEPTS

An attempt to understand the application of major marketing concepts to the medical care services sector is very revealing. The market as we know it is a relationship between buyers and sellers resulting in an exchange of goods or services. Marketing activities include initial communication about services or products and then an exchange of these goods or services for money or a promise to pay.

The market relationship operates best in an atmosphere where communication and exchange take place freely and openly. Ideally the buyer should know what he is purchasing and should recognize the amount of positive value acruing to him through the purchase. The buyer of medical care services, however, does not really know what he is buying. Furthermore, his choice from the wide range of goods and services provided in this sector of our economy is restricted by both the necessity to act through an agent (usually a doctor), and the acuteness of his need.

Quality of medical care services is difficult to assess. Health professionals and students of medical care seldom can agree on what actually constitutes quality. Yet, obvious differences in quality do exist and are to some extent evident to the discerning consumer. Also, to some extent competition based on quality does exist between major medical centers.

Many persons feel that medicine is an exact science. They believe they are purchasing, when they seek a physician's services, an exact diagnosis and cure for a specified physical complaint. Actually, medicine can be considered both an art and a science. Considering it an art refers to the fact that good medicine is dependent, in part, on an individual's intuition. It is possible that two equally trained and equally experienced doctors will have entirely different opinions on the same case. There are many examples of what, to the layman, appears to be a diagnosis inferring exact knowledge but which is, in effect, a naming of a symptom. There are also many examples, particularly in the realm of drug therapy, where symptoms are treated but the cause of the disease remains unknown and/or untouched. In some cases, eventual realization of the true nature of these services leads to disillusionment and a reduction in the value the consumer will place upon them in the future.

At first glance the medical care service sector appears as a vast array of different services. There are 298 health occupation specialties in 134 occupations in 32 basic functional categories as listed in *The Health Manpower Sourcebook*.[8] There is, however, an important unifying feature. The majority of the services offered to the consumer by those serving in these occupations do so through an intermediary. This intermediary could be referred to as a primary care delivery agent. This agent is an individual or organization employing individuals who make initial contact with the consumer and shepherd him through the maze of available services.

Physician as Agent

In most cases the initial contact is made through a physician who is a private practitioner. Even when a hospital emergency room provides the initial contact, the consumer is usually referred to his own physician or supplied with one as quickly as possible. In poverty areas where the private practitioner is rare, the hospital, through its outpatient department, is taking over the function of primary care delivery agent. After the initial contact, the physician, acting as an agent for the consumer, chooses the proper mix of relevant goods and services. Consider the relationship between the consumer, the physician, and the medical laboratory. The physician decides whether or not laboratory tests are needed, which ones are needed, and which laboratory will do them. The consumer may well be aware that the laboratory work at the local hospital is well-controlled and of good quality. Yet, the physician may have a contract with a laboratory in a different state and the consumer would have no knowledge of the institution or the quality of work done there.

The consumer exercises some choice in the selection of a physician, very little in choosing a specialist (appointments by referral only), a service, or even a hospital.

Coordinating Mechanisms

The number and diversity of individual marketing units and the services they render create a need for coordinating mechanisms: control, cooperation, and competition.[9] In most sectors of a market economy, competition plays a primary role by offering the consumer a range of choice and by establishing price and quality of the goods or services. In the medical care sector, however, the key coordinating mechanism is control. As we have noted, the physician as the key element in the medical care system is able to direct the marketing activities of almost all other providers of medical services. Medical care can be viewed as a team effort and the physician as the team leader.

The origin of physician control can probably be traced back to the Flexner Report of 1911.[10] This report was an exposé on the sorry state of American medicine. Many medical schools were little more than diploma mills, educational standards were very low, state licensing standards were lax, and the public was being treated by poorly trained physicians. In effect, the free market situation existed with free competition, free entry, and a great deal of consumer choice. The Flexner Report was used by the medical profession as the opportunity to achieve control of its own educational institutions and of state licensing standards. Since then the medical profession has continually pushed for higher standards.

Professional control has had three major results. The first is that the consumer is much less likely to encounter a truly incompetent physician today than in the time the free market system existed. Secondly, American medicine can be represented as islands of excellence separated by geographic and economic gaps in the delivery of needed care.[11] This is caused mainly by the relatively small number of practitioners who continue to practice as individual marketing entities serving a population growing in size with increasing expectations. Thirdly, physicians' services are seldom utilized efficiently. Despite highly sophisticated training, he spends much of his time treating minor ailments and in some cases well people.

The second most important coordinating mechanism in the medical care sector is cooperation. Professionals work and cooperate with each other through their rigidly defined roles. For example, the general practitioner, on behalf of the patient, orders a bacterial culture from a laboratory, asks for a consultation from an internist, and writes a prescription for an antibiotic which is filled by a pharmacist. It is highly probable that in a situation of severe emergency, any one of the four individuals involved could have treated the illness if antibiotics were available. Yet, role requirements, reinforced by licensing laws, insure cooperation.

Competition, a coordinating mechanism of prime importance in other sectors of the economy, is restricted in the medical service field. Some competition exists between certain professional groups; for example, medical doctors vs. chiropractors or osteopaths and optometrists vs. ophthalmologists. Competition also exists between hospitals. It is a decided advantage for a hospital, even a necessity, to maintain a high daily patient census. The marginal costs of maintaining a full bed compared with an empty bed are minimal; however, the full bed contributes revenue to operating expenses. In an area with more than one hospital and an excess of beds, it is necessary to create an attractive atmosphere for the private practitioner. In this way the practitioner is influenced to admit his patients to one hospital rather than another. It is for this reason, and for reasons of increasing prestige, that expensive and often under-utilized equipment is introduced into a specific institution. The cost is, of course, ultimately passed on to the consumer.

The Marketing Mix

Careful examination of the medical care marketplace reveals that individuals, particularly providers of care, react as though they were in a perfectly competitive environment. While no marketplace exhibits the conditions for such an environment in a strict sense (no barriers to entry, freely fluctuating prices, perfect knowledge on the part of buyers and sellers, unrestricted competition), the medical care marketplace seems to be as far away from such conditions as any field. This becomes particularly evident when we look briefly at the formulation and implementation of marketing policy. Traditionally called the marketing mix, this includes four variables: product, promotion, price, and place.[12] These four variables, of course, depend to a large extent on the goals which each provider of medical service determines. In the case of the physician, it may be to maximize his financial/psychological income; a hospital's goal may be to operate at 90 percent occupancy or above, or perhaps merely not to operate at a loss.

Individual provider goals are formed and influenced by early training, personality, socialization in medical or professional school, income expectations and needs for self-gratification. Institutional provider goals are influenced by community/patient needs (the development of ethnic hospitals), governmental policy (education and research support), reimbursement policies of financial intermediaries, and the needs of the medical profession.

A provider's product line will in large measure be dependent upon the choice of goals. A hospital, for example, may discourage outpatient testing or ambulatory care to achieve its occupancy goal. A general practitioner may practice surgery as well as medicine to increase his income. Alternatively, a hospital concerned that all residents in its surrounding area may not receive services may decentralize its outpatient services into storefront clinics to increase accessibility. Further breadth may be added with preventive care and multiphasic screening including a day-care center to care for children while parents receive treatment. A hospital may consider depth to be important to its research or teaching program and offer an impressive line of back-up services for acute care. The desire to distinguish among buyers may lead to market segmentation as exemplified by a private or semi-private hospital room or the specialty hospital.

Promotional activities are drastically curtailed by the ethical framework of the medical profession. The advertisement of medical services is approved by the medical profession if and only if such advertising is in the interest of the profession as a whole. Thus, while "Fight cancer with a checkup and a check" is considered ethical, an individual physician is forbidden to advertise that he is highly trained or well-equipped to provide that "checkup." This is one of the factors which leads to the restricted market and its resultant lack of consumer knowledge. Strong pressure is exerted to enforce this ethic by organized medicine. This is accomplished through restricting local medical society membership which in some cases is a prerequisite for hospital privileges. (While recently the courts ruled that this was not permissible, the practice may still continue.) Informal controls run the range from exclusion in social relations to the inability to establish referral relationships and coverage for vacations and weekends.

In the past, price differentiation has played a large part in medical service pricing decisions. Scaling fees to the income of patients has been a common practice. Although medical care was thought to be very important the state was often unwilling to provide it for the indigent, and doctors usually did not refuse a patient because he was unable to pay. Differential pricing of medical services was the inevitable result. Price competition (price cutting) is forbidden and strictly controlled internally by the profession, usually through the local medical societies. Many areas of public health use a penetration pricing policy to solicit broad use of services, for example, innoculations at low cost. Insurance companies have been paying hospitals on a cost-plus basis, but as prices continue to rise, hospitals are finding external forces more and more shaping their pricing policies. As government gets deeper in the financing of these services, pricing discretion is likely to decrease.

Finally, decisions of place—distribution channels and location—are closely connected to marketing targets or goals. The characteristics of the consumer to be served—where he lives, how mobile he is, his personal income—as well as characteristics of place itself—transportation networks—will play a major role in this decision.

FOOTNOTES

1. Barbara Coleman, "Rising Medical Costs Spur Ideas for a National Health Insurance," *Times Herald* (Olean, New York), 21 September 1970; Barbara Coleman, "Federal Financial Aid Would Eliminate Rising Medical Costs," *Times Herald* (Olean, New York), 11 March 1971.

2. Irving J. Lewis, "Government Investment in Health Care," *Scientific American* 224 no. 4 (April 1971), p. 19.

3. Lee E. Preston, *Markets and Marketing—An Orientation* (Glenview, Illinois: Scott, Foresman and Company, 1970), p. 81.

4. James R. Jeffers, et al., "On the Demand Versus Need for Medical Services and the Concept of 'Shortage'," *American Journal of Public Health* 61 no. 1 (January 1971), pp. 46-47.

5. Preston, op. cit., p. 82.

6. Boisfeuillet Jones, ed., *The Health of Americans* (Englewood Cliffs, N.J.: Prentice-Hall, Inc., 1970), p. 170.

7. Preston, op. cit., pp. 72-73.

8. *Health Manpower Source Book,* sec. 21, "Allied Health Manpower, 1950-1980," (Washington, D.C.: U.S. Government Printing Office, Public Health Service Publication, no. 263, sec. 21, 1970).

9. Preston, op. cit., p. 55.

10. The Carnegie Foundation for the Advancement of Teaching, *Medical Education in the United States and Canada,* Bulletin No. 4 (The Foundation, 1910).

11. Miles C. Hardie, "Islands of Excellence," *Hospital Administration* 14 no. 3 (Summer 1969), pp. 42, 51.

12. Preston, op. cit., p. 155.

11

MARKETING BUSINESS SERVICES

In this final chapter, attention is directed to those services included under SIC classification 73 in Appendix A; the reader is advised to review this classification before proceeding. They may be defined as a group of specialized, external, and independent services not elsewhere classified which are intended to facilitate the production and marketing of goods and services by profit-making enterprises, private institutions, and public bodies when called upon to do so.

In a sense, this is a residual group of services. Communications, transportation, financial, and legal services also facilitate the production and marketing functions. The use of the term "business" is an acknowledgment of custom rather than reality since demand for business services can originate from any source other than the ultimate consumer. The service characteristic resides in their specialized and external nature and in the fact that they are "on call."

Unless required by law to make use of an external service (public stock offerings or the auditing of financial accounts of publicly-owned corporations), whether to utilize a business service firm is essentially a make or buy decision. A firm or agency may either depend on its in-house resources or hire them or call on the outside specialist. Some prefer to be self-sufficient, others desire flexibility. The decision is not unlike that of manufacturers who must decide whether to make their own parts or assemble those made by others or whether to acquire their own raw material resources or buy them from others. In any case, marketing is involved only when services or goods are purchased rather than performed or produced internally.

Decisions to buy business services occur under two situations. First, a decision can be made to *replace* an activity currently being performed internally or to purchase a new service rather than incorporate it within the organization. For example, a university terminates its own food-dispensing activities and contracts with a food service firm; a retail chain purchases the services of a protection agency rather than hire its own guards. Second, a firm, institution, or government agency may wish to *supplement* its present activities. For example, a firm may have its own organizational planning department but it may also seek the guidance of a management consulting firm to broaden its decision-making inputs on organization issues.

As a generalization, business service firms perform staff activities. At the extreme, it is conceivable that a firm could delegate all staff responsibilities to independent, external service firms and confine its own efforts to line responsibilities alone. As a second generalization, it can be noted that business services can redress competitive imbalance. Because of their in-being nature, the smaller, weaker, or more troubled competitor can call upon professional skills and technical talents approaching, equal to, or greater than the in-house capacities of the large, strong, and prosperous competitor.

Business service is a growth industry of recent origin. In the nineteenth century there were very few make or buy decisions of this sort. Either the conditions of production and marketing were so simple that there was no need for specialized business service or their need was not evident to the prevailing entrepreneurial manager.

What has occurred to bring business services to the fore? First, both the increasing complexity of production, marketing, and management and the increasing body of knowledge designed to keep pace with complexity have made it difficult for one man, one group of men, or one firm to be all-knowing. Hence, the demand for specialized know-how on call. Technological and cost benefits of specialization are a second reason. For example, a service firm specializing in creating sales contests should do a better job than a firm's marketing management which is inexperienced in this area of sales promotion. And economies of scale permit a marketing research firm to conduct a field survey more economically than a manufacturer. A time factor is a third reason. Business managers and, for that matter, the managers of institutions and government agencies, no longer operate at a pedestrian pace. Changes in markets, technology, and regulations occur more frequently and the firm must react with equal frequency. Sometimes, it cannot afford the luxury of a long lead time to tool up. The firm, therefore, calls for the help of a business service in being. Fourth, the contemporary business firm must assume new responsibilities previously considered quite peripheral to its economic mission—responsibilities for which there are no historical guidelines or internal competence. One new responsibility is in the area of human relations, particularly the firm's responsibilities to its employees. Another is what is currently termed the social responsibility of business. The more a firm's responsibilities broaden beyond its central functions and goals, the greater the need for specialized counsel in these previously unrecognized needs for managerial competence.

In addition, much of the growth in business services can be ascribed to the business service industry itself. Nowhere is the observation that one firm's problem is another firm's opportunity more appropriate. Many business services have resulted from a combination of entrepreneurship, risk-taking, and ability to see an unmet need. Consider the following illustrations. Big business and big government have difficulty finding qualified people to fill top management positions. Result: the executive recruiting firm.[1] Many firms lack the financial means to buy a variety of capital goods. Result: the specialist organization which leases everything from computers and machine tools to cash registers and shipping pallets.[2] Manufacturers, real estate developers, banks, consultants, and public agencies are interested in the New Town development. Result: a firm developing a New Town conducts five-day seminars on the subject; the fee is $750.[3] A number of firms are establishing plants on the Mexican side of the border. Result: industrial service companies lease or build plants, hire personnel, and undertake all the operational and administrative tasks; the client manufacturer furnishes capital equipment, technical staff, and raw materials.[4] There has been a substantial growth in computer accessory equipment produced primarily by small manufacturers who have difficulty maintaining the equipment they sell. Result: a third-party computer maintenance service industry.[5] European firms have difficulty exporting their technology to the United States. Result: an American consultant who analyzes American markets, makes licensing arrangements with American firms, and assists in establishing American subsidiaries.[6] Industry, large and small, is concerned about productivity. Result: a publisher sponsors a nationwide closed-circuit television conference linking meetings in twenty cities; panelists include top specialists from industry, labor, and government.

COMPONENTS OF DEMAND FOR BUSINESS SERVICES

All producers are prospects for business services. While the business community is the core market, both the public and nonprofit sectors are recognizing the contribution of business services. This increasing interest is the result of acknowledgment that good management principles and practices are as important in public administration and in nonprofit institutions as they are in business. For example, a substantial percentage of income of leading consulting firms comes from governments. Of particular interest is a growing recognition of the need for marketing tools and concepts in nonmarket areas. Government agencies and enterprises, political parties, and charitable and religious organizations are expanding their use of advertising and marketing research services, for example.

The location of demand within the organization is found at three levels. First, in the case of routine or low-value, action-type services, buying decisions are made by functional specialists—the purchase of photofinishing, blueprinting, and photocopying services, for example. Decisions to buy the services of commercial testing laboratories, marketing research firms, and building maintenance organizations, for example, are made at the middle management level. Finally, decisions to buy service products which may have organization-wide application, where the need for the service is difficult to define, and where experience is of little value in the buying decision, are made at the top management level: a decision to change advertising agencies or to buy the services of a consulting group, for example.

Demand for business services is often characterized as being highly sensitive to cyclical trends. This generalization is not necessarily true. In the first place, business services whose demand originates from many industries and from the public as well as the private sector are less likely to experience extreme fluctuations in contrast with business services whose demand is confined to a single industry. In the second place, business services which have *replaced* internal operations are less susceptible to demand erosion during depressed economic conditions because of their higher variable cost component. That is, it is easier to pattern the purchase of facilitating services to economic conditions than it is to modify internal human and capital resources devoted to performing the service. On the other hand, it is true that business services which *supplement* internal operations, consulting for example, are among the easiest to reduce or eliminate during recessions. (Because it is easy does not necessarily make it a wise decision.) Demand for some services may be countercyclical: protection and temporary help agencies, for example.

Buying Motives

Reasons for buying which are associated with conventional industrial goods marketing are equally applicable to services. Some are economic, others are behavioral in their origin. Motives for buying from one service firm rather than another, the patronage motives, are also present. However, the significance of buying motives varies according to the purpose of the purchase: to substitute an outside service for internal performance or to supplement internal operations. Consider the following examples of economic motives.

1. A variety of services are purchased rather than performed internally in order to reduce costs. This is particularly true of the many auxiliary or indirect activities the modern manufacturer must carry on. The cost reduction motive also accounts for the purchase of infrequent services in place of maintaining a standby internal arrangement.[7] In addition, unexpected crises such as antitrust action or a serious strike may call for supplemental services.
2. A desire to increase the firm's productivity and overall market

performance is a primary economic buying motive for purchasing the supplemental services of consultants, marketing research organizations, or industrial behavioral scientists.

3. With the advent of social responsibility and ecological impact as variables in the decision-making process, inexperience and confusion are potent motives for supplementing the managerial competence of the firm with external, specialized advice. Similarly, a major reason for the increasing demand for business economists' services is the desire for a better reading of the increasingly complex and rapidly changing future environment of the firm.

While nonrational or behavioral buying motives are supposedly less in evidence in producer buying decisions in contrast with those of ultimate consumers, current marketing thought assigns a greater role to them. They may be even more important in the purchase of business services. Consider the following examples.

1. The manager with a preference for order and directness of effort and an impatience in reacting to new demands is likely to prefer the alternative or replacement type of service to diversifying his own employee group and building up a new staff organization.

2. Some supplemental services are purchased in order to improve the image of the buyer: it is the thing to do. Patronage motives are also at work here: well known advertising agencies, marketing research organizations, research and development laboratories and business consultants enhance the image of their clients.

3. It is argued that the services of consultants are often obtained in order to reinforce or confirm the views and plans of client management, and that this is a rather shortsighted utilization of the consultant's competence. However, it is argued here that this type of confidence-bolstering is quite understandable, especially if the stakes are high. Of course, if the consultant's recommendations are not reinforcing it would be shortsighted to dismiss them.

4. Supplemental advice is often purchased because of conditions of extreme uncertainty in proposed courses of action, and risk reduction may be a major buying motive. While economic considerations are important, a significant behavioral component is also present; not only the economic fortunes of the firm but the future status of the decision maker is at stake.

COMPONENTS OF BUSINESS SERVICES SUPPLY

A major characteristic of business services supply is ease of entry. Service industries are not oligopolistic, for the most part. While there are a few "Big Fives" and "Big Eights" in business services there are also successful regional competitors which capture a significant portion of the market. Also, patents do not protect the established service firm from new competition. And their human-intensive character lowers capital requirements for entry. Some measure of the openness of business services supply can be deduced from the fact that the Census shows that in 1967, 59.9 percent of all business service establishments had no payroll. Ease of entry has produced important results. First, reaction time to service needs of the business community is shorter; in fact, service entrepreneurs see needs as opportunities before their potential customers or clients. Second, because almost anyone can hold himself forth as a service expert, freedom of entry results in a wide disparity in quality of performance. (This is less true where examinations must be passed—public accounting, for example.) Ease of entry also means a relatively high attrition rate although statistical evidence is not available on this score.

Trends in Business Services

The Census shows that receipts for business services in total were up 49 percent, 1967 over 1963. This was significantly greater than the growth in receipts of all other services as well as the increase in retail sales and in value added by manufacturing.

Table 11.1 discloses a quite mixed pattern of growth in the *number* of service establishments with payrolls; eight of the service industries showed a decline. In every industry, *receipts* increased. The "Statistical and Computer Services" industry was one of the larger components in 1967 but was not even included in the Census data for 1963—some evidence of the sensitivity of business services to the needs of its market. The reader is urged to review this table with the objective of explaining variations in the direction and rate of change in number and receipts of the various services categories.[8]

Classification of Business Services

The total supply of business services is extremely heterogeneous. As a result, the only meaningful means of developing a comprehensive supply model is a series of continuums along which each service type can be plotted. The more meaningful differentiating features appear to be as follows.

1. Nature of seller—ranging from the purely professional to the purely commercial. Example: consultants and accountants are professional sellers; building maintenance and duplicating service firms are commercial sellers.

Table 11.1
SIZE AND CHANGE IN SELECTED BUSINESS SERVICES: 1963-1967

SIC Code	Kind of Business Service	Number[1]			Receipts (thousands)		
		1963	1967	Percent Change	1963	1967	Percent Change
7311	Advertising Agencies	4,820	5,747	19.2	5,786,839	7,587,231	13.1
7312	Outdoor Advertising Services	1,233	1,144	7.2-	241,768	278,252	11.5
7313	Radio & Television Representatives	1,004	290	32.3-	182,027	64,607	5.8
7313	Publishers' Representatives		389			128,010	
7319	Miscellaneous Advertising	649	615	5.2-	88,766	102,825	15.8
7341	Window Cleaning	1,663	1,491	10.3-	75,873	90,880	19.8
7342	Disinfecting & Deodorizing Services	304	236	22.4-	16,014	18,553	15.9
7342	Pest Control & Exterminating	3,255	3,495	7.4	219,214	296,580	35.3
7349	Miscellaneous Services to Buildings	6,949	9,675	39.2	499,985	883,990	76.8
7392	Business, Management Consulting Services	7,793	9,037	17.0	1,114,772	1,738,187	55.9
7392	Statistical & Computer Services[2]		1,825			793,983	—
7392	Public Relations	1,677	1,598	4.7-	141,210	164,088	16.2
7392	Interior Decorators	1,123	1,792	59.6	91,479	155,536	70.0
732	Adjustment & Collection Agencies	5,609	3,517	4.2	437,494	399,773	54.6
732	Mercantile Reporting Agencies		483			125,708	
732	Consumer Credit Reporting Agencies		1,847			151,060	
733	Duplicating, Mailing, Steno. Services	1,864	5,428	191.2	110,556	771,636	598.0
736	Private Employment Agencies	3,490	4,471	28.1	138,191	258,364	87.0
7391	Commercial Research Development Labs	1,154	1,437	24.5	895,830	1,067,550	19.2
7397	Commercial Testing Labs	1,415	1,253	11.4-	156,615	208,501	33.1
7393	Armored Car Services	309	344	11.3	67,244	90,600	34.7
7393	Detective, Protective Services	2,169	2,547	17.4	281,158	431,778	53.6

SIC							
7394	Leasing, Rental Heavy Construction Equipment		2,999			462,041	66.8
7394	Leasing, Rental Other Equipment	5,660	3,917	22.2	791,094	857,746	73.8
7395	Photofinishing Labs	1,533	1,715	11.9	394,631	685,767	6.4
7396	Trading Stamp Services	923	315	65.9-	717,709	763,325	
7398	Temporary Office Help Supply Services	816	1,227	50.4	159,074	331,419	108.3
7398	Temporary Help Supply Service Except Office	443	802	81.0	100,491	331,374	229.8
7399	Telephone Answering Service	1,979	2,184	10.4	84,609	121,987	44.2
7399	Water Softening Services	1,251	2,062	64.8	90,764	226,458	149.5
7399	Packaging, Labeling Services	521	758	45.5	120,447	175,008	45.3
7399	Other Business Services	7,322	8,241	12.6	910,274	1,386,593	52.3
	All Selected Services	504,336	521,410	3.4	41,023,378	55,527,000	35.4
	Retailing	1,628,139	1,668,856	2.5	237,998,133	302,591,447	27.1
	Manufacturing	306,617	305,680	.3-	192,082.9³	261,983.8³	36.4

[1]Services establishments with payroll.
[2]Not included in 1963.
[3]Value added.

Source: U.S. Census of Business and Manufacturing.

2. Character of performance—some are purely advisory whereas others are purely action. Example: the result of marketing research services is typically a series of recommendations; the result of temporary help services is an accomplished act.

3. Significance of service product to buyer—ranging from major to minor. Example: the services of a consultant or a research and development laboratory can have a major impact on the future of the client; photocopying and window-cleaning services are of minor importance.

4. Immediacy of benefits—some service benefits evolve over the long term whereas others are felt over the short term only. Example: benefits derived from architectural services are long-term; those of a collection agency are short-term.

5. Visibility of results—some results are hidden, others are quite apparent. Example: the services of management consultants are not visible to the senses; the services of employment and advertising agencies are visible.

6. Labor input—ranging from pure knowledge to pure skill content. Example: research and development and testing laboratories stress knowledge input; photofinishing laboratories and outdoor advertising services stress skills.

7. Buyer-seller relationship—may be continuing or intermittent. Example: armored car and protection services and the services of advertising agencies illustrate continuing buyer-seller relationships; testing and executive search services are typically called upon only as needed.

Each business service category can be plotted at some point on each continuum; within each category it is likely that competing service firms will fall at different points in recognition of the great variety of policies and practices which characterize services in general.

An interesting and useful classification is illustrated in Figure 11.1.[9] The diversified multiple service firm offers many services to a wide variety of clients. The institutional specialist offers a variety of services to a narrow market: hospitals, universities, or banks, for example. A certified public accounting partnership which limits its services to auditing and tax work is an example of a functional specialist. Some public accounting firms concentrate their work in one industry only: hotels and motels, for example. Such a firm is classed as an institutional and functional specialist. The reader would find it a productive exercise to consider the advantages and disadvantages of each cell from the standpoint of both the seller and buyer.

<table>
<tr><td rowspan="2"></td><td colspan="2" align="center">Number of Services</td></tr>
<tr><td align="center">Many</td><td align="center">Few</td></tr>
</table>

		Number of Services	
		Many	Few
Number of Clients or Customers	Many	Diversified Multiple	Functional Specialist
	Few	Institutional Specialist	Institutional and Functional Specialist

Figure 11.1 *MATRIX CLASSIFICATION OF BUSINESS SERVICES*

Government Services to Business

Both local, state, and national governments provide a variety of services to business. At the local and state level they are often offered as inducements to locate in competition with other political bodies. The services of the federal government to assist small business and to facilitate export expansion are particularly noteworthy.

Many government services are "free." Yet research by the author shows that the Department of Commerce sold technical and professional services in 1971 amounting to over 32 million dollars. Receipts included fees for patent applications, charges for work of the National Bureau of Standards, and sales of a variety of statistical and technical services.

The Small Business Administration provides technical assistance and individual counseling on problems of business management such as marketing, accounting, product analysis, production methods, and procurement; it conducts and co-sponsors business management training programs; and provides a variety of support activities including publications and films.[10]

MARKETING ISSUES IN BUSINESS SERVICES

The balance of this chapter is confined to the marketing of professional services, primarily management consulting services. The variety of marketing practices is so great and the degree to which they vary from the conventional view of marketing is so unequal that inclusive treatment would be too complex. Also, this limitation provides an opportunity for a background analysis supporting the more detailed reading that follows.

The Professional Service Product

For the most part, every professional service-client relationship results in a unique product. Although some consultants stress a uniform, "packaged" approach, standardized products are foreign to the meaning of professional services.

On a conceptual plane, Wittreich believes the reduction or minimization of uncertainty to be the basic product of the professional service organization. This means that the organization is capable of rendering the service (which is quite different from holding forth the capacity to render a service). This concept also assumes the organization's capacity to *understand* a client's problem as contrasted with problem-solving ability.[11]

On a more pragmatic plane, McManus identifies the following products of professional service organizations: problem-solving; system diagnosis and analysis; system design; conducting programs, conferences, and seminars; performing specific tasks in the client's environment; and providing information.[12]

It should be remembered that professional services are *supplemental* in nature. They can be and are performed within the firm. It is only when a decision is made to go outside that a service product comes into existence.

Systems marketing is growing in the field of professional services. Consulting firms, architects, accountants, and financial institutions are broadening their product lines with the inevitable result of controversy and competition. The task of buying professional services also becomes more difficult. Is it more productive to buy segments of professional service or more inclusive service packages? (This is a lively issue in advertising.) Will the marketer of a broad line of professional services have the capacity to understand the firm's problem or will the specialist identify the wrong problem? Can the systems marketer maintain his objectivity? (In the case of consulting services offered by commercial banks, at the moment the Federal Reserve Board has said no.)[13]

The sources of ideas for new professional service products are quite conventional. What do our clients need which we cannot provide? What resources do we now have which have not been offered in the market-place? What are our competitors doing?[14]

Pricing Professional Services

In general, pricing is not a significant factor in the professional business service firm's marketing strategy. In addition, the method used in setting the price is generally uniform within the various professional services industries.

Some of the characteristics of professional services which influence pricing include the following:

1. There is a reluctance to overtly compete on the basis of price because of a widely held belief that it is contrary to the concept of a profession.

2. The price is typically set in advance of performance whether for a specified project or on a retainer basis. As a result, the buyer is concerned about what he pays and what he receives whereas the seller is concerned about unforeseen costs for which he will not receive compensation.

3. Varying levels of professional competence are involved; presumably, two buyers of the same model of machine tool or television set receive equivalent products; no such standardization can be assured in the marketing of professional business services.

4. The worth or value of many professional services emerges long after their performance; cost-benefit analyses are therefore difficult.

5. The relative significance of the service to the buyer may be substantial or modest. For example, a consultant may spend a day with one client regarding a merger proposal involving many millions of dollars and a day with another client regarding modification of an assembly line. Should the price charged each client for the day's work be the same?

In general, price levels are a function of elapsed time and professional competence. In Figure 11.2, the highest price would fall in the upper left cell and lowest in the lower right cell.

Pricing Formulas

Different professional services in the past have met the pricing complexity with a variety of formulas. The auditing services of accounting firms are priced on a cost-plus basis. Advertising agencies utilize fixed prices: fifteen percent of billings. Consulting firms tend to price according to the value of the problem they are called upon to solve. Architec-

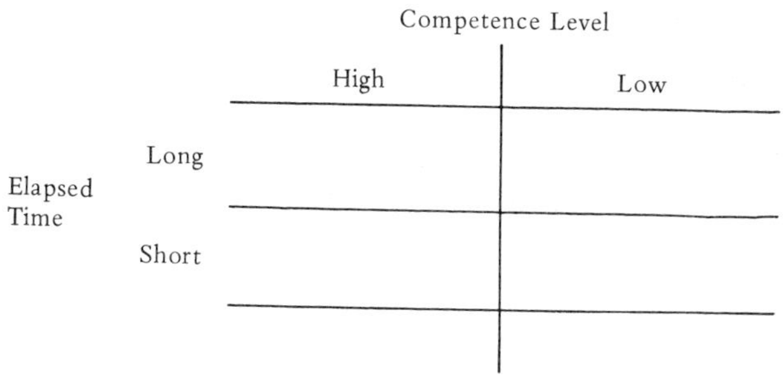

Figure 11.2 *VARIABLES IN PRICING PROFESSIONAL BUSINESS SERVICES*

tural services are priced on the basis of a percentage of the actual or estimated project construction cost and, in consideration of the size and complexity of the project. There are exceptions, of course, and the pricing of professional business services is in a state of flux. For example, the pricing of advertising agency services is shifting from a flat commission to a fee basis related more directly to cost inputs and value to client. Many architects are dissatisfied with the risks inherent in their pricing method. Essentially, newer approaches are attempting to relate price more directly to the variables in Figure 11.2.

Finally, the price of professional services is not influenced by results of services performed. Not only is it considered unethical, but the basically advisory nature of the service means that the client implements and therefore determines the results.

Price Elasticity

There are interesting variations in the price elasticity of demand for professional services. Demand is generally price-inelastic on the downward side. Price reductions would not expand demand, and, in fact, might reduce it because of the buyer's suspicions regarding the quality of performance. On the other hand, demand could be elastic on the upward side because of the supplemental nature of most professional services. If prices rise, the buyer is tempted to "make" rather than "buy," unless services are mandated by custom or law (advertising and auditing, for example).

Communications in Professional Business Services

The role of promotion in the marketing of professional business services falls somewhere between the intensely self-regulated professions of law and medicine and the purely commercial services. For example, the American Institute of Certified Public Accountants proscribes advertising and personal selling absolutely. Within the management consulting profession, attitude and practice vary from prohibition of overt promotion to its acceptance if it does not reflect unfavorably on the profession. As would be expected, advertising agencies find no conflict between true promotional advertising and their professional standards. Yet, all professional business services carry on promotional communications. The distinction lies in the degree to which conventional promotional techniques are used in contrast with the more subtle but professionally acceptable methods.

Among conventional techniques are personal selling; advertising in business and technical journals and trade papers; direct mail; and public relations. Wittreich has identified the major themes utilized in conventional promotion as follows: persuasion by method, that is, by extolling the character of the firm's service; persuasion by personnel, that is, stressing the reputation of key personnel; and persuasion by success story, that is, stressing benefits already gained by the service firm's clients.[15]

The more subtle and professionally acceptable promotional practices include meeting the right people at the right time at the right place—for example, an informal meeting of the principal of a professional service firm and a member of a potential client's top management on the golf course or at a private club. Participation at professional meetings, writing professional articles, and the publication of professional house organs for appropriate distribution are acceptable. In other words, stress is on exposure rather than overt promotion.

Because of the inherent need to purchase professional business services on faith, diffusion of a firm's reputation in the market through "word-of-mouth" advertising is undoubtedly the most effective form of promotional communication even though it is beyond the control of the seller. Of course, whether it is, in fact, promotional, depends upon the sellers' performance record.

Finally, the *manner* in which the buyer-seller relationship is carried on has an important effect on the communications element in the marketing of professional business services. It must be remembered that top management is often involved, that the performance of the service by the outside professional is expected to be superior to that which could be accomplished by the firm's own personnel, and that a substantial portion of the service must be performed, literally and figuratively, within the client firm. As a result, all contacts between client and seller are a form of promotional communication. To the extent that they demonstrate proficiency, are conducted in a professional manner, and reflect an understanding of the sensitive nature of the relationship, they promote continuing business and new business. Deficiencies in these areas communicate a negative reaction.

Channel and Location Considerations in Professional Business Services

A short, direct marketing channel is mandatory. As noted, each service product is unique and must be developed and purchased through direct contact; there is no role for an agent intermediary.

With regard to location, much of the professional service product is performed at the location of the buyer. For the advertising account executive, public accountant, architect, or management consultant, the central effort in terms of creativity and problem definition and solution must be conducted on the premises of the buyer; only details are worked out at the seller's place of business. An interesting departure from conventional marketing practice is observed here. In the marketing of goods, the flow of promotional effort is from seller to buyer; in the case of professional business services, there is a reluctance to follow this pattern and a preference for the buyer to come to the seller on the basis of reputation and referral, that is, word-of-mouth or diffusion. The traditional view of marketing channel and location is to emphasize convenience for the buyer in reaching the seller; in the case of professional business services the problem is resolved by eliminating the need for the buyer to go anywhere once the initial contact is made.

PROFESSIONAL BUSINESS SERVICES FROM A MARKETING PERSPECTIVE

New Perspectives from Marketing

Like so many other services, professional business services are shifting from a pioneering era to a more mature stage of development. This transition can be facilitated through wider acceptance of marketing concepts and practices. First, goals must be established and plans made to achieve them. Automatic but unorganized growth which is characteristic of all pioneering industries can no longer be depended upon. Yet, no meaningful goals or plans are prepared without thorough consideration of the market and the means of cultivating it. Second, increasingly, efforts must shift from the creation of primary to the creation of selective demand. Since it is no longer necessary to sell the idea of professional services, the professional business service firm must look to its own interests by focusing demand on *its* services (not on services in an abstract sense). In other words, the reality of competition must be faced. Third, it follows that it is no longer sufficient to, figuratively, wait for the client to come to the seller; the seller must seek out the buyer by accepted means. In this regard, the history of bank marketing offers an appropriate parallel. Finally, the fact that marketing is more than selling must be recognized. Problem-oriented consultants and advertising agencies are aware of this distinction, of course.

Marketing's Impact on Professional Business Services

Marketing has already made a substantial impact in a number of areas. First, sellers seek to determine why industry, institutions, and government buy their services—a recognition of the marketing concept. Second, through the application of marketing research, more complete coverage of the market is being achieved. Third, acceptance of the place for product development in services has advanced the concept of systems of services. Fourth, accepting the reality of marketplace competition and the need for marketing has resulted in the more widespread use of capital goods, particularly the computer, to improve productivity.

Problem Areas

Viewing professional business services from a marketing perspective suggests several problem areas requiring attention. (While it is much easier to isolate problems than to propose solutions, it would be presumptuous at this time and place to so propose.) First, there is the difficulty in evaluating performance in many professional services. What is good or poor performance? Against what standard is performance measured? Second, there is the specter of regulation, not self-regulation but government regulation; some of the difficulties to which reference has been made make professional business services susceptible to regulation to "protect the user." Such regulation would be most unwise. Professional associations have a key responsibility to take steps to eliminate need for regulation and to develop a justification for continuation of market control. Third, internal functional and managerial competence is growing; the entrepreneur is giving way to the professional manager. As a result, the marginal advantage of the external professional is declining. Fourth, much has been made of the need to expand marketing in the professional services field. However, it must not be adopted without qualification. Rather, it must be adapted to a professional environment; marketing concepts and practices should be modified to maintain consistency with professional standards.

FOOTNOTES

1. "Executive Recruiting: a Growth Business," *Business Week,* 27 January 1973, pp. 58-59.

2. "He Put Leasing on a Sound Footing," *Business Week,* 17 June 1972, p. 67.

3. "The Race Is On for New Towns," *Business Week,* 13 March 1971, p. 130.

4. "A Business Boomlet on Mexico's Border," *Business Week,* 22 January 1972, p. 36.

5. "Service Contracts for Computers," *Business Week,* 19 February 1972, pp. 40-41.

6. "Multinational: The U.S. Market for Europe's Technology," *Business Week,* 22 July 1972, p. 35.

7. For an interesting discussion of buying motives see Harry I. Greenfield, *Manpower and the Growth of Consumer Services* (New York: Columbia University Press, 1966), pp. 37-46.

8. A number of important business services are classified elsewhere by the Bureau of the Census: accounting, engineering, legal, and of course, communications, transportation, finance, etc. Also excluded are those services associated with the sale of goods: installation, maintenance, training of operatives, etc.

9. Mr. Lawrence W. O'Brien developed the matrix while a student in the author's course in service marketing.

10. *Review of Small Business Administrations's Programs and Policies—1971* (Washington, D.C.: U.S. Government Printing Office, 1971), pp. 57-61.

11. Warren J. Wittreich, "How to Buy/Sell Professional Services," *Harvard Business Review* (March-April 1966), pp. 128-129.

12. From research by Michael L. McManus, a doctoral candidate at Cornell University.

13. "Consulting Is Not a Banker's Business," *Business Week,* 24 June 1972, p. 122. (For background reading on "systems" see also, "Consultants Clash Over Ownership," *Business Week,* 27 November 1971, pp. 66-71.

14. See Aubrey Wilson, *The Marketing of Professional Services* (Maidenhead, England: McGraw-Hill Book Company U.K. Ltd., 1972), pp. 142-154.

15. Warren J. Wittreich, op. cit., pp. 132-133.

MARKETING BY CONSULTING FIRMS

H. Justin Davidson

A classic and unique assessment of professional consulting within the framework of the marketing mix.

For our purposes here, consulting firms will be defined as *organizations* that sell *professional,* personal services. Although the term *professional* is much misused, it is used here in the classic sense. Thus, we exclude from the scope of our discussion personal service organizations such as beauty shops, baseball teams, and firms supplying temporary clerical manpower. Similarly, *organization* is used to exclude individual proprietorships. Our discussion will focus on firms that employ a number of professional consultants.

Even with this limited definition, a variety of organizations can be classed as consulting firms. Doctors, lawyers, certified public accountants, architects, management consultants and engineering consultants—when practicing in group form—are all consulting firms. The following discussion is most applicable to management and engineering consultants, but has some applicability to all of the above.

We look at the marketing practices of consulting firms from four perspectives: pricing, product, promotion, and planning. We begin with pricing since it leads to understanding the basic economics of consulting.

PRICING

In simplest terms, consulting firms sell time: the time of skilled professional people. Indeed, the slogan of the consulting industry might well be *People are our most important product.* This emphasis on the time of people is reflected in the way consulting firms commonly sell their services: *time and expenses* (or time and materials).

The author is Dean of the Graduate School of Business and Public Administration, Cornell University and was formerly a partner in management advisory practice.

The client of a consulting firm typically receives a bill itemizing these two categories in more or less detail. The actual hours that professional members of the firm have worked are extended by billing rates (prices) for each member's time to obtain a time charge. Expenses directly related to the client engagement, such as travel and lodging, are accumulated to obtain the expense charge. Since expenses are typically a *pass-through* to the client, the pricing question for the consulting firm is that of setting billing rates for its professional staff.

Within a consulting firm, billing rates are usually set through a two-stage process. First, in a macro look at the economics of the firm, a standard billing-multiple is determined. Second, in a micro process, billing rates based on the standard multiple are calculated for individual staff consultants, and then adjusted to reflect market and other factors. We look first at the macro process.

Macro Pricing

Consulting firms are professional organizations. They are also business organizations. They return a profit to their partners, principals, or shareholders to compensate for the time, investment and risks involved. In the following discussion, we assume a one-partner firm to illustrate the factors involved in making an adequate consulting return. The analysis applies, however, to a firm of any size

In managing the firm to make a profit, the partner must deal with the following more or less controllable factors.

Number of Professional Staff. A larger staff (a larger staff/ partner ratio) leads to increased returns. But the nature of the consulting practice affects the number of staff that a single partner can manage. Generally, we shall assume the partner employs N consultants and, for numeric illustration in this example, 10.

Average Staff Compensation. Average staff compensation depends not only on the salaries paid for differing levels of consulting expertise, but also on the mix of consulting levels. We assume the partner pays his professional consulting staff an average compensation of S dollars per hour for a standard work year of 2,000 hours.[1] (Annual salary is thus 2,000 S.) For numeric illustration, we assume S is $10.

Overhead. Consulting firm overhead includes such items as secretarial and clerical staff, office space, professional dues, insurance and all other miscellaneous expenses required to support the firm. For the most part these expenses tend to be proportional to the salaries of the professional consulting staff. Thus, we assume an overhead cost equal to an overhead or burden rate, B. For numeric illustration, we assume B is 0.50, or 50 percent of staff salaries.

Average Staff Productivity. We have assumed each staff consultant is paid for a 2,000-hour year. But the average staff consultant will not be able to work for and bill clients for 2,000 hours each year. To maintain his professional skills, each consultant must spend some time in continuing education. Assignments cannot be scheduled perfectly. Time may be spent in developing new business. Finally, as professional people, consultants spend freely of their time in civic and professional affairs. Thus, a significant portion of a consulting staff's time cannot be billed to clients.

Generally, we shall express the productive portion of the consulting staff's time as a fraction, P, of the standard 2,000-hour year. For numeric illustration, we assume average staff productivity, P, is 0.70, that is, the average staff member will bill 2,000 P hours to clients each year.

Average Billing Multiple. A cost-based approach to pricing relates price as a ratio to cost. In the macro view, pricing of consulting services is essentially cost-based. Billing rates are determined as a multiple of salary costs. We assume an average billing multiple, M. That is, the billing rate of consultants is M times average staff compensation, S. For numeric illustration, we assume M is 2.5.

Given these factors and the numeric values assumed above, we can compute the profit or return of the partnership.

Revenues of the partnership are computed as the average hourly billing rate of the consulting staff, MS, multiplied by the average productive time billed to clients each year, 2,000 P, multiplied by the number of consultants, N.

$$\text{REVENUE} = 2,000 \text{ NMSP}$$
$$= 2,000 \ (1)(2.5)(\$10)(0.70)$$
$$= \$350,000$$

Professional salary costs of the partnership are the number of consultants, N, multiplied by their average salary cost, 2,000 S.

$$\text{PROFESSIONAL SALARY COSTS} = 2,000 \text{ NS}$$
$$= 2,000 \ (10)(\$10)$$
$$= \$200,000$$

Overhead costs are equal to the overhead rate, B, multiplied by professional salary costs, 2,000 NS.

OVERHEAD = 2,000 NBS
         = 2,000 (10)(0.50)($10)
         = $100,000

Subtracting salary ($200,000) and overhead costs ($100,000) from revenues ($350,000) leaves the partnership with a profit or return of $50,000.

In this example we have assumed values for the various control factors, including the billing multiple, that determine consulting return and computed that return. In practice, our example would be inverted. The partnership sets a target return, plans the various control factors (except for the billing multiple) and then computes the billing multiple.[2]

The reader is warned that the numbers used above in the example are illustrative. Except for a few publicly held firms, data on the finances of consulting firms are not commonly available. Nevertheless, the numbers are believed to bear order-of-magnitude resemblance to reality. For example, billing multiples of 2.5 to 3.5 are commonly cited for most consulting practices.

Micro Pricing

Given a target billing multiple for the firm, target billing rates for individual staff consultants are easily computed. If 2.5 is the multiple, a consultant's target billing rate is 2.5 times his hourly salary. Target billing rates are subjectively adjusted, however, for a variety of factors. The most common adjustments involve the market, rounding, and scaling.

After the partner has computed the target billing rate for a staff member, the next questions that he asks are, "Will the market bear it? Will the client buy it? Is the staff member worth it?" The partner assumes that clients see each staff consultant with a price tag on his lapel. Based on his judgment, the partner revises the target billing rate up or down.

An interesting side effect of this market test frequently takes place. Billing rates are most often revised in conjunction with reviewing the staff consultant's salary. If the target billing rate can be adjusted upward or downward, the target salary for the consultant may be similarly adjusted. With a large downward adjustment in view, the services of the staff consultant may be terminated. Thus, at the macro level, consulting prices are cost-based; at the micro level, consulting costs are price-based.

Another adjustment to billing rates is rounding. A target rate of $21.53 will be rounded to $22. Billing rates may also be rounded to maintain internal or external equity. If the target billing rates for two staff consultants are $24 and $22 respectively and if both bear similar responsibilities, their billing rates are apt to be equalized at $23.

A final adjustment to target billing rates tends to be scaling. Billing rates of senior staff consultants are frequently scaled down from target and those of juniors scaled up. The practice is market-based in that it recognizes client resistance to higher billing rates. Insightful clients sometimes recognize and take advantage of this practice. They demand a rich mix of senior staff consultants on engagements to realize the comparative price advantage.

PRODUCT

At the simplest level, we have described the consulting product as the time of skilled people. The answer becomes more complex when the client asks, "What can the consultant do for me?" The answer of the consultant is still simple. "Make money for you." But the good consultant makes money for the client in any one or combination of the following ways.

Shrinking Time

Organizational life is full of situations where time is of the essence. A project must be finished at a time certain to avoid penalties. Substantial gains may be realized by completing a project at an early date. If the time dimension of project planning has been inadequate or if plans have gone awry, the consulting firm can provide a buffer inventory of skilled people to recapture time that has been lost.

As an e. ample, consider a company installing a new accounting system. Before year end, they determine that system implementation is behind schedule and that year-end reports to stockholders may be delayed—with substantial damage to stockholder relations. A reasonable course is to use consultants to recapture the lost time.

Leveling Staffing

Organizations often face situations that involve peak staffing. Costs savings may be realized by leveling the peak and thus reducing associated hiring, training, and firing costs. Installation of a new computer system, for example, will typically require more systems analysts than will be needed for routine systems maintenance. Consultants may save the company money by absorbing and buffering this peak load.

Uncertainty Reduction

All successful organizations take risks. Yet all organizations attempt to reduce risk to reasonable levels. Through experience and expertise, consultants can reduce risk. Consider a steel company introducing a new technology such as continuous casting. While its engineering staff may be competent, the company may reduce its uncertainty by seeking counsel from an engineering consultant familiar with continuous casting.

With few exceptions, all consulting engagements involve one or more of these basic services that consultants provide. Two combination situations merit special mention.

The Expert

The reasons for an organization hiring the "expert" usually decompose into the twin reasons of uncertainty reduction *and* leveling. By his knowledge and experience, the expert can reduce uncertainty. But his use also levels staffing—since the alternative to an outside expert is an inside expert. Much legal consulting falls into the expert category. Depending upon the size of the organization and the rarity of the legal question, we find both inside and outside legal experts.

The Implementer

The implementer, the consultant who gets things done, usually reduces uncertainty *and* shrinks time. An example is the consultant in manpower reduction. He reduces uncertainty by shoring up the resolve of the manager—who probably knows that the reduction is necessary. He shrinks time by adding peak staff to help with the sorting process of deciding who must go.

All of these services that consultants provide for clients can be summarized in another way. Consultants provide alternatives. They provide an organization with the alternative of doing a project with them to compare with the alternative of doing the project without them. A sensible way for a company to evaluate purchase of the consulting product is to compare these alternatives—to look at their respective cash flows, rate of return and risks. An equally sensible way for a consultant to promote his services is to present the same comparison.

PROMOTION

Promotion, selling of its services, is crucial to the economic well-being of the consulting firm. The product that it sells, a project, is unique. The firm will never repeat the same project for the same client. As soon as it develops one project, it must look forward to developing another. Without a backlog of projects (booked and prospective), the consulting firm finds its productivity ratio falling dangerously.

Promotion of nearly all consulting services takes place within the context of professionalism. With the aim of protecting the public, professionals are regulated by codes of ethical behavior. Those codes nearly always enjoin the professional from soliciting business in an unseemly manner—in order to protect the public from the exaggerated claims of the unprincipled. The question is sometimes raised if these codes of "professional" ethics run more to preserving monopoly than to preventing unscrupulous competition. The question is largely moot. Reasonable competition appears to exist in practice.

Some of the unique characteristics of promoting and marketing consulting services flow from the professional ethic.

Consulting firms do not advertise. Restrictions on advertising vary among legal, accounting, medical, and management consulting firms. But one seldom sees newspaper or magazine ads or television commercials for consulting firms. Advertising is indirect: by the sign on the office door, telephone listings, word of mouth from satisfied clients, publications in trade or scholarly journals and participation in civic and professional affairs. Members of consulting firms appear at more conferences, serve more as members of community projects, write more articles and belong to more clubs and professional organizations than perhaps any other comparable group of people in the country.

Consulting firms do not solicit. It is bad form to ask a potential client, particularly if he is someone else's client, to consult for him. Consultants can't initially ask for the order! But in all cases, the consultant is free to respond to an invitation by a potential client to submit a proposal. Since no one has been able unambiguously to define what constitutes a request for a proposal—especially when it takes place in an informal setting, the behavior of individual consultants with prospective clients varies.

Consulting firms do not bid, they propose. Lawyers, doctors, CPAs and management consultants usually flinch when asked to bid, especially on a fixed-price basis. The flinch, however, is legitimate. An invitation to bid on consulting services generally raises the following warning signals:

The prospective client may want something for nothing. If so, he's apt to end getting nothing for a little—with resulting bad publicity for all consulting organizations.

The prospective client may not know what he wants. If so, the consultant can't intelligently respond to the request without great risk either to himself or to the client.

With a bid request, consulting organizations will try to persuade a prospective client to let them do what they should always do:

First, define the problem. Reach agreement with the client about the problem, and objectives and scope of the project that will solve it. Consulting organizations will often invest some resources in defining the problem. There are, however, situations where the problem is defining the problem. Most consulting firms won't do this for free.

Second, plan the project. The work plan should include the tasks involved, task timing, task staffing (both by the client and the consultant) and milestones (evidence) of task completion.

Third, agree on project organization. Authority, reporting, and communication channels should be specified.

Fourth, estimate project cost and agree on billing arrangements. Three types of billing arrangements are common. Time and expenses is most common. Consulting firms prefer this approach as it minimizes their risk and permits due professional care for the quality of the project. From the client viewpoint, time plus expenses has a drawback. Project cost remains an estimate and not a firm commitment. Without a hard target for total cost, the consultant may *gold-plate,* build more quality than needed into the project.

When a cost target is of concern to the client, most consulting firms will propose on the basis of "time and materials not to exceed a specified total cost." This approach permits the client to plan and offers some protection against gold-plating. By building an adequate contingency factor into the not-to-exceed figure, the consulting firm can maintain emphasis on project quality without undue financial risk. The financial risk not borne by the client is borne either by the consulting firm or, more likely, redistributed in the long run among its clients through increased billing rates.

A third billing arrangement is the fee contingent upon results. Few reputable consulting firms will enter into a contingent fee arrangement that is variable both up and down. While risk makes contingent-fee arrangements undesirable to the consulting firm, a critical negative factor for both parties is the difficulty of defining the contingency. For example, a fee contingent upon a certain cost reduction is meaningless unless great care is taken to define what constitutes a cost reduction and the constraints (such as a work force that is not demoralized) to be observed in achieving the reduction. A more common contingent fee arrangement is contingent-up. The consulting firm will bill time and expenses plus an add-on for spectacular success.

Finally, reduce all of the above agreements to writing. This proposal procedure often seems tedious to the consultant and to the client. The human tendency is to try short-cuts. Any consultant with experience, however, has a few scars that came from short-cutting the proposal procedure. And many clients have bitter views of consulting firms because they ducked their responsibility to insure clear understanding of the consulting project that they asked be performed.

The proposal phase is where consulting projects are sold. The consulting firm has the opportunity to demonstrate its competence or incompetence. The client has the opportunity to evaluate. If the client rejects the proposal, the client can turn serially to another consulting firm for another proposal.

PLANNING

Planning marketing strategy is no different for a consulting firm than for any other business organization. Three facets of planning for consulting firms deserve special mention.

Product Lines

As with consumer and industrial markets, consulting product lines come and go. Estate planning may be a hot item today and a slow-mover tomorrow. New product lines must continually be added and old product lines dropped if a consulting firm is to prosper and grow. A critical problem for the consulting firm is the development of new products and the timing of their introduction.

In one sense a consulting firm never develops a new product. Consultants can correctly be described as transfer agents who stand between current real-world practice and the keen, cutting edge of research taking place in universities and other institutions. With one foot in the world of research and one in the world of practice, the consulting firm pulls its clients forward toward tomorrow's improved practice. Consulting firms rarely do basic research, they package the findings of basic research so that they can be applied in practice.

An excellent example of this transfer role is afforded by inventory control. In the early fifties, academia made great strides in developing new and improved theories for controlling inventory. Although there was limited experimentation with application, university emphasis was clearly on theory. In the late fifties, management consulting firms began to experiment with applying these theories in practical settings. From this experience, practical approaches began to be developed. A number of firms packaged these approaches and began to promote them. By the middle sixties, inventory control was a booming product line for consultants. Today inventory control is a stable, low-volume product line. The same cycle of research, packaging, boom and decline is evident for other product lines—as old as work measurement and as new as matrix management.

To be successful in catching the boom period, the consulting firm must carefully time introduction of its packages. Contrary perhaps to experience with industrial and consumer product lines, consulting firms most often err on the side of introducing product lines too soon. Several firms introduced inventory control in the late fifties, found little demand and de-emphasized the line. In the middle sixties, they viewed competitors who were profiting from being late. From the seminal research idea, the new consulting product line typically requires a long gestation period.

People

Behind old and new consulting product lines are people. Planning product lines requires people planning. The consulting firm has two alternatives. It can plan on acquiring people who bring new product lines with them. Or it can plan for its existing people to package new product lines. Both planning approaches are used.

When existing people are used to develop product lines, they are usually assigned to "research." This research typically includes maintaining communications with basic researchers to provide early recognition of new developments, adapting these new developments for practical use, and testing the resulting approach or package in client situations. This research is a factor lowering the billing productivity of a firm.

The need for manpower or people planning in consulting firms is difficult to overemphasize. Although there is some evidence that the situation may have changed, a history of rise and decline of individual consulting firms suggests that internal manpower planning has been inadequate. Consulting firms have often been the lengthened shadow of one or two people, a shadow which disappeared when the one or two retired.

Image

Consulting firms continually fuss about their image. The tendency may be due to the professional's proclivity to worry about status and prestige. But part of the concern is important. Images of consulting firms vary. Images contribute to or detract from success.

The question for a consulting firm, "What image should we have?" is essentially the question, "What mix of product lines should we be in?" There is no general answer to this question, and none will be attempted. One quick method of gaining insight about a consulting firm's image can, however, be noted.

The method consists simply of listing the values of economic factors that affect consulting success. Consider the following:

	Firm	
	A	B
Staff/Partner Ratio	8	10
Average staff compensation	$25,000	$20,000
Productivity	0.60	0.70
Billing Multiple	3.0	2.5

These numbers tell a great deal about firms A and B. The consultants of Firm A are supervised more, perhaps because they operate in high technology. If price reflects quality, Firm A has more highly qualified people. The lower productivity ratio indicates a combination of more research, training, scheduling, promotion, and public relations costs of Firm A. The billing multiple at Firm A indicates that they are near the top of price line.

None of these numbers argue that Firm A is better than Firm B. To use a retailing analogy, they indicate that Firm A operates in the select end of the line like a Tiffany. Firm B operates more toward the mass merchandising end like a Woolworth. Depending upon what one wants, either may be the right store.

Image results from many factors other than those listed above— size of firm, length of history, quality of clients and many others. But the image that a firm wishes to project cannot stray too far from the economic realities of its practice.

Summary

We have briefly described the pricing, product, promotion and planning characteristics of consulting firms. In placing this description in perspective, the reader is enjoined to remember two things.

Consulting is an old profession. Kings had their astrologers who reckoned the influence of stars on future actions. Emperors had their priests who counseled on right actions leading to success here and in the hereafter.

Consulting is a young profession. Large legal, medical, architectural, accounting, engineering, and management consulting firms that provide professional services to other large organizations are a development of the twentieth century.

One characteristic appears common to consultants of yesterday and today. They have been reticent about the management of their operations. We hope this article makes a small contribution and leads others to contribute to knowledge about a growing and significant part of our society.

FOOTNOTES

1. We do not imply that consultant firms hire their professional staff by the hour. Indeed, consultants are normally hired at an annual rate.

2. For those who are inclined to formulae, the billing multiple is computed directly:

$$M = (1/P)(Z/2,000 \ NS + B + 1)$$
where Z is the planned profit in dollars.

APPENDIX A

MAJOR SERVICE INDUSTRIES

Arranged by SIC (Standard Industrial Classification) numbers

48 *Communications*
  4811 Telephone
  4821 Telegraph
  4832 Radio broadcasting
  4833 Television broadcasting
  4899 Communications services, not elsewhere classified
  7351 News syndicates

73 *Consulting and Business Facilitating*
  7311 Advertising agencies
  7312 Outdoor advertising services
  7313 Radio, television, and publishers' advertising representatives
  7319 Miscellaneous advertising
  7321 Consumer and mercantile credit reporting agencies, and adjustment and collection agencies
  7331 Direct mail advertising services
  7332 Blueprinting and photocopying services
  7339 Stenographic services
  7341 Window-cleaning
  7342 Disinfecting and exterminating services
  7349 Miscellaneous services to buildings
  7361 Private employment agencies
  7391 Commercial research and development laboratories
  7392 Business, management, administrative, and consulting services
  7393 Detective agencies and protective services
  7394 Equipment, rental and leasing services
  7395 Photofinishing laboratories
  7396 Trading stamp services
  7397 Commercial testing laboratories
  7398 Temporary help supply service
  7399 Business services, not elsewhere classified

8911 Engineering and architectural services
8931 Accounting, auditing, and bookkeeping services
071 Agricultural services
072 Animal husbandry services
1213 Coal mining services
138 Oil and gas field services
148 Nonmetallic minerals services

82 *Educational (excluding totally tax supported)*
8211 Elementary and secondary schools
8221 Colleges, universities, and professional schools
8211 Junior colleges and technical institutes
8231 Libraries and information centers
8241 Correspondence schools
8242 Vocational schools
8299 Schools and educational services, not elsewhere classified
8921 Nonprofit educational and scientific research agencies

60 *Financial*
601 Federal Reserve banks
602 Commercial and stock savings banks
603 Mutual savings banks
604 Trust companies not engaged in deposit banking
605 Establishments performing functions closely related to banking
611 Rediscount and finance institutions for credit agencies other than banks
612 Savings and loan associations
613 Agricultural credit institutions
614 Personal credit institutions
615 Business credit institutions
616 Loan correspondents and brokers
621 Security brokers, dealers, and flotation companies
622 Commodity contracts, brokers, and dealers
623 Security and commodity exchanges
628 Services allied with the exchange of securities or commodities
671 Holding companies
672 Investment companies
673 Trusts

80 *Health*
8011 Offices of physicians and surgeons
8021 Offices of dentists and dental surgeons
8031 Offices of osteopathic physicians
8041 Offices of chiropractors

8061 Hospitals
8071 Medical laboratories
8072 Dental laboratories
8092 Sanatoria and convalescent and rest homes
8099 Health and allied services, not elsewhere classified

49 Household Operations

491 Electric companies
493 Combination companies and systems
495 Sanitary services
496 Steam supply
721 Laundries, laundry services, and cleaning and dyeing plants
762 Electrical repair shops
764 Reupholstery and furniture repair
881 Domestic service performed in private households
0731 Horticultural services

65 Housing

6513 Operators of apartment buildings
6514 Operators of dwellings
6531 Rental agents
7011 Hotels, tourist courts, and motels
7031 Trailer parks

63 Insurance

631 Life insurance
632 Accident and health insurance
633 Fire, marine, and casualty insurance
635 Surety insurance
636 Title insurance
639 Insurance carriers not elsewhere classified
641 Insurance agents, brokers, and services

81 Legal

811 Legal services

72 Personal

723 Beauty shops
724 Barber shops
725 Shoe repair shops, shoe shine parlors, and hat cleaning shops
726 Funeral services
727 Garment pressing, alteration, and repair
729 Miscellaneous personal services
763 Watch, clock, and jewelry repair

78 *Recreational*
    781   Motion picture production and distribution
    782   Motion picture service industries
    783   Motion picture theaters
    791   Dance halls, studios, and schools
    792   Theatrical producers, bands, orchestras, and entertainers
    793   Bowling alleys and billiard and pool establishments
    794   Sports promoters, commercial operators, and recreation services (golf courses and clubs, skating rinks, race track operation, etc.)
    841   Museums and art galleries
    842   Arboreta, botanical, and zoological gardens

4 *Transportation*
    40   Railroad transportation
    41   Local and suburban transit and inter-urban highway passenger transportation
    42   Motor freight transportation and warehousing
    44   Water transportation
    45   Transportation by air
    46   Pipeline transportation
    47   Transportation services
    751   Automobile rentals
    752   Automobile parking
    753   Automobile repair shops
    754   Automobile services, except repair

86 *Miscellaneous*
    861   Business associations
    862   Professional membership organizations
    863   Labor unions
    864   Civic, social, and fraternal associations
    865   Political organizations*
    866   Religious organizations*
    867   Charitable organizations*
    899   Services, not elsewhere classified (ghost writers, weather forecasters, cloud seeding, etc.)

*If formally organized and offering memberships and services for which fixed charges are made. Even so, inclusion may be questionable.

Source: *Standard Industrial Classification Manual* (Washington, D.C.: U.S. Government Printing Office, 1967).

BIBLIOGRAPHY

As nearly as possible this compilation is limited to material on services in general. Written works relating to specific service industries which are not subject to broader application are excluded.

Alderfer, E.B. "SCORE." *Business Review,* Federal Reserve Bank of Philadelphia, March 1967, pp. 12-15.

"American Repairman: a Vanishing Breed?" *U.S. News and World Report,* 13 September 1965, pp. 88-90.

"America's Huge Catered Affair." *Newsweek,* 4 September 1967, pp. 60-62.

Armor, L.A. "Skills in Demand: Market for Business Services is Burgeoning Mightily." *Barrons,* 7 November 1960, p. 3.

Arnould, R.J. "Pricing Professional Services: a Case Study of the Legal Service Industry." *Southern Economic Journal* 38 (April 1972), pp. 495-507.

"Battle for Industry's Travel Dollar." *Dun's Review and Modern Industry* 85 (June 1965), pp. 136-37.

Bell, J.E. and D. Appel. "The Service Gap—Marketing's Crisis in the Seventies." *Southern Journal of Business* 5 (July 1970), p. 10.

Belth, J.M. *The Retail Price Structure in American Life Insurance.* Bloomington, Indiana: Bureau of Business Research, Indiana University, 1966.

Bennett, K.W. "Service Industries: A New Frontier." *Iron Age* 203 pp. 78-79.

Berkwitt, G.J. "Big Staff Services Spinoff." *Dun's Review* 99 (April 1972), pp. 70-72.

_____. "Rise of the Service Conglomerates." *Dun's Review* 90 (December 1967), pp. 67-68.

Bickelhaupt, D.L. "Trends and Innovations in the Marketing of Insurance." *Journal of Marketing* 31 (July 1967), pp. 17-22.

Compiled by Phillip A. Hines with updating by Hernan H.G. Etcheto, doctoral candidates, Cornell University.

Borst, G.E. "Service Industries See Chances Now to Expand Their Distribution and Marketing Methods in Germany." *International Commerce,* 15 June 1970, pp. 8-9.

Bower, M. "Personal Service Firms Venture Abroad." *Columbia Journal of World Business* 3 (March, 1968), pp. 49-58.

Brown, W.F. and R. Cassady, Jr. "Guild Pricing in the Service Trades." *Quarterly Journal of Economics* 61 (February 1947), pp. 311-338.

Broy, A. "Kinney—In the Forefront of the Service Industry Boom." *Magazine of Wall Street,* 29 April 1967, pp. 23-26.

Burck, G. "The Still Bright Promise of Productivity." *Fortune* 78 (October 1968), pp. 134-136.

_____. "There'll be Less Leisure Than You Think." *Fortune* 81 (March 1970), pp. 86-89.

"A Builder 'Packages Everything.' " *Business Week,* 2 November 1968, pp. 146-148.

"Business Know-how Fertilizes the Farm." *Business Week,* 14 September 1968, pp. 64-74.

"Buying for Profit: Supplies and Services." *Purchasing,* 1 May 1969, pp. 294-295.

Cates, D.C. "Services Industries, Clarifications for Investors." *Commercial and Financial Chronicle,* 23 November 1961, p. 2283.

Cobleigh, I.U. "Kinney Service Corporation." *Commercial and Financial Chronicle,* 6 September 1962, p. 1015.

Codner, B. "New Concepts for Improving the Marketing of Services by Department Stores." *Oregon Business Review* 25 (January 1966), pp. 1-4.

"Commercial Services on the Rise." *Monthly Business Review,* Federal Reserve Board, Cleveland, August 1960, pp. 2-6.

Conrad, E. "An R&D Approach for Service Industry." *Business Horizons* 11 (October 1968), pp. 73-78.

Crawford, W.L. "Do-It-Yourself Solves Some Problems of Rapid Growth; Shaler Township." *American City* 85 (Spring 1970), p. 90.

"Creeping Capitalism; Private Operation of Public Services." *Forbes,* 1 September 1970, pp. 22-26.

"Decline of Durables." *Time,* 8 September 1961, p. 79.

Dhrymes, P.J. "Comparison of Productivity Behavior in Manufacturing and Service Industries." *Review of Economics and Statistics* 45 (February 1963), pp. 64-69.

Diamond, D.E. "Negroes and the Service Industries." *Challenge* 13 (December 1964), pp. 33-35.

_____. "The Shift to Services: What Does it Mean?" *Challenge* 10 (July 1962), pp. 40-43.

Donovan, J.E. "Greater Economic Role of Service Industries." *Financial Analysts Journal* 19 (March-April 1963), pp. 89-91.

Duncan, J.H. "Role of the Industrial Engineer in a Service Economy." *Insurance,* 4 October 1969, p. 27.

Ellwood, P.M. Jr. and M.E. Herbert. "Health Care: Should Industry Buy It or Sell It?" *Harvard Business Review* 51 (July-August 1973), pp. 99-107.

"Expansion Phase for Service Industries." *Financial World,* 16 November 1960, pp. 114-115.

French, H.E. "The New American 'Instant' Civilization." *American Review* 11 (December 1961), pp. 92-103.

"From Factory to Service Employment." *Monthly Business Review,* Federal Reserve Bank of Cleveland, May 1960, pp. 3-7.

Frye, J. "Advertising a Service Business." *Electronics World* 86 (July 1971), pp. 52-53.

Fuchs, V.R. "The Growing Importance of the Service Industries." *Journal of Business* 38 (October 1965), pp. 344-373.

_____. *The Service Economy.* New York: National Bureau of Economic Research, 1968.

Fuchs, V.R., ed. *Production and Productivity in the Service Industries.* New York: National Bureau of Economic Research, 1967.

Fuchs, V.R. and J.A. Wilbern. *Productivity Differences Within the Service Sector.* Occasional Paper No. 102. New York: National Bureau of Economic Research, 1967.

Goldstein, L.J. "Service Industry Stocks Are Exceedingly Attractive." *Commercial and Financial Chronicle,* 28 December 1967, p. 2407.

"Good Growth for Services." *Financial World,* 11 November 1970, p. 9.

Greenfield, H.I. *Manpower and the Growth of Producer Services.* New York: Columbia University Press, 1966.

"The Growth of Consumer Services." *Business Review,* Federal Reserve Board of Chicago, November 1960, pp. 5-10.

"Growth Potential in Service Firms; With Data on Leaders." *Financial World,* 11 October 1961, p. 6.

Guss, L.M. "The Care and Feeding of Marketing Consultants." *Journal of Marketing* 30 (July 1966), pp. 6-8.

Gutmann, P.M. "Service Sectors." *Magazine of Wall Street,* 23 May 1970, p. 32.

Guzzardi, W. Jr. "Consultants: the Men Who Came to Dinner." *Fortune* 71 (February 1965), pp. 138-141.

Haggerty, P.E. "Productivity: Industry Isn't the Only Place Where It's a Problem." *Forbes,* 1 February 1971, pp. 43-45.

Haig, B.D. "Measurement of Real Expenditure and Production of Goods and Services." *Economic Record* 42 (December 1966), pp. 520-535.

Hanning, G.M. "Rising Costs Mold Changing Pattern in Service Maintenance Business." *Air Conditioning, Heat and Refrigeration News,* 4 May 1970, p. 3.

Hauk, J.G. *Technical Services in the American Economy: A Problem in Market-*

ing Management. Michigan Business Studies, vol. 16, no. 1. Ann Arbor: University of Michigan, 1962.

Hecksher, A. "Reflections on the Manpower Revolution." *American Scholar* 33 (Autumn 1964), pp. 568-578.

"Here Is a Company That's Cleaning Up." *Business Week,* 26 October 1968, pp. 176-180.

"High Cost of Services." *Forbes,* 15 January 1969, p. 57.

Hollander, S.C. *Management Consultants and Clients.* East Lansing: Division of Research, Graduate School of Business Administration, Michigan State University, 1973.

"How Growth of Services Is Changing America," *U.S. News and World Report,* 9 November 1970, pp. 34-35.

"How to Make a Last-place Product a Banner Success." *Sales Management,* 16 April 1965, pp. 34-36.

"Inflation and the Service Sector." *OECD Observer,* 59 (August 1972), pp. 27-29. pp. 27-29.

"Is the Shift to Services Really a Drag?" *Business Week,* 9 September 1972, pp. 84-87.

Johnson, E.M. *An Introduction to the Problems of Service Marketing Management.* Newark, Delaware: Bureau of Economic and Business Research, University of Delaware, 1967.

———. "Services Industry by 1970 May Hit $200 Billion Level." *Commercial and Financial Chronicle,* 24 September 1964, sec. 2, p. 51.

Judd, R.C. "Case for Redefining Services." *Journal of Marketing* 28 (January 1964), pp. 58-59.

———. "Similarities or Differences in Product and Service Retailing." *Journal of Retailing* 43 (Winter 1968), pp. 1-9.

Kann, S.W. "How Non-Merchandise Exports Bolster Our Overseas Trade: Services Now Account for an Increasingly Large Slice of U.S. International Business." *Export Trade,* 14 January 1963, pp. 10-13.

King, W.R. "Systems Analysis at the Public-Private Marketing Frontier." *Journal of Marketing* 33 (January 1969), pp. 84-89.

"Kinney Spreads Umbrella Wider." *Business Week,* 16 April 1966, pp. 101-102.

Knowles, J.W. "A New Source of Employment Stability? The Shift to Services." *Challenge* 8 (July 1960), pp. 46-50.

Kotler, P. and S.J. Levy. "Broadening the Concept of Marketing." *Journal of Marketing* 33 (January 1969), pp. 10-15.

———. "A New Form of Marketing Myopia: Rejoinder to Professor Luck." *Journal of Marketing* 33 (July 1969), pp. 55-56.

Lengelle, M. *The Growing Importance of the Service Sector in Member Countries.* Paris: Organization for Economic Cooperation and Development, 1966.

Lewis, V. "Dial S for Service." *Dun's Review* 93 (March 1969), pp. 98-99.

Linden, F. "Business of Services." *Conference Board Business Record* 18 (February 1961), pp. 41-43.

_____. "Consumer Market in 1980: Services." *Conference Board Record* 9 (May 1972), pp. 50-52.

_____. "What's Ahead for Consumer Services." *Conference Board Record* 4 November 1967), pp. 32-35.

Lindholm, R.W. "Taxing Retailing and Services with the Value Added Tax." *Conference Board Record* 9 (February 1972), pp. 17-20.

"Linking Up a Chain: While You Wait." *Business Week,* 9 October 1965, p. 148.

Luck, D.J. "Broadening the Concept of Marketing Too Far." *Journal of Marketing* 33 (July 1969), pp. 53-55.

_____. *Service Industry Study of the Illinois Statewide Economic Study.* Urbana: Bureau of Economic and Business Research, University of Illinois, 1967.

Lynes, R. "Great Service Swindle." *Harpers* 236 (March 1962), p. 24.

MacDonald, D. "Arriving: The Household Professional." *House Beautiful* 111 (March 1969), pp. 88-89.

Machlup, F. *The Production and Distribution of Knowledge in the United States.* Princeton: Princeton University Press, 1962.

Malabre, A.L. Jr. "Shift in Spending." *Wall Street Journal,* 24 October 1963, p. 1.

_____. "Consumer Expenditures: Service Spending Levels Off." *Management Review* 53 (January 1964), pp. 30-33.

"Management Seminars Fade Fast in Popularity as the Economy Slows." *Wall Street Journal,* 18 June 1970, p. 1.

McDonald, H.E. and T.L. Stromberger. "Cost Control for the Professional Service Firm." *Harvard Business Review* 47 (January-February 1969), pp. 109-121.

McGarr, C.J. "Definitive Operating Concept for Service Organization." *Systems and Procedures Journal* 16 (May 1965), pp. 44-50.

"Name It, He'll Get It; François Lanos' Paris Planning Service." *Newsweek,* 18 December 1961, p. 94.

"A New Industry's Wild Ride." *Business Week,* 24 May 1969, pp. 64-78.

"New York V-P For Everybody." *Business Week,* 3 November 1962, p. 140.

"Next the Hospitality Conglomerate." *Business Week,* 12 June 1971, p. 61.

Nicholson, H. "New Inflation Hidden in G.N.P. Shows Up in the Run-Away Cost of Services." *Magazine of Wall Street,* 13 July 1963, pp. 432-435.

"No Place Like House Calls." *Newsweek,* 14 March 1966, pp. 95-96.

"Offbeat Services Ride a Trend." *Business Week,* 15 October 1960, pp. 103-104.

"Office Procedures of a Small Manufacturer." *Office* 66 (November 1967), pp. 100-101.

"Office Services." *Dun's Review and Modern Industry* 88 (September 1966), pp. 157-158.

"Office Services Include Everything from Laundromat and On-Line Data Centers to Temporary Help and Employee Food Services." *Dun's Review and Modern Industry* 86 (September 1965), pp. 166-167.

Ofur, Gur. *The Service Industries in a Developing Economy*. New York: Frederick A. Praeger, 1967.

"One Stop Center for Services." *Business Week,* 11 June 1960, p. 52.

Oshin, E.S. "How to Escape the Serviceman Syndrome." *House and Garden* 127 (June 1965), pp. 140-141.

Parker, Donald D. *The Marketing of Consumer Services*. Business Studies Series no. 1. Seattle: University of Washington, College of Business Administration, Bureau of Business Research, 1960.

Passer, H.C. "Growth in the Service Sector." *Conference Board Record* 9 (May 1972), pp. 38-43.

"Plan for Value: Supplies and Services." *Purchasing,* 30 October 1971, pp. 207-247.

Prasow, P. "Manpower Development and Requirements in Our New Service Economy." *California Management Review* 11 (Fall 1968), pp. 91-93.

"Professions on Trial." *Economist,* 1 June 1963, pp. 906-907.

Rathmell, J.M. "What is Meant By Services?" *Journal of Marketing* 29 (October 1966), pp. 32-36.

Regan, W.J. "Economic Growth and Services." *Journal of Business* 36 (April 1963), pp. 200-209.

_____. "The Service Revolution." *Journal of Marketing* 27 (July 1963), pp. 57-62.

"The Renting Kick." *Sales Management,* 7 September 1962, pp. 44-46.

Rolland, L.J. "Boom Marks Service Fields." *Financial World,* 23 January 1963, pp. 7-8.

"Savings and Loan Owned Service Corporations." *Savings and Loan News* 90 (February 1969), pp. 24-28.

Senninger, E.J. Jr. "A Service Classification of Michigan Cities." *Michigan Academy of Science, Arts, Letters, and Papers* 49 (1964), pp. 433-443.

"Service Companies and the Values in Them." *Dun's Review and Modern Industry* 83 (February 1964), pp. 117-119.

"Service Companies—Growth Field." *Financial World,* 23 August 1966, pp. 6-12.

"Service Companies; Should They or Shouldn't They?" *Forbes,* 1 June 1965, p. 40.

"Service Economy." *Scientific American* 220 (April 1969), pp. 48-49.

"The Service Economy Grows—But Does It." *Business Week,* 15 February 1969, p. 126.

"Service Industries." *Commerce Today,* 30 November 1970, pp. 39-40.

"Service Industries, New Glamour Field With Data On Leaders." *Financial World,* 14 March 1962, p. 13.

"The Service Sector—Where the Action Is." *Business Review,* Federal Reserve Board of Kansas City, March 1970, pp. 3-11.

"Services for Profits." *Financial World,* 10 February 1965, pp. 13-14.

"Services Grow While the Quality Shrinks." *Business Week,* 30 October 1971, pp. 50-57.

"Services in the U.S. Economy." *Business in Brief,* no. 84 (February 1969), pp. 5-7.

"Servicing for the Seventies." *Investor's Reader,* 10 July 1963, pp. 12-17.

Shapiro, B. *Marketing in Nonprofit Organizations.* Cambridge, Massachusetts: Marketing Science Institute, 1972.

————. "Marketing for Nonprofit Organizations." *Harvard Business Review* 51 (September-October 1973), pp. 123-132.

"Ship Line Charts New Course." *Business Week,* 8 February 1969, pp. 106-112.

Sibson, R.E. "Pricing by Product Type—A Service." in *Creative Pricing,* edited by Elizabeth Marting. New York: American Management Association, 1968.

Skan, L. "Procurement of Technical Services." *Purchasing,* 13 June 1968, pp. 63-64.

"Soaring Services." *Wall Street Journal,* 12 October 1970, p. 1.

Sparrough, M.E. "Service Industry Wage Changes and Fringe Benefits." *Monthly Labor Review* 91 (February 1968), pp. 35-39.

"Spiraling Services." *Wall Street Journal,* 31 August 1958, p. 1.

"Supplier Technology Sparks VA Ideas—Supplies and Services." *Purchasing,* 18 April 1972, pp. 205-209.

Survey of Selected Management Practices of the Personal Service Type of Business in the Memphis Area. Memphis: Memphis School of Business Administration, Memphis State University, 1961.

Taylor, G.B. "Services and the City Region." *Town and Country Planning* 32 (May 1964), pp. 215-221.

Taylor, T.C., "Changing Markets: Selling the Services Society." *Sales Management,* 6 March 1972, pp. 23-30.

————. "New Shifts Shaping Industry Markets." *Sales Management,* 1 November 1963, pp. 45-46.

"Their Servicemen Are Women." *Sales Management,* 16 February 1962, p. 80.

"They Board Up the Windows." *Business Week,* 1 May 1971, p. 90.

"Thriving in Business Without Any Sales." *Business Week,* 13 March 1963, pp. 140-141.

"Training in Service Occupations." *Monthly Labor Review* 89 (May 1966), pp. 523-527.

Turner, E.B. "Marketing Professional Services." *Journal of Marketing* 33 (October 1969), pp. 56-61.

"United Charts a New Flight Plan." *Business Week,* 14 August 1965, p. 128.

United States House Committee on Government Operations, Special Studies Subcommittee. "A Cost Profile for Support Services." 23-25 April 1968, 90th Congress, 2nd Session.

United States House Committee on Science and Astronautics, Subcommittee on NASA Oversight. "Support Service Contracting by the National Aeronautics and Space Administration." Proceedings, 11 July 1968, 90th Congress, 2nd Session.

United States Senate, Committee on Government Operations. "Government Policy and Practice With Respect to Contracts for Technical Services." Hearings, 22 March-17 April 1967, 90th Congress, 1st Session.

United States Senate, Committee on Government Operations. "Government Policy and Practice with Respect to Contracts for Technical Services: Status Report." 17 May 1968, 90th Congress, 2nd Session.

Warshaw, M.R. "Effective Marketing—Key to Public Utility Growth." *Michigan Business Review* 14 (November 1962), pp. 16-20.

Weiss, E.B. "Face of the Future: New Source of Profit Under Controlled Marketing." *Advertising Age*, 15 February 1971, p. 44.

_____ . "Marketers: Don't Ignore Our Growing Service-Oriented Society." *Advertising Age*, 5 May 1969, p. 104.

_____ . "Service Industries Promise More Than They Give." *Advertising Age*, 10 March 1969, p. 55.

Weiss, T. "Urbanization and the Growth of the Service Workforce." *Explorations in Economic History* 8 (Spring 1971), pp. 241-258.

"What Price Service?" *Business Review*, Federal Reserve Board, San Francisco, January 1964, pp. 10-14.

"Where Inflation Takes Its Toll: The Soaring Cost of Services." *U.S. News and World Report*, 19 January 1970, pp. 30-31.

"Why Customers Complain: The Breakdown in Service." *U.S. News and World Report*, 1 December 1969, pp. 50-52.

"Why Service Workers Are Less Productive." *Business Week*, 14 November 1964, p. 156.

Wickens, A.J. "Competition Between Actual Goods and Services." *Commercial and Financial Chronicle*, 13 July 1961, p. 167.

Wilson, A. *The Marketing of Professional Services*. London: McGraw-Hill Book Company U.K. Ltd., 1972.

Winston, C. "Retail Trade and Use of Services." *Survey of Current Business*, 41 (May 1961), pp. 22-28.

Winter, E.L. "How to License a Service." *Columbia Journal of World Business* 5 (September 1970), pp. 83-85.

_____ . "A New Horizon for Service Industries." *International Trade Revue* 36 (November 1962), pp. 30-31.

Wittreich, W.J. "How to Buy/Sell Professional Services." *Harvard Business Review* 44 (March-April 1966), pp. 127-138.

Zaltman, G. and I. Vertinsky. "Health Service Marketing: A Suggested Model." *Journal of Marketing* 35 (July 1971), pp. 19-27.

Zikmund, W.G. and W. J. Stanton. "Recycling Solid Wastes: A Channels-of-Distribution Problem." *Journal of Marketing* 35 (July 1971), pp. 34-39.

NOTE:

1. The best source for current and comparative statistics on services is the *Survey of Current Business.*

2. The Intercollegiate Case Clearing House Volume XIV contains a special section devoted to cases on the management of nonprofit organizations.

INDEX